THE WINE LOVER'S BUCKET LIST

First published in the United States of America in 2020 by
Universe Publishing, A Division of
Rizzoli International Publications, Inc.
300 Park Avenue South
New York, NY 10010
www.rizzoliusa.com

2020 2021 2022 2023 / 10 9 8 7 6 5 4 3 2 1

ISBN: 978-0-7893-3901-0
Library of Congress Control Number: 2020937084

Visit us online:
Facebook.com/RizzoliNewYork
Twitter: @Rizzoli_Books
Instagram.com/RizzoliBooks
Pinterest.com/RizzoliBooks
Youtube.com/user/RizzoliNY
Issuu.com/Rizzoli

Conceived, designed, and produced by
The Bright Press, an imprint of the Quarto Group
The Old Brewery
6 Blundell Street
London N7 9BH
United Kingdom
T 00 44 20 7700 6700
www.QuartoKnows.com

Publisher: James Evans
Art Director: Katherine Radcliffe
Editorial Director: Isheeta Mustafi
Designer: Tony Seddon
Managing Editor: Jacqui Sayers
Project Editor: Rica Dearman
Senior Editor: Caroline Elliker
Editorial Assistant: Chloe Porter
Picture Researcher: Charlotte Rivers

Printed and bound in China

THE WINE LOVER'S BUCKET LIST

1000 AMAZING ADVENTURES IN PURSUIT OF WINE

SIMON J. WOOLF

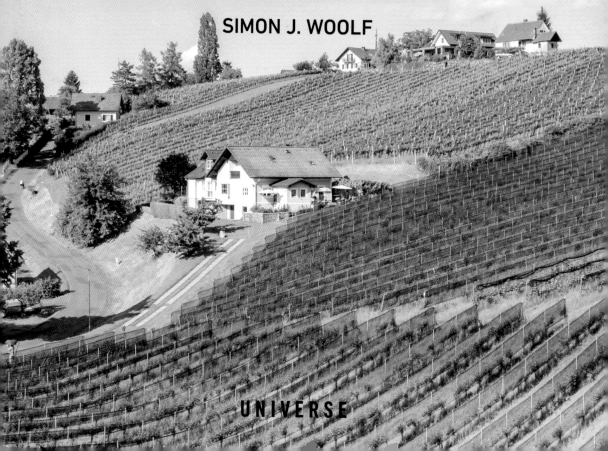

UNIVERSE

Contents

HOW TO USE THIS BOOK

This book is organized by areas of the world. Within each chapter you will then find entries arranged under individual countries—or in the case of North America, states, provinces, and territories. If you have a specific vineyard in mind, simply turn to page 406 to search for it in the index.

A note about opening hours

Due to the changing nature of establishments, we haven't included details of opening times, but would advise you to visit a company's website or contact them directly for this and any other information. This is also the case for events such as wine festivals—dates will vary from year to year, so be sure to check in advance. You may also wish to check the price with the organizers and how far in advance you will need to purchase tickets.

Color code

Each entry number in the book has been given a color that relates to one of six categories, as shown below, allowing you to select activities based on the type of element you are interested in, e.g. a winery or an event.

Color key

- ■ tastings/vineyard tours
- ▨ journeys/adventures/hotels
- ▨ festivals/annual events/new skills
- ■ bars/restaurants
- ▨ shops/history/culture
- ▨ top lists

Foreword

A bottle of good wine is nothing if not a travelogue. The best examples invite you along for the journey.

Taste the salt-sprayed flavors of a Getariako Txakolina, and they convey you to Spanish Basque Country, where the grapes are lashed by a constant wind off the Bay of Biscay. Sip a fine Etna Rosso, and in the stony push-pull between sweet and bitter, you can practically sense the nervous energy of the volcano smoking and rumbling in the distance.

This ability of wine to transmit not only its place of origin but often the culture that produced it is extraordinary. Yet receiving these messages is not a passive act. It requires knowledge of where a wine comes from, who produced it, and why. Otherwise, you are drinking blind, which, for some people, is pleasant enough.

But for those who crave understanding, wine is not only transporting, but it inspires travel. And when you arrive at your destination, you can do yourself no better favor than to have in hand a copy of this book, expertly compiled by Simon J. Woolf and company.

The key to a fulfilling travel experience—you will not be surprised to hear—is knowing where to go. Avoiding the tourist traps and finding the best, most representative cafés, restaurants, vineyards, shops, and bars—this is what separates the merely enjoyable from the indelible.

It helps that wine regions are often among the most beautiful and interesting parts of the world, whether the ridiculously steep vineyards of the Mosel, the volcanic lump that is Santorini, or the moody crags that mark the Sonoma Coast.

This bucket list does not restrict itself to famous wine-producing areas. It will introduce you to the little-known and the yet-to-be-discovered. It also ventures into urban destinations, where the challenge is to find the best and most distinctive wine-oriented refreshment.

You can have no better guide than Mr. Woolf, author of one of the most interesting books on wine, *Amber Revolution*, which trekked far beneath the surface in chronicling the orange wine renaissance.

It's the duty of any guide to go beyond the factual to the inspirational. This book, like a good bottle, will help you discover where you need to go.

Eric Asimov
Chief wine critic for *The New York Times* and author of *How to Love Wine: A Memoir and Manifesto* and *Wine with Food: Pairing Notes and Recipes from The New York Times*

Left: La Stoppa, a cult winery based in the Trebbiola Valley in Piacenza province, Italy

Introduction

What is it that makes great wine so magical? Perhaps that, unlike craft beer or artisanal spirits, wine is by its very nature location-specific. Grapes only prosper in certain climatic conditions, and harvest comes just once a year. To make exceptional wine, vineyard and winery need to be as close to each other as possible. Even a globetrotting winemaker annually crossing continents will struggle to make wine more than eighty times in their life—compare that to the average brewer, who might create more than twenty beers a year, and you start to see why wine is so precious and so profound.

There's a fringe benefit to wine's finicky location requirements—the places where wine is made are usually outstandingly beautiful! Furthermore, this delicious beverage acts as a catalyst, wherever you travel. Head to long-established regions of production and wine is inextricably tied to culture: tapas in Logroño is nothing without a glass of joven, "*un verre du vin*" is practically a basic human right in France. Viticulture can permanently shape the landscape too, as with Portugal's dramatically terraced Douro Valley.

In compiling this book, I had two main aims. First, to share some of my favorite wine experiences, and second, to stimulate you to look off the beaten track. Anyone can find their way to a top winery with a global brand, and anyone with a fat enough wallet can walk into a restaurant and point at the most expensive wine on the list. These are not true bucket list items, and you don't need this or any other book to find them.

The most precious wine experiences are those you have to dig a little deeper to find—or to understand. That's where this book comes in. Discover a vibrant wine scene that you never knew existed in Slovakia. Be amazed that the cult wine selection on offer in a Tokyo wine bar far exceeds anything you'll find in Europe. Visit lesser-known corners of Italy where time holds its breath so you can better enjoy the wine—and the view.

Many of the wineries profiled in this book are family affairs where the tour guide, winemaker, and managing director are one and the same person. So, if the owners need to go shopping, or happen to be in a separate country promoting their wine, you may find it impossible to visit. Contact wineries and make a reservation in advance to avoid a wasted journey.

Ultimately, wine provides the perfect justification to travel to some of the world's most idyllic retreats, and to meet and talk with local people who are usually delighted to meet someone who shares their passion. Drink adventurously, let the liquid in the glass inspire your travel, and be amazed where it takes you.

Simon J. Woolf

Note: Information about wineries and their wines was accurate at the time of publication, but can be subject to change.

Right: RAW WINE in Berlin is a celebration of natural, organic, and biodynamic wines (*see page 111*)

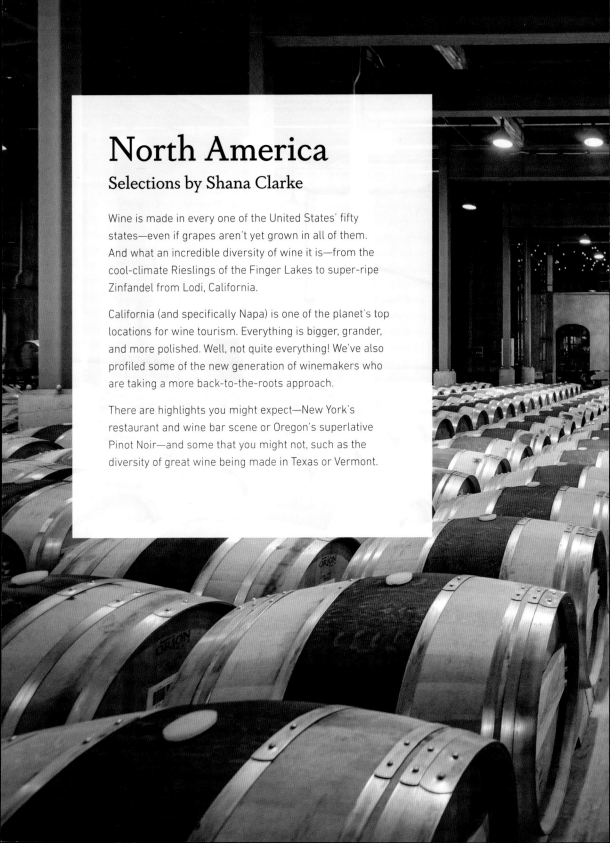

North America
Selections by Shana Clarke

Wine is made in every one of the United States' fifty states—even if grapes aren't yet grown in all of them. And what an incredible diversity of wine it is—from the cool-climate Rieslings of the Finger Lakes to super-ripe Zinfandel from Lodi, California.

California (and specifically Napa) is one of the planet's top locations for wine tourism. Everything is bigger, grander, and more polished. Well, not quite everything! We've also profiled some of the new generation of winemakers who are taking a more back-to-the-roots approach.

There are highlights you might expect—New York's restaurant and wine bar scene or Oregon's superlative Pinot Noir—and some that you might not, such as the diversity of great wine being made in Texas or Vermont.

BETHEL, VERMONT

1 Rethink hybrids courtesy of these winemakers

Hybrids and *vitis labrusca* (American indigenous varieties) are valued for their hardiness but are rarely considered the basis for fine wine. Winemakers Deirdre Heekin and Caleb Barber of La Garagista Farm + Winery aim to change that; their small-production Vermont wines have caught national attention for their elegance and sophistication. Find out how they challenge many preconceived notions about grapes like Frontenac Noir and Marquette.

STOWE, VERMONT

2 Relax with a great glass in Stowe

Enjoy an imaginative selection of artisanal US and European wines with hearty food at Cork Wine Bar & Market. The ambiance invites you to linger. And the market part? There's a small store on the premises that sells the same delicious wines that you'll find on the restaurant list.

HUDSON VALLEY, NEW YORK

3 Taste history at the United States' oldest winery

Unlike other winemaking operations, Brotherhood Winery was able to survive Prohibition by producing sacramental wine for the Church. The cellars established in the winery's formative years are still in use today—explore the underground caves before embarking on a tasting flight in the art-filled tasting room.

1 *Above:* La Garagista Farm + Winery uses organic, permaculture, and biodynamic practices

Visit the wineries of Long Island

4 Channing Daughters Winery

Owner and sculptor Walter Channing's impressive works are on display at this winery—dramatic pieces sit in the middle of the vineyards. Winemaker Christopher Tracy makes the most of the cool Atlantic climate, and vinifies a number of cuvées. Try those produced from northern Italian grape varieties and made as "orange wines" (white grapes fermented with their skins, giving the wine a darker hue).

6 Bedell Cellars

At Bedell Cellars the connection between art and wine runs deep. Check out the tasting room—a converted barn that is adorned with artwork from high-profile artists. Many of these commissioned pieces also make an appearance on the wine labels. Work from artists like Chuck Close and Mickalene Thomas—who painted former First Lady Michelle Obama's official portrait—grace the bottles, turning each wine into a collector's piece.

8 Wölffer Estate Vineyard

This rosé specialist's tasting room is open year-round, and Friday and Saturday evenings in the warmer months are the most memorable. Lay your blanket on the lawn, listen to live music, and enjoy the sunset over the vineyards while sipping one of the winery's choice cuvées.

5 Paumanok Vineyards

Family-run Paumanok Vineyards was one of North Fork's pioneering wineries, and today it's one of the best places to explore Long Island's expressions of Bordeaux blends, Chardonnay, and Chenin Blanc. Built on top of a barrel cellar, the tasting room offers expansive views of the vineyards. In nice weather you can venture out onto the patio to enjoy flights of wine.

7 Sparkling Pointe

In this little piece of Champagne in North Fork, the winery puts a singular focus on traditional method sparkling wine. Whether sitting on the outdoor patio, or under the magnificent chandelier in the whitewashed tasting room, you can absorb the air of luxury and celebration. Don't miss the caviar and sparkling wine pairing.

8

9 Kick back with natty wines in Brooklyn

Wine bar June is a cozy space in Cobble Hill, with an Art-Deco feel to the decor. Manager Lena Mattson stamps her unique bubbly character on the proceedings. Check out the all-natural wine list—it's sizable, frequently changing, and especially strong with Austrian, Italian, and orange wine options. There's a small but well-conceived food offering, too.

10 Drink a drop or two from France

Hugely popular, and deservedly hyped, The Four Horsemen is a tiny wine bar and Michelin-starred restaurant owned by James Murphy (of LCD Soundsystem). The massive natural wine list is overwhelmingly French-focused, with a smattering of excellence from elsewhere. If you want to drink Selosse Champagne, Chateau Rayas Châteauneuf-du-Pape, or back vintages of Yvon Métras, then this is your go-to.

11 Taste wine on an urban waterfront

An industrial neighborhood in a remote part of Brooklyn may seem an unlikely place for wine production, but Red Hook Winery has been crafting some of the state's best wines for more than a decade. Sourcing from vineyards in the Finger Lakes and Long Island, the wine is made at the waterfront-warehouse-turned-winery. Not one but three winemakers contribute to the lineup. Take in views of the Statue of Liberty rising over the East River in the welcoming tasting room.

12 Join a group of natural winemakers

The excitement over natural wine is rising to a fever pitch, thanks largely in part to the RAW WINE fair, one of the world's largest showcases of natural wine producers. The traveling event brings together winemakers from all over the world who follow low-intervention, organic, or biodynamic principles in their viticulture and winemaking. During the two-day fair, you can interact with hundreds of passionate winemakers and taste thousands of wines.

13 Learn from a young master sommelier

When is a wine bar more than a wine bar? When it's Corkbuzz, a self-described wine "studio." Created by Laura Maniec Fiorvanti, one of the world's youngest master sommeliers, this social spot aims to meld fun and education. Get involved in the daily blind tasting flights, wine classes, and events. Most notably, every evening from 9 p.m. until closing, the venue hosts "Champagne Campaign," where all bottles of the French bubbly are half price.

14 Go back to the roots at Racines NY

Restaurant Racines NY aims to bring a little Parisian flair to Manhattan and serves wines "with a story to tell." Current wine director Pascaline Lepeltier presides over a vast list of goodies. France, and specifically the Loire, has the strongest representation; California is also well covered. The list dips its finger into exotic pockets such as Georgia (the republic) and Greece. On Mondays, Racines NY allows you to BYOB with no corkage fee. But with this kind of wine list, why would you?

15 Stock up on small-production, artisanal wines

There is no more iconic wine shop anywhere in Manhattan than Chamber Street Wines. Since its opening in 2001, David Lillie and Jamie Wolff's temple to real, artisanal wine has maintained an amazing diversity and quality in its selections. Attend one of the regular tastings and events with visiting winemakers or authors.

16 Take a deep dive into Riesling

It's no secret that Riesling is the signature variety for the Finger Lakes, and Boundary Breaks in Lodi is deeply devoted to the grape. It creates various expressions—from bone-dry to sweet ice wine—to show off Riesling's versatility. At its off-the-beaten-path tasting room, enjoy unparalleled views of Seneca Lake while sipping the winery's complex, age-worthy wines.

17 Taste the creations of a pioneering immigrant

Along with Dr. Konstantin Frank and Charles Fournier, German emigrant Hermann J. Wiemer was one of the first to realize the winemaking potential of the Finger Lakes region. Seeing the similarities in climate between his native Mosel and this area of upstate New York, he began planting Riesling vines. Today, you can sample single-vineyard Rieslings, along with other cool-climate whites and reds, in Hermann J. Wiemer Vineyard's tasting room in Dundee.

17 *Above:* Hermann J. Wiemer Vineyard can be found on the western slopes of Seneca Lake

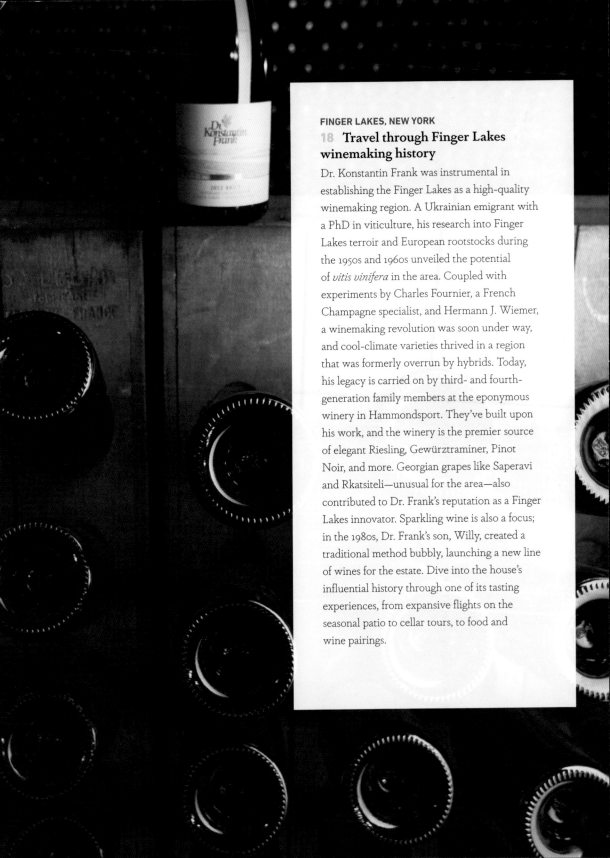

18 Travel through Finger Lakes winemaking history

Dr. Konstantin Frank was instrumental in establishing the Finger Lakes as a high-quality winemaking region. A Ukrainian emigrant with a PhD in viticulture, his research into Finger Lakes terroir and European rootstocks during the 1950s and 1960s unveiled the potential of *vitis vinifera* in the area. Coupled with experiments by Charles Fournier, a French Champagne specialist, and Hermann J. Wiemer, a winemaking revolution was soon under way, and cool-climate varieties thrived in a region that was formerly overrun by hybrids. Today, his legacy is carried on by third- and fourth-generation family members at the eponymous winery in Hammondsport. They've built upon his work, and the winery is the premier source of elegant Riesling, Gewürztraminer, Pinot Noir, and more. Georgian grapes like Saperavi and Rkatsiteli—unusual for the area—also contributed to Dr. Frank's reputation as a Finger Lakes innovator. Sparkling wine is also a focus; in the 1980s, Dr. Frank's son, Willy, created a traditional method bubbly, launching a new line of wines for the estate. Dive into the house's influential history through one of its tasting experiences, from expansive flights on the seasonal patio to cellar tours, to food and wine pairings.

FINGER LAKES, NEW YORK

19 Meet the collaborators of an inauguration day wine

A joint effort from three different wineries—Fox Run Vineyards, Anthony Road Wine Company, and Red Newt Cellars—the TIERCE Riesling Release Party is one of the most highly anticipated of the year. Look out for the party that rotates among the three estates and is the first opportunity for fans to get their hands on this sought-after wine. It's not just legendary in the Finger Lakes; the 2010 vintage was poured at the 2013 Presidential inauguration luncheon.

FINGER LAKES, NEW YORK

20 Pair wine with culinary know-how

While it doesn't take much to appreciate a good glass of wine, a little bit of education can enhance the enjoyment. Attend New York Kitchen's classes and events, such as Wine 101 and "how to pair" sessions, which elevate wine to the next level. For a less-formal approach, the New York Kitchen's tasting room encourages sampling flights of local wine, beer, and spirits.

FINGER LAKES, NEW YORK

21 Tour a gold-certified sustainable winery

Winemakers Nancy Irelan and Mike Schnelle of Red Tail Ridge aren't afraid to push boundaries. Their winery was the first in New York State to be awarded Leadership in Energy and Environmental Design's (LEED's) gold certification for its sustainable and environmental conservation operations, such as the use of geothermal energy, water management, and use of recycled materials in the building's construction. The duo constantly experiment in both the vineyards and in the cellar. Working with grapes like Teroldego and Dornfelder, they aim to unlock the region's potential for growing grapes beyond what's currently cultivated. They play with skin ferments and native yeasts during vinification and study various traditional sparkling production methods. Seek out the small-lot releases of sparkling Teroldego or a Riesling pét-nat (Pétillant Naturel).

FINGER LAKES, NEW YORK

22 Chow down on gourmet hot dogs and top-notch wines

A roadside hot dog stand may seem an unlikely place to find grand cru Burgundy, but this highbrow-lowbrow approach to dining is what makes F.L.X. Wienery unique. Master sommelier Christopher Bates—who pulls double duty as a winemaker at his Element Winery—pairs gourmet burgers, dogs, and fries with an extensive wine list that wouldn't be out of place at a white-tablecloth restaurant. A bonus: local wines don't get charged a corkage fee! F.L.X. Wienery in Dundee has spawned a mini-empire in the region: in addition to F.L.X. Table, a fine-dining, tasting-menu concept, and F.L.X. Fry Bird, a fried chicken joint, Bates operates a tasting room featuring sixty local wines, as well as a catering company. Come with a healthy appetite and palate.

FINGER LAKES, NEW YORK

23 Travel the Seneca Lake Wine Trail

Wineries encircle all of the Finger Lakes' major bodies of water, but the highest concentration is the thirty members of the Seneca Lake Wine Trail. Spend a day visiting these tasting rooms and don't miss the east side, which is nicknamed "the banana belt," due to the climate's proclivity to run a few degrees warmer than elsewhere in the region. Whether it's folklore or proven fact, the wine culture that has developed over the years is undeniable.

23 *Above:* Thirty winery members make up the Seneca Lake Wine Trail

TEXAS

Dive deep into the world of Texas wine at these four locations

24 William Chris Vineyards

When a winegrower with thirty years' experience and an up-and-coming winemaker joined forces, Texas wine would never be the same. Sourcing from both the High Plains and Texas Hill Country, the duo at William Chris Vineyards offers a range from varietal bottlings to a standout pét-nat. They were the first to own Galileo tanks—spherical concrete tanks—in the United States. Sip their wines at the vineyard's serene farmhouse.

26 Cabernet Grill

To taste the depth and breadth of what the Texas wine industry has to offer, head to Fredericksburg's Cabernet Grill, with its all-Texas wine list. Curated selections feature the best of nearly every winery in the state. From sparkling wines to dessert options, there's a wine for every course. Thoughtfully created flights give diners the chance to compare and contrast varieties.

25 Duchman Family Winery

Texas Hill Country may have more in common with the rolling hills of Tuscany than one might think, and there's no better place to explore the connection than at Duchman Family Winery. It dabbles in grapes from all over Italy: Sangiovese, Dolcetto, and Vermentino. Taste a bit of Texan dolce vita at the winery's Tuscan villa-inspired tasting room.

25

27 Pedernales Cellars

Like six degrees of separation, many of Texas's winemakers can trace their training back to David Kuhlken at Pedernales Cellars. After taking over the winery from their parents in 2005, David and his sister, Julie, turned the grape-growing operation into a full-fledged winery. Whether cutting their teeth on Albariño or learning the nuances of Tempranillo, members of the Texas wine community honed their craft under the tutelage of David. Soak in beautiful views at the Pedernales tasting room while sampling their wines.

MADISON, VIRGINIA

28 See why Virginia is for (wine) lovers

One of the best places to discover the burgeoning Virginia wine scene is at Early Mountain Vineyards. Founded by Jean Case and her husband, former AOL CEO and chairman Steve Case, in 2010, the winery is on a mission to bring prominence to the state's viticulture. Sidle up to the tasting bar and try Cabernet Franc, Petit Manseng, and a pét-nat rosé.

DENVER, COLORADO

29 Drink canned wine

The Infinite Monkey Theorem is an urban winery that defies nearly all winemaking conventions. One of the pioneers of Colorado winemaking, and a recent arrival to the Texas scene (in Austin), it not only looks to newer regions for grapes, but it was one of the leaders in canned wines. Stop by one of the "wine taprooms" for a taste of its innovations.

WALLA WALLA, WASHINGTON

30 Get a wine education in this old schoolhouse

If you're looking to learn more about Washington State wines, there's no better place than L'Ecole No. 41's tasting room. The converted 1915 schoolhouse retains its classroom charm—old chalkboards and a children's mural adorn the walls—but the lessons here focus on grapes and vines. As the third-oldest winery in the state, L'Ecole No. 41 has a lot to teach you about Cabernet Sauvignon, Syrah, and Chardonnay.

WALLA WALLA, WASHINGTON

31 Walk and sip your way through this town center

The quaint town of Walla Walla has become an epicenter of wine tourism in Washington State—the downtown area boasts around forty tasting rooms. Amble down Main Street and sample cuvées from some of the state's top producers, such as Rotie Cellars and nearby Seven Hills Winery and Charles Smith Wines.

WALLA WALLA, WASHINGTON

32 Try top Syrah from a former New York sommelier

Master sommelier Greg Harrington was so convinced by Syrah's potential in Washington State that he gave up New York City life to move across the country and make wine. Today, you can try the Gramercy Cellars' wines—which now include varieties such as Grenache and Cabernet Sauvignon—in the Walla Walla tasting room.

32 *Above:* Gramercy Cellars makes only 8,000 cases of wine a year

RED MOUNTAIN, WASHINGTON

33 Visit a French château in a biodynamic vineyard

When Champagne native Ann-Marie Liégeois married Washington resident Tom Hedges in 1976, neither could have imagined that their union would give birth to one of Washington State's most revered wineries, Hedges Family Estate. Today, their children also work in the business: daughter Sarah is head winemaker, and son Chris is general manager. In 2008, the winery converted to biodynamic farming and became one of the few Demeter-certified Biodynamic establishments in the country. Upon your visit, you'll notice that the estate's French roots run deep: the château-inspired winery and tasting room, located in the middle of vineyards, converts the grounds into a parcel of French countryside.

WOODINVILLE, WASHINGTON

34 Drink blends in an old beer brewery

After twenty-five years of producing luscious Bordeaux blends, DeLille Cellars moved its ever-growing operation to an old brewery—now a sleek new facility—in Woodinville. Here, you'll find a three-floor tasting room that offers various wine flights, tours, and tasting experiences. The rooftop deck has firepits and a fireplace area, beckoning drinkers year-round.

SEATTLE, WASHINGTON

35 Celebrate Washington State wines

The four-day Taste Washington extravaganza brings wine and food purveyors throughout Washington State to Seattle for a celebration of all things in the Pacific Northwest. Seminars about winemaking and wine styles, tastings, and other events fill the packed calendar. During the various evening events, taste some of the most exclusive wines from winemakers' cellars.

35 *Above:* More than 200 wineries can be found at Taste Washington

36 Meet the world's first Certified B Corp winery

Started by four veterans of the Oregon wine industry, A to Z Wineworks was created with the goal of creating high-quality, high-value wines. However, behind the fun and accessible label lies a more serious mission: in 2014, A to Z was the first winery in the world to become Certified B Corp. Businesses that achieve this recognition strive to create social change through their business practices, taking into account the three tenets of sustainability: people, planet, and profit. Both A to Z and its sibling winery, REX HILL, carry the Certified B Corp seal. Learn more about their practices—and taste top-tier Willamette Valley Pinot Noir, Chardonnay, and sparkling wine—at REX HILL's newly renovated tasting room.

37 Sample coveted Pinot Noirs

Coveted by the sommelier community, Bergström Wines has become a compass point for Oregon Pinot Noir and Chardonnay. Oregon-born, Burgundy-trained winemaker Josh Bergström came home to his family's burgeoning winery in 1999 and worked alongside his parents to turn their small vineyards into a full-fledged winemaking operation. Taste Bergström's award-winning wines at the winery's tasting room or book an appointment to tour the vineyards.

38 Explore an old farmhouse while tasting Pinot Noir

At Dominio IV's converted farmhouse, the connection between wine and agriculture becomes crystal clear. The one-hundred-year-old structure, now converted into a tasting room and event space, is a bucolic setting for tasting the winery's sustainably grown Pinot Noir, Tempranillo, and Syrah. Wander the fields with a glass of wine in hand or settle in with a bottle of wine on the wraparound porch.

WILLAMETTE VALLEY, OREGON
39 Wander in lavender fields

At King Estate Winery, you can have your Pinot two ways: red and white. The Pinot Noir and Pinot Gris specialists carefully cultivate the grapes as part of the 1,033 acre (418 ha), Demeter-certified Biodynamic property. While wine is the focus, there's much to explore: fruit orchards, gardens, even a lavender field. Book a reservation at the on-site restaurant, where the land's bounty makes its way to the table.

WILLAMETTE VALLEY, OREGON
40 Indulge in three days of Pinot Noir

For Pinot Noir lovers, the three-day-long International Pinot Noir Celebration is the ultimate wine experience. Mingle with professionals and aficionados from all over the world and meet the winemakers behind some of the most renowned labels. You'll also get the opportunity to tour some of Oregon's best Pinot Noir vineyards, and numerous tasting events abound. More than seventy wineries showcase their craft over the weekend.

WILLAMETTE VALLEY, OREGON
41 See the homestead of Oregon Pinot

The Eyrie Vineyards is a winery of firsts: founder David Lett was the first to plant Pinot Noir in Willamette Valley and the first to plant Pinot Gris in the United States. His plantings set off a revolution that have reverberated throughout the country. Tour the cellars and see where the Pinot story began.

WILLAMETTE VALLEY, OREGON
42 Bid on some of Oregon's best Pinots

Willamette Valley makes top-notch Pinots, but to get your hands on some ultra-exclusive bottles, the annual Pinot Noir Auction should be at the top of your list. Every year, each participating winery—about ninety in all—crafts a special wine, which will then be auctioned off to top bidders. Don't miss the event, which includes tastings, seminars, and parties, all celebrating the popular grape.

39 *Opposite:* King Estate Winery produces 350,000 cases of wine annually

43 Meet the artist making his own amphorae

Many winemakers may dream of owning custom barrels for their cellars, but Andrew Beckham of Beckham Estate Vineyard made this vision a reality. Drawing upon his experience as a potter, Beckham started making bespoke amphora, modeled after traditional Georgian fermentation vessels (*qvevri*). Liking the results, he experimented with various sizes and shapes. These large-scale couture tanks help Beckham craft his ideal style of wine. His creations have quickly caught on within the winemaking community; other low-intervention or natural winemakers have requested vessels for themselves. An appointment at the winery not only encompasses a tour of the vineyard and a wine tasting, but you can also view Beckham's extensive gallery of ceramics.

44 Go "rogue" with a visit to Oregon's southern half

In southwestern Oregon's Rogue Valley, a new breed of winemakers is providing an interesting counterpoint to the well-known Willamette Valley. While the northern appellation draws strong comparisons to Burgundy, Leah Jørgensen, winemaker at her eponymous winery, looks to the Loire for inspiration. Discover her Cabernet Franc and the rare and delicious Blanc de Cabernet Franc.

45 Taste explosively good wines from volcanic terroir

Grape growing is challenging at Obsidian Ridge; the high-elevation, volcanic-soil vineyards challenge winemakers on a regular basis. However, this unique terroir creates some of the most expressive Cabernets in the region. Obsidian Ridge also stands out with its use of Tokaj oak barrels, produced at its proprietary cooperage in Hungary.

43 *Above:* Beckham Estate Vineyard's Andrew Beckham makes bespoke amphora pots

ANDERSON VALLEY, CALIFORNIA

46 Play with dogs while sipping Pinot

Have a penchant for pooches? Then this is the place for you. The winery dogs that nuzzle against your legs as you sit on the porch of Witching Stick Wines' tasting room seem eager to taste the elegant Chardonnay and Pinot Noirs that sit in the glass. The unassuming winery obtains fruit from some of the best sites in Anderson Valley, but the relaxed setting belies the serious winemaking that goes into these finely finessed wines.

46 *Above:* Witching Stick Wines is located in downtown Philo

ANDERSON VALLEY, CALIFORNIA

47 Dine at a restaurant favored by winemakers

Chef Janelle Weaver's restaurant, The Bewildered Pig, with its seasonally inspired menus, straddles the line between fine dining and neighborhood hangout. It's not unusual to find area winemakers gathered together at tables and drinking bottles from her well-curated wine list. You'll find the staff are equally passionate about wine and might actually be winemakers-in-training themselves.

ANDERSON VALLEY, CALIFORNIA

48 Drink Pinot two ways

Discover the incredible lineup of wines that comes from just two grapes: Pinot Noir and Pinot Gris. Lichen Estate specializes in sparkling wines modeled after the great bottles of Champagne, but the still wines also exhibit an elegance and purity that linger in the mind. Be sure to try the white Pinot Noir, a crystalline version of the traditional red wine.

ANDERSON VALLEY, CALIFORNIA

49 Wine, dine, and sleep in this complex

Sleepy Anderson Valley is becoming the new "it" region for cool-climate expressions of Pinot Gris, Chardonnay, Pinot Noir, and Syrah. At the Madrones complex, a hybrid hotel-dining–tasting room complex, explore what's causing so much buzz. Smith Story Wine Cellars, run by husband and wife Eric and Alison, features wines from both Anderson Valley and Sonoma, while Drew Family Cellars focuses on cool-climate expressions of Pinot Noir. It's also here that Long Meadow Ranch opted for its first foray out of Napa; its tasting room doubles as an event space for wine-savvy patrons. Spend a night in one of the Madrones' guest rooms, grab lunch or dinner at the on-site restaurant, and revel in the potential of this laid-back American Viticultural Area (AVA).

ANDERSON VALLEY, CALIFORNIA

50 Pair homemade wine and cheese

Navarro Vineyards paved the way for Anderson Valley winemakers, and today, Sarah Cahn Bennett, the daughter of Navarro's founders, is forging a new path in the region. Pennyroyal Farm is a dairy, winery, and farm that works symbiotically to produce sustainable offerings. The sheep—whose milk is used for cheese production—roam the vineyards and eat troublesome weeds. Their manure, along with the dairy cows', fertilizes the fields. Soil compost from the nearby farm also provides nutrients to the vineyards, and cover crops eliminate the need for tilling soil. All of these edibles and potables are available at Pennyroyal's tasting room. Pair wine flights with a cheese board, or opt for a full lunch made with ingredients direct from the farm.

51 Discover new cuvées from some old vines

Many winemakers pay keen attention to terroir when selecting vineyards, but for Morgan Twain-Peterson and Chris Cottrell of Bedrock Wine Co., terroir is only half the story. The duo intentionally seeks out old vines throughout California with the goal of revitalizing sites. As champions of old-vine Zinfandel, Carignan, Mourvedre, Sémillon, and more, Twain-Peterson (son of famed Ravenswood Winery winemaker Joel Peterson) and Cottrell look to preserve a piece of the past through their innovative, award-winning bottlings. The label started as a passion project for Twain-Peterson in 2007. Initially working out of a converted chicken coop, he moved production to another facility, and it continued to flourish. Twain-Peterson also holds the unique Master of Wine title, of which there are only 396 in the world (at the time of writing). Arrange a tasting at the historic General Joseph Hooker House.

SONOMA, CALIFORNIA

52 Eat, shop, and drink at an artisanal complex

Industrial design is juxtaposed against the sunny California sky at outdoor market complex The Barlow. Home to a number of craftsmen, eateries, and artists, The Barlow is also the base for some of Sonoma's most buzzed-about wineries. Kosta Browne produces its highly allocated wines at a facility located within the complex, and in 2018, opened The Gallery, its tasting experience for wine club members. At the more democratic Pax Mahle Wines tasting room, sip on flights from this Syrah specialist in the wood-paneled space. Other up-and-coming winemakers, such as Martha Stoumen, often work out of Pax's winery and use the public-facing space for meetings and tastings.

SONOMA, CALIFORNIA

53 Taste dueling wines from this duo

A love for Italian varieties—and each other—is at the core of Ryme Cellars, created by husband-and-wife team Ryan and Megan Glaab. The pair find new expressions of grapes like Aglianico in California terroir, and their playful take on Vermentino is much anticipated in each vintage: purchase their "his" and "hers" versions, done with different vinification techniques.

SONOMA, CALIFORNIA

54 Dance the day away

Immerse yourself in good music, top wine, and great vibes at the family-friendly Huichica Music Festival! Bring a blanket, grab a glass of wine, and chill out to a lineup of bands at Gundlach Bundschu Winery's amphitheater, or sway to the music inside the Old Redwood Barn.

SONOMA, CALIFORNIA

55 Get crafty while drinking

In 2016, Katie Bundschu, sixth-generation legacy of Gundlach Bundschu, created her own project, Abbot's Passage. She sources her grapes from overlooked vineyard sites in Sonoma, while her tasting room also serves as a retail store and a "maker's workshop." Drop in to try the exquisite wine collection.

SONOMA, CALIFORNIA
56 Pretend you're in a movie

Francis Ford Coppola made his name in the movies, but his eponymous Sonoma winery is no less cinematic. A movie gallery displays memorabilia from the director's numerous films, including the automobile from the film *Tucker: The Man and His Dream*. A number of touring experiences—from a guided walk through the facilities to a scavenger hunt—showcase the many facets of the estate. After working up an appetite, grab one of the wood-fired specialties at Rustic, the on-site restaurant. Be sure to bring the kids, as family is a big part of the experience. Swimming in the large pool or playing bocce on the court is a kid-friendly way to pass the afternoon.

SONOMA (AND PASO ROBLES), CALIFORNIA
57 Sample small-production wines

Stemming from the term for small-lot winemakers in Bordeaux who refused to follow the rules, the Garagiste Wine Festival honors and promotes California producers—all of whom make fewer than 1,500 cases a year. At this traveling event, which stops in several regions throughout the year, sample wines from these artisan winemakers in a festive and pretension-free atmosphere.

SONOMA, CALIFORNIA
58 Indulge in local wines and s'mores

As an idyllic Sonoma resort, the Farmhouse Inn could tempt you with its welcoming luxury, soothing spa treatments, and firepit (ideal for after-dinner s'mores) alone. However, this retreat also houses a delectable farm-to-table restaurant with an outstanding wine list. Pore over the extensive, well-curated local wine offerings and sip some of California's best bottles.

SONOMA, CALIFORNIA

59 Try some natural wine from California

While Ruth is not an actual person, she embodies the spirit Evan Lewandowski wants to express in his Ruth Lewandowski Wines. His winemaking trajectory is fairly unusual; after stints making wine around the world, he returned to Salt Lake City to start a winery, and then moved it to Healdsburg in California. Be sure to taste his fantastic skin-fermented Cortese or Arneis.

WEST SONOMA COAST, CALIFORNIA

60 Watch the fog lift at this Pinot Noir specialist

Just 3 mi (4.8 km) away from the Pacific Ocean, and at 1,500 ft (457 m) in elevation, Hirsch Vineyards truly exemplifies the extreme Sonoma Coast. David Hirsch started off by selling his grapes to some of Sonoma's most revered wineries, but in 2002, he built his own winery. He and his daughter, Jasmine, make stunning single-vineyard Pinot Noirs and Chardonnays from the fog-enshrouded vineyards along the craggy coast. Although the treacherous, winding roads to the vineyards are inaccessible to most people, the Hirsches recently opened a tasting room in Healdsburg, so you can enjoy their wines, sans four-wheel drive.

Above: The family-owned Farmhouse Inn sits in the heart of the Russian River Valley

WEST SONOMA COAST, CALIFORNIA

61   Sleep and sip in this oceanside retreat

Experience the perfect respite from Sonoma Coast wine country travels at the sleek, modern Timber Cove Resort. Oceanside walking trails speak to the outdoorsy lifestyle of the area, but the restaurant's extensive, locally focused wine list and lobby bar pay homage to the flourishing wine industry. Bring a glass up to your private balcony and listen to the waves while sipping your nightcap.

WEST SONOMA COAST, CALIFORNIA

62   Take in sweeping views

The tiny Fort Ross-Seaview is an AVA and home to one of the most scenic wineries on the far Sonoma Coast. At Fort Ross Vineyard & Winery, grab a seat on the patio overlooking the expansive landscape, and taste through wine flights. Pinot Noir and Chardonnay are a focus, but the winery was also one of the first to plant Pinotage—a nod to the owners' South African heritage—in the United States.

WEST SONOMA COAST, CALIFORNIA

63   Scale new heights on the West Sonoma Coast

High on a hilltop on the extreme Sonoma Coast sits Peay Vineyards. Just 4 mi (6.5 km) away from the Pacific Ocean, and constantly encased in fog, the hard-to-access site produces some of the region's most expressive Pinot Noir, Syrah, Viognier, and Chardonnay. The cold ocean winds and fog mean grapes slowly ripen, developing complex flavors and great acidity. Spend an afternoon at one of its spring open days to taste the wines.

61 *Above:* Timber Cove Resort perches on the edge of a cliff above the Pacific Ocean

NAPA, CALIFORNIA

64 Saddle up for a wine-tasting experience

See how horses and vines peacefully coexist at this pastoral Napa estate. Tamber Bey Vineyards not only produces Bordeaux- and Burgundy-inspired wines, the property is also home to an equestrian training facility and horse sanctuary. Watch the animals roam the ranch as you taste your way through Tamber Bey's cuvées.

NAPA, CALIFORNIA

65 Meet a Napa (and Cabernet) trailblazer

Cathy Corison has long defied convention; she has steadfastly hung on to her style of Cabernet, a ripe yet restrained version that was valued by winemakers decades ago. Although the pendulum has swung in multiple directions over the years—particularly toward bolder, denser Cabs—her style has always remained a classic. After thirty-plus years, she's still receiving awards and accolades. Visit her Napa winery and the famous Kronos Vineyard (the source of some of her most scarce and thus most sought-after bottles), which yawns expansively toward the horizon.

64 *Above:* Tamber Bey Vineyards is home to the largest horse rescue organization in Napa

NAPA, CALIFORNIA

66 See where high design meets sustainability

Cabernet specialist Silver Oak not only shows the influence of Napa and Sonoma terroir in its award-winning wines, it became the first US winery to own an American oak cooperage (in 2015). Innovation does not end in the cellar; its LEED's platinum-certified winery makes Silver Oak a leader in sustainable engineering, as you'll discover when you visit its tasting room.

NAPA, CALIFORNIA

67 Dine on local Napa cuisine

Long Meadow Ranch's popular restaurant, Farmstead, is the true definition of farm to table. Most of the ingredients in the dishes come directly from Long Meadow Ranch's farm, while the wine list is a compilation of offerings from the ranch's various vineyards. Enjoy drinks and snacks on the lively patio or pass around plates and bottles in the homey indoor space.

NAPA, CALIFORNIA

68 Discover beautiful old vines

Much of California's Chardonnay revolution can be traced back to Stony Hill Vineyard's mountainous roots: the first vines of the famous white variety in Napa were planted in 1948 on a converted goat farm on the eastern side of the Mayacamas Mountains. One of the key traits of Stony Hill's Chardonnays are their ability to age; often, they reveal their full expression after several years in the bottle. Riesling and Gewürztraminer also build on the winery's reputation for elegant, complex white wines. You'll forget the harrowing drive up to the winery once you settle onto the patio with its mountain views and sip on these exquisite wines.

NAPA, CALIFORNIA (AND NEW YORK, TEXAS, AND SINGAPORE)

69 Enhance your wine knowledge

There's no better place to learn about wine than in the epicenter of US wine country. While the Culinary Institute of America turns out world-renowned chefs and wine professionals, the school welcomes enthusiasts and aficionados in its recreational classes. From pairings and regional comparisons to deep dives into wine styles, there are numerous ways to deepen your wine knowledge.

NAPA, CALIFORNIA

70 Taste the new Napa in downtown Napa

Amid the marquee wineries in Napa, the Outland tasting room spotlights under-the-radar producers directing the next wave of California wine. It's a collaborative tasting space, where you can try POE's Burgundy- and Champagne-inspired bottles; Forlorn Hope's minimal-intervention Barbera, Picpoul, and Pinot Gris; and Farella Vineyard, one of the first Coombsville AVA-designate Cabernets. Cheers!

68 *Above:* Stony Hill Vineyard can be found on the northeast slope of Spring Mountain

NAPA, CALIFORNIA

71 Indulge in boutique wines from a legend

Frolic with the numerous winery dogs or explore the gardens at Julie Johnson's Tres Sabores winery. Johnson's wine influence can also be felt at Frog's Leap winery and the nonprofit organization Women for WineSense—both of which she was a cofounder. But it's at Tres Sabores, her certified organic boutique winery, that this Cabernet and Zinfandel specialist's personality really comes through.

NAPA, CALIFORNIA

72 Taste a personal project from a leading Napa winemaker

What started as a side project for Larkmead's winemaker Dan Petroski has become one of California's most sought-after labels. Inspired by his family's Italian roots, the crisp, low-intervention white wines of his Massican label became a counterpoint to Petroski's Cabernet winemaking. Look for his wines in local restaurants.

72 *Above:* Dan Petroski's Massican wines can be found in local restaurants

NAPA, CALIFORNIA

73 Fall asleep in wine country

As one of Napa's preeminent luxury hotels, the Auberge du Soleil experience wouldn't be complete without a meal at its Michelin-starred restaurant. Enjoy quintessential wine-country cuisine on the scenic outdoor patio, accompanied by a wine from the 15,000-bottle cellar.

NAPA, CALIFORNIA

74 Revel in a three-Michelin-starred meal

Three-Michelin-starred The Restaurant at Meadowood is the culinary jewel of this luxury resort. Let the local ingredients shine with a pairing from the extensive and well-curated wine list. For a less formal experience, sip on a refreshing local cuvée while sitting poolside. A plethora of activities on the grounds, from golf to hiking, is sure to work up a thirst.

NAPA, CALIFORNIA

75 Open bottles in Napa

Charter Oak, chef Christopher Kostow's slightly more casual spin-off from The Restaurant at Meadowood, emphasizes the importance of community. Despite the extensive bottle list, the restaurant waives the corkage fee for your first bottle of wine brought in as a nod to Napa's wine-centric residents.

NAPA, CALIFORNIA

76 Tour the Golden Road Part I

Set out on the Silverado Trail, which is paved in "winery gold"—many of Napa Valley's most exclusive wineries reside along this two-lane road linking Napa and Calistoga. Stag's Leap Wine Cellars, Joseph Phelps, Duckhorn Vineyards, and Clos Du Val are just a few of the marquee names you'll find along this thoroughfare.

NAPA, CALIFORNIA
77 Laugh yourself silly in a winery

Napa's oldest winery, established in 1861, doesn't take itself too seriously. At Charles Krug's monthly comedy nights, laugh along with the area's funniest comics while drinking some of the estate's choice cuvées. In warmer months, outdoor events such as live concerts make the winery an entertainment destination in wine country.

NAPA, CALIFORNIA
78 Tour the Golden Road Part II

California's *other* star-lined street, Highway 29, is a main route through seven AVAs in Napa County. Along the journey you'll encounter tasting room after tasting room from some of California's most recognized names in wine, such as Robert Mondavi Winery, Inglenook, Heitz Cellar, and Twomey.

77 *Above:* Charles Krug is the oldest winery in Napa

NAPA, CALIFORNIA

79 Drink wine for a good cause

Started in 1981 by several community-minded wineries, Auction Napa Valley is a philanthropic four-day event that benefits local nonprofit organizations. A range of events—from dinners to barrel tastings, to the grand auction—bring together wine lovers and professionals alike. Bid on exclusive lots of wine from some of Napa's winemaking luminaries.

NAPA, CALIFORNIA

80 Become a master blender

Dreams of becoming a master blender can come true at Hess Collection's blending sessions. You'll learn about the craft from the experts, then blend and sip your way to your ideal cuvée. Afterward, you can design a label for your wine, which can result in a completely bespoke bottle.

NAPA, CALIFORNIA

81   Fuel up with wine

Roll up to this converted 1930s-era gas station and fill 'er up not with gas, but with wine. Tank Garage Winery's tasting room—provocatively dubbed the "Lubrication Bar"—features easygoing cuvées from Napa and beyond. The tongue-in-cheek vibe extends to the bottles, with retro, graphic labels.

NAPA, CALIFORNIA

82   Drink wine in a cave

To see Hourglass's winery and tasting room, you need to go to the mountainside, literally—the estate created a cave *inside* a mountain. Wander the various rooms, with design touches such as fur throws and chandeliers, through one of the most unique wineries in Napa.

81   *Above:* Tank Garage Winery offers various group tastings

NAPA, CALIFORNIA
83 Swill wine in an outdoor cabana

Officially established as a bonded winery in 1933, Louis M. Martini became one of Napa's first wineries post-Prohibition, and an influential estate for the region. As an early adaptor of innovations such as controlled fermentation and the use of wine machines to fight frost, the Martini family is regarded as an industry leader. In 2019, the seminal winery received a multimillion-dollar makeover and reestablished its place as Napa royalty. The spacious property boasts multiple tasting rooms, and you can take your pick of experiences from venue tours to seated library tastings. Martini Park, a large outdoor space, is dotted with cabanas for private parties, an outdoor patio, and a culinary pavilion.

NAPA, CALIFORNIA
84 Hang like a rock star

Cliff Lede Vineyards is a little bit (wine) country, a little bit rock 'n' roll. The estate vineyards are named after the founder's favorite rock songs, and the Backstage Tasting Lounge is like a green room for VIPs. Make a reservation to taste flights of the limited-production wines and view the rotating art collection.

NAPA, CALIFORNIA
85 Pop a cork in a "château"

The French château-style winery is an impressive setting for a tasting of Domaine Carneros's wines. It was founded by the Champagne Taittinger family, and sparkling wine is a focus here. Pair your flight with caviar or cheese and take in the manicured grounds from a terrace table, or revel in the elegance of the indoor salon.

NAPA, CALIFORNIA

86 Visit the estate of an early female winemaker

Freemark Abbey is considered one of Napa's most historical wineries, but it was also an estate ahead of its time. In 1886, widow Josephine Tychson built a cellar and became one of the first officially recognized female winemakers in California. After World War II, it opened a "sampling room," a precursor to the modern tasting room. Try some of the well-crafted Cabernets and Chardonnays.

NAPA, CALIFORNIA

87 Splash out at a gastronomic temple

If you want to splurge, the sky's the limit at the three-Michelin-starred The French Laundry. Thomas Keller's cuisine needs no introduction, and the wine program is every bit its equal. This is a list that sticks mostly to the classics, although there are eclectic pockets here and there. Château Margaux 1961, anyone?

LODI, CALIFORNIA

88 Behold the world's oldest Cinsault vines

Old-vine wines are revered for their concentrated, complex fruit, but Bechthold Vineyard takes this to a new level. Planted in 1886, the Cinsault that thrives in the vineyard is considered to be some of the oldest in the world. Whether used as a blending grape or as a stand-alone bottling, fruit from this site is used by some of the country's best winemakers.

LODI, CALIFORNIA

89 Travel the Lodi Wine Trail

Old-vine Zinfandel is the calling card for this California wine region, and today, about eighty wineries thrive in the AVA. Step back in time as you visit some of these historic vineyards along the Lodi Wine Trail or stroll through downtown Lodi and sip some choice bottles in the urban tasting rooms.

BERKELEY AND OAKLAND, CALIFORNIA

90 Drink wine in urban warehouses

The Bay Area's wine scene mixes urban edginess with California's penchant for quality winemaking. Boutique winemakers, many following a low-intervention philosophy, have set up shop across the water from San Francisco. Donkey and Goat's and Broc Cellars' presence on Fifth Street in Berkeley paved the way for a number of other producers. Fanning out from this epicenter are protégé labels such as Blue Ox Wine Co. and Windchaser Wine Co. Over in Oakland, labels like Dashe Cellars and Rosenblum Cellars make up part of the city's collective of wineries. One-man operations like Prima Materia and family-run Côte West are also making names for themselves with their handcrafted, small-production offerings. Spend an afternoon walking through the different wine neighborhoods and exploring the next generation of California wine.

90 *Above:* Housed in an old ink factory, Donkey and Goat is a winery, retail store, and tasting room

SAN FRANCISCO, CALIFORNIA

91   Sample wines made from the United States' heritage grape

A celebration of what's considered to be the United States' heritage grape, the Zinfandel Experience brings together producers from all over to exhibit their Zins. Seminars educate about the history of the grape, winemaking considerations, and Zinfandel's place on a global scale. You can partake in a dinner, auction, and a Grand Tasting, which feature wineries' best offerings at this three-day event.

SAN FRANCISCO, CALIFORNIA

92   Drink from the tap

Jamber Wine Pub is adamantly a pub and not a bar. All the wines are served on tap (nothing in a bottle) and locally sourced in California. Choose from more than twenty choices, where the concept is not only ethically switched on, but also delicious. Local craft beers are also on tap, and the menu offers comfort food to soak it all up.

SAN FRANCISCO, CALIFORNIA

93   Go wine clubbing

Lounge in the spacious, clubby comfort of bar and restaurant The Hidden Vine and enjoy wines from just about every corner of the globe. The strongest selections are from California and France, but there are nice, eclectic options from Slovenia, Portugal, and Greece.

CARMEL-BY-THE-SEA, CALIFORNIA

94   Surf and then sip wine

Quaint oceanside village Carmel-by-the-Sea is a showcase for Monterey's wineries. Nearly twenty tasting rooms from estates across the vast region cluster nearby on an easy-to-walk wine trail. Spend the morning surfing or swimming at Carmel Beach, then wander through the town—known for its hidden courtyards—and sip wine at places like Albatross Ridge, Wrath, and Silvestri Vineyards.

91 *Above:* The Zinfandel Experience takes place at three San Francisco locations

TOP 3

SANTA LUCIA HIGHLANDS, CALIFORNIA

Discover three of the best Santa Lucia Highlands wineries

95 Hahn Family Wines

Monterey County has long been considered "the salad bowl" of the nation, but Hahn Family Wines saw potential for more than just produce. After several successful vintages, the family lobbied for the creation of the Santa Lucia Highlands (SLH) AVA. Taste its high-quality Pinot Noirs and Chardonnays at the SLH tasting room.

96 McIntyre Vineyards

Great wine isn't the only goal for winemaker Steve McIntyre of McIntyre Vineyards; sustainability in all aspects of business is a top priority. In 2008, he cofounded the SIP Certified program (Sustainability in Practice), which focuses on the "three Ps": people, planet, and profit. You'll find the commitment to better practices shines through in the Chardonnays and Pinot Noirs.

97 Double L Estate

Morgan Winery's Double L Estate vineyard is one of the leading sites in the Santa Lucia Highlands AVA. It's the first—and only—certified organic vineyard in the region. Planted in 1997—before SLH was even recognized as an AVA—the Pinot Noirs and Chardonnays from the vineyard are some of the most coveted in the area, so be sure to try some.

95

CENTRAL COAST, CALIFORNIA
98 Reenact scenes from *Sideways*

The influence of movie *Sideways* on Merlot may have finally waned, but The Hitching Post II's supporting role has made it a popular stop for wine country diners. Barbecue dominates the food offerings, and local wines round out the beverage list. In addition to highlighting Santa Barbara wineries, the restaurant features its own proprietary cuvées.

CENTRAL COAST, CALIFORNIA
99 Become a Rhône Ranger

Grenache, Syrah, Mourvedre, and other Rhône varieties are the focal point of the multiday Hospice du Rhône wine festival. Vintners from across the world come together for seminars, lunches, and tastings that spotlight the myriad of styles being produced. A highlight of the weekend is the live auction, where you can bid on exclusive wines.

SANTA BARBARA, CALIFORNIA
100 Sip Syrah

When you drink Syrah, you can help to support vineyard crews. Stolpman Vineyards' expansive Ballard Canyon property not only produces some of California's top Syrah, its 2 acre (0.8 ha) "La Cuadrilla" block serves as a training platform for the vineyard crew. Proceeds from the La Cuadrilla cuvée go to the workers as a year-end bonus, and through the La Cuadrilla Foundation, a nonprofit extension of this program, workers and their families receive medical and educational support.

SANTA BARBARA, CALIFORNIA
101 Fall in love with Grenache

Angela Osborne's quest to make Grenache (which didn't grow well in her native New Zealand) took her around the world until she finally found the potential she was looking for in California's vineyards. Seek out her label, A Tribute to Grace, where she focuses on single-vineyard expressions of the grape, sourcing from sites located throughout the state.

101 *Above:* A Tribute to Grace is based in the Sierra Madre Mountains

102 Listen to music under the stars

The Santa Maria Valley climate is not just ideal for growing Pinot Noir, Chardonnay, and Sauvignon Blanc; warm, starry evenings and ocean breezes create the perfect backdrop for concerts at Presqu'ile Vineyard's amphitheater. The intimate venue hosts major headliners throughout the year, and you can enjoy the winery's offerings while taking in the music wafting through the air.

103 Add these wines to your collection

Winemakers Mike Roth and Craig Winchester (together, Lo-Fi Wines) may strive to produce quaffable and fun wines, but they take their process very seriously. Working in a low-intervention, natural style of winemaking, they embrace the resulting nuances and variations in each bottle. Sample the Lo-Fi Wines at their Los Alamos tasting room.

104 Discover wines in an industrial park

From the outside, it looks like any industrial park, but Lompoc Wine Ghetto—and its surrounding area—is an epicenter of Santa Barbara winemaking. Sashi Moorman, the winemaker with a venerable empire to his name—Piedrasassi, as well as Domaine de la Côte and Sandhi Wines, his labels in partnership with celebrity sommelier Rajat Parr—calls the area home. Palmina Wines by Steve Clifton focuses solely on Italian varietals, while Greg Brewer highlights the region's influence on Chardonnay and Pinot Noir at Brewer-Clifton. Affordable rents make the area a draw for young upstarts, and you'll find labels with just a few hundred cases to their name vinifying alongside these established names. Tasting room experiences vary widely: some are bare-bones spaces, while others are outfitted with sleek tasting bars.

MALIBU, CALIFORNIA

105 Go wild on a Malibu Wine Safari

The 1,000 acre (405 ha) Saddlerock Ranch is
more than just vineyards: zebras, bison, and even
a giraffe call this Southern California landscape
home. Ride in an open-air vehicle on the Malibu
Wine Safari and see the various creatures, many
of which were movie stars in a former life.
Complete the excursion with a tasting of
local wines.

LOS ANGELES, CALIFORNIA

106 Meet a nomadic winemaker

Scholium Project, Abe Schoener's experimental,
low-intervention cuvées, garnered accolades
over time, but for years he never had a winery
of his own. The wandering vintner joined forces
with well-known sommelier/winemaker Rajat
Parr at a new Los Angeles facility that you can
visit. Here, they collaborate on a new label and
new cuvées.

LOS ANGELES, CALIFORNIA

107 Taste rare back vintages

Aged and collectible wines are the cornerstone
of Augustine Wine Bar's impressive list.
A rotating collection of highly sought-after
rarities are offered by the glass, and the bottle
selection includes vintages dating back to 1860.
Far from stuffy, the atmosphere is cozy and
inviting—pair your selection with the famous
tater tots.

LOS ANGELES, CALIFORNIA

108 Broaden your taste buds in Los Feliz

Lou Wine Shop has brought artisanal and natural
wines to Los Feliz in a big way, and since its
opening in 2014 is now well established. Check
out the themed tastings and look out for
Lou the owner on the floor—his advice is
always invaluable.

109 Match Thai food with natural wine

Chef-owner Kris Yenbamroong describes Night + Market, his mini-empire of three Thai restaurants, as "California chill meets Bangkok frenzy fueled by natural wine." The food wins many plaudits, and the wine list matches perfectly with the cuisine. Make a reservation at WeHo (West Hollywood) or Sahm (Venice), and just turn up at Song (Silver Lake).

110 Drink slowly at this event

Slow Wine, the enological offspring of Slow Food, started in Italy as a way to judge wines based on their sustainable practices and respect for tradition rather than a generic quality-rating system. Over the years the number of exhibitors at this showcase has grown, and wines from all over the world sit alongside the Italian contingency—look out for it when it comes to your area.

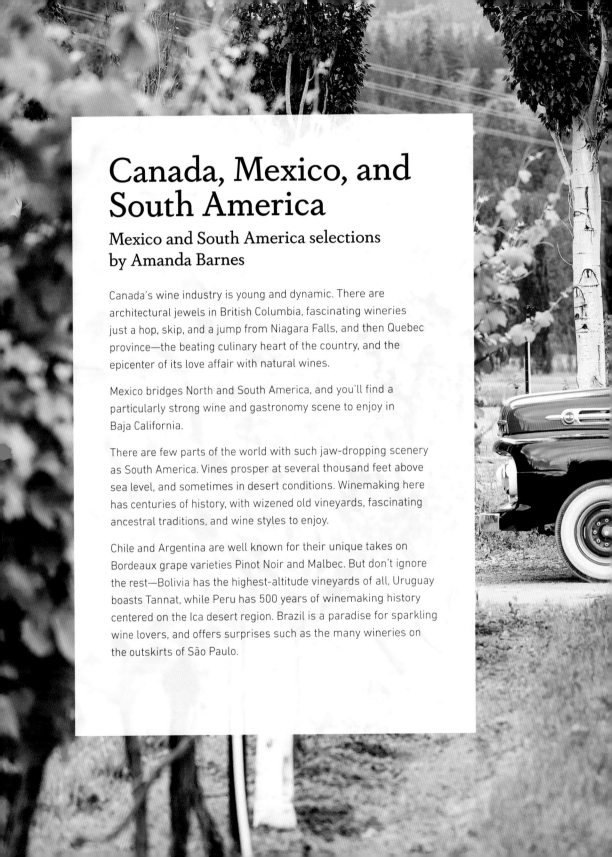

Canada, Mexico, and South America

Mexico and South America selections by Amanda Barnes

Canada's wine industry is young and dynamic. There are architectural jewels in British Columbia, fascinating wineries just a hop, skip, and a jump from Niagara Falls, and then Quebec province—the beating culinary heart of the country, and the epicenter of its love affair with natural wines.

Mexico bridges North and South America, and you'll find a particularly strong wine and gastronomy scene to enjoy in Baja California.

There are few parts of the world with such jaw-dropping scenery as South America. Vines prosper at several thousand feet above sea level, and sometimes in desert conditions. Winemaking here has centuries of history, with wizened old vineyards, fascinating ancestral traditions, and wine styles to enjoy.

Chile and Argentina are well known for their unique takes on Bordeaux grape varieties Pinot Noir and Malbec. But don't ignore the rest—Bolivia has the highest-altitude vineyards of all, Uruguay boasts Tannat, while Peru has 500 years of winemaking history centered on the Ica desert region. Brazil is a paradise for sparkling wine lovers, and offers surprises such as the many wineries on the outskirts of São Paulo.

NOVA SCOTIA, CANADA

111 Put some Nova Scotia sparkle in your day

Nova Scotia certainly has a cool climate, but plenty of sun—and that's perfect for making sparkling wines, as has been happening at Benjamin Bridge. If the wine tasting alone doesn't tempt you, the views over the valley from the tasting room terrace are stunning.

QUEBEC, CANADA

112 Enjoy views of the old port

Écho Buvette is a French bistro in Quebec City that punches well above its weight, with a perfectly executed small-plates concept. The wine list is enjoyably quirky, with classic French regions well represented, and a strong European selection in general. Look out for the sprinkling of Quebecois bottles.

QUEBEC, CANADA

113 Try Quebec's answer to Champagne

Domaine Bergeville makes traditional method sparkling wines (the same method as used in Champagne), but with a twist—it grows only cold-climate grape varieties such as Frontenac Gris or Marquette, giving its crisp, fresh wines a very specific Quebecois twang. Visit the Hatley estate—it has both organic and biodynamic certification—during the winter.

QUEBEC, CANADA

114 Overnight at a picturesque winery

Vignoble Clos Ste-Croix de Dunham is in a very pretty location, with space for a picnic and accommodation in a historic villa built in 1842. Drink the award-winning wines that are made from French varieties and modern crossings such as Maréchal Foch, Vidal, and Seyval Blanc.

QUEBEC, CANADA

115 Hang out at a food and natural-wine joint

If you're a fan of earthy pét-nats or funky orange wines, Le Vin Papillon is the address you'll want to have in Montreal. Drop into this cozy natural-wine bar for a tipple. The bar is an offshoot from the iconic Joe Beef restaurant, but with a lighter style of cuisine focused on vegetables and seafood—and a lively, informal atmosphere.

QUEBEC, CANADA

116 Explore the birthplace of Quebec wine

The signposted Brome-Missisquoi Wine Route covers around twenty wineries across Quebec's picturesque eastern townships. Drive or cycle around the Appalachian foothills to visit the wineries, and don't miss the hundred or so *Amis de la Route des vins*"—restaurants, hotels, spas, and other attractions that all add to the experience.

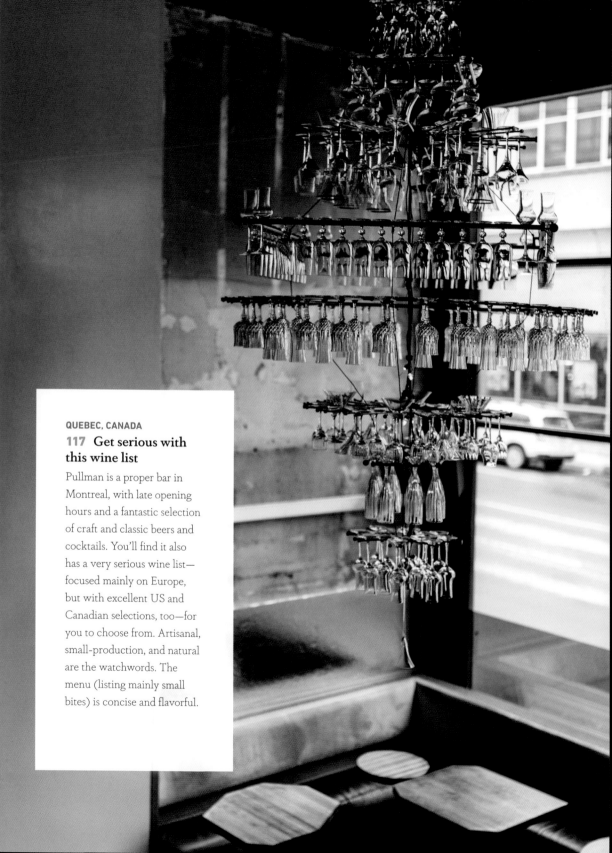

QUEBEC, CANADA

117 Get serious with this wine list

Pullman is a proper bar in Montreal, with late opening hours and a fantastic selection of craft and classic beers and cocktails. You'll find it also has a very serious wine list—focused mainly on Europe, but with excellent US and Canadian selections, too—for you to choose from. Artisanal, small-production, and natural are the watchwords. The menu (listing mainly small bites) is concise and flavorful.

ONTARIO, CANADA

118 Visit a pioneering estate

When Caroline Granger started making wine in Prince Edward County, she was almost on her own. Grange of Prince Edward Winery has pioneered serious wine production in the county, and continues to push itself to new levels of quality each year. Taste the wines that are very much handmade, showing considerable vintage and terroir expression.

ONTARIO, CANADA

119 Try wines made from new grape varieties

Vines need to be hardy to survive in Prince Edward County, so boutique Karlo Estates winery is researching the use of modern hybrid grape varieties that are better able to resist the cold winters. Try the juicy Petite Pearl and Marquette reds, which are proving the success of this strategy. The estate's Pinot Noir is also noteworthy.

119 *Above:* The tasting room at Karlo Estates winery inside the renovated nineteenth-century barn

TOP 3

TORONTO, ONTARIO, CANADA

Treat yourself to quality wines at these three Toronto venues

120 Archive

The space might be small, but the wine list at Archive offers a massive selection of interesting, lo-fi delights from across Europe and beyond. You'll feel very welcome if you're a true wine adventurer—no pretensions or posturing here. The option of small pours or tasting flights broadens the possibilities for further experimentation.

120

121 Edulis Restaurant

Edulis Restaurant has become famous for its exquisite tasting menus that are focused on seafood and seasonal produce such as mushrooms—and also for its warm, unpretentious service. Truffles also make a regular appearance in season. Check out the enjoyably eclectic, well-priced, and fairly Eurocentric wine list.

122 Paris Paris

The name plus the 1980s and 1990s hits soundtrack seems kitsch, but Paris Paris is nothing of the sort. There's a seriously upmarket food offering (especially in the evenings), plus one of Toronto's best small-production, natural-wine lists. Look for the sprinkling of homegrown goodies among the European and New World selections.

123 *Above:* Hidden Bench Estate Winery can be found in the heart of Beamsville Bench

ONTARIO, CANADA

123 Enjoy a curated tasting at a top Niagara winery

Niagara has enough wineries that are happy to provide an undemanding experience to bachelorette parties and other casual tourists. Hidden Bench Estate Winery isn't among them— the ethos and the winemaking are very serious, with a focus on French grape varieties and French classicism in every way. Sample wines made from 100 percent organic estate-grown grapes.

ONTARIO, CANADA

124 Taste cult wines from Niagara

Is Pearl Morissette a winery or a restaurant? It's both, and neither plays second fiddle. The wines are made with great care and minimal intervention by Burgundy-trained François Morissette, and are constantly sold out. Enjoy true fine dining at the restaurant with a nine-course tasting menu—and try those elusive wines!

ONTARIO, CANADA

125 Relax with a dream Ontario wine list

A few restaurants bake their own bread, but not many also do their own butchery and farm their own vegetables. Backhouse in Niagara-on-the-Lake aims for ultra-local sourcing and to celebrate the produce of the local community. You'll find it's all used to stunning effect in the restaurant's creative and intricate tasting menus. Its quality commitment also extends to a mind-blowing list of wines and verticals from Ontario producers—plus a few hundred options from leading artisans' wineries around the world, just in case you need some variety. Executive chef and owner Ryan Crawford also makes his own wine under the name of the Crawford Wine Project.

ONTARIO, CANADA

126 Discover Niagara's biodynamic pioneers

Experience the passion of owner Bill Redelmeier, as he explains his vision at Southbrook Vineyards. The winery building and surroundings are carefully designed to minimize environmental impact and to promote nature and diversity. Southbrook now farms biodynamically—a holistic theory that goes beyond organics. The wines are expertly made by Ann Sperling.

ONTARIO, CANADA

127 Take a gastronomic tour of Niagara's wineries

November weekends are extra special in Niagara-on-the-Lake. Taste the Season is an initiative by the Wineries of Niagara-on-the-Lake where each of around twenty-five participating wineries offers a top wine-and-food pairing. Purchase a single, well-priced ticket, which is valid for the whole month and allows you to visit them all.

ONTARIO, CANADA

128 Explore the Wineries of Niagara-on-the-Lake

Niagara-on-the-Lake has a deserved reputation as one of Canada's top food-and-wine destinations. More than twenty wineries promote themselves together as "Wineries of Niagara-on-the-Lake." There's a huge variety, from famous names such as Inniskillin to boutique biodynamic estates like Southbrook. All are within minutes of one another. Use the dedicated website to plan a day's itinerary and to check on opening times or special events.

ONTARIO, CANADA

129 Visit the coolest place in Ontario's wine country

Niagara is famous for its ice wines—made from grapes picked when the temperature falls below 18°F (-7.8°C), and Peller Estates is one of its biggest names for this style. Chill out in its 10 Below Peller Icewine Lounge, fashioned out of ice, and taste the wine in the same environment that the grapes were picked.

128 *Above:* One of the Wineries of Niagara-on-the-Lake's vineyards, with Lake Ontario in the background

BRITISH COLUMBIA, CANADA
130 Stop by one of Canada's top winemakers

Ann Sperling is one of Canada's most experienced and respected winemakers. She's a consultant winemaker for a Niagara property, but her home base is Sperling Vineyards in Kelowna. Visit to learn about the importance of organic viticulture, and be sure to taste the natural Amber Pinot Gris.

BRITISH COLUMBIA, CANADA
131 Visit an iconic Okanagan winery

You'll find fortresslike gates, a bell tower, and an amphitheater that seats 1,200—but the architecture at Mission Hill Family Estate is modern. It's a hugely impressive complex, with commanding views over Kelowna. Various tour options allow you to understand the Okanagan terroir and taste the wines. Don't miss the opportunity to have lunch in the Terrace Restaurant.

131 *Above:* Mission Hill Family Estate offers a variety of experiences and tours

BRITISH COLUMBIA, CANADA

132 Taste some beautiful free-form wines

The supermodern Okanagan Crush Pad Winery in Summerland was built as a custom-crush facility for winemakers without their own wineries, but the team also makes its own sensational wines under the labels Free Form, Haywire, and Narrative. Discover the wild fermentations and additive-free winemaking.

BRITISH COLUMBIA, CANADA

133 Base yourself in wine country

Spend a few days in Penticton—it's the perfect base to visit the eighty or more wineries within a twenty-minute drive of the city limits. Don't miss the multitude of scenic excursions around lakes Okanagan and Skaha.

TOP 3

VANCOUVER, BRITISH COLUMBIA, CANADA

Dine and drink at these three Vancouver venues

134 Salt Tasting Room

Salt Tasting Room allows you to build your own meat-and-cheese platter, from its ever-changing list of ten small-batch cured meats, ten artisanal cheeses, and ten condiments. The staff will match your choices with wine or even a tasting flight—or you can select from the concise but well-thought-out list, featuring plenty of local producers.

135 Burdock & Co

Andrea Carlson's concept at Burdock & Co restaurant focuses on locally farmed or foraged ingredients, which take center stage in the creative cuisine. You won't be disappointed with the wine list—it may be short, but it is imbued with the same sustainable ethics as the food. It includes wines such as Jean-Paul Brun, A&A Durrmann, and Escoda-Sanahuja.

136 Grapes & Soda

The main event may be the food when you dine at Grapes & Soda—a small-plates concept where every dish packs a punch and looks sensational—but the wine list won't let you down. Choose from excellent organic and minimal-intervention selections from Europe, plus a few local gems.

BRITISH COLUMBIA, CANADA

137 Spend a week immersed in wine

During the last week of February, the Vancouver
International Wine Festival transforms the city
into a melée of visiting winemakers (from close
to twenty countries), gala dinners, and wine
tastings. An impressive 750 wines can be tasted
at the main event. Sign up early for the smaller
seminars and tastings, as they sell out quickly.

BRITISH COLUMBIA, CANADA

138 Go local at an idyllic BC winery

Tilar Mazzeo and Robert Miles believe
passionately in keeping it local, so their winery
and farm in Saanichton, Parsell Vineyard, is
extremely self-sufficient, even experimenting
with locally grown oak for the barrels. Buy
Parsell's wines—including organically farmed
Ortega and an Amber Pinot Gris—from the
cellar door or at a local market. The couple also
runs a luxury bed-and-breakfast.

BRITISH COLUMBIA, CANADA

139 Try farm-fresh bites and wine

Covert Farms Family Estate was established
during the 1950s, and grows organic fruit and
vegetables as well as making delicious wines.
Enjoy the beautiful setting during a visit to the
winery in Oliver, or while picking your own
produce in season—or kick back on the patio
with a glass and some snacks.

BRITISH COLUMBIA, CANADA

140 Pair high-class tapas with great sherry

Bodega is a tapas restaurant in Victoria, so
understandably the wine focus is on Spain—
but the twist is the inclusion of wines from other
countries where Spanish grapes are used. You'll
also find a couple of BC wines make it onto the
list. Be sure to try the large selection of sherries
in all styles.

139 *Opposite:* Covert Farms Family Estate serves up charcuterie and cheese boards featuring small bites from the farm

BAJA CALIFORNIA, MEXICO

141 Explore Tecate's oldest vines

Just over the border from San Diego is the wine region of Tecate. Here, you'll find some of the oldest vines and the leading natural-wine producer in Mexico. Drop into Bichi and try the artisanal, small-production wines from old vines, including the very first grapes to be planted in the New World—Listán Prieto, aka the Mission grape.

BAJA CALIFORNIA, MEXICO

142 Go back to school at La Escuelita

La Estación de Oficios del Porvenir (known locally as La Escuelita) is the most important training ground for the growing community of wine producers in Guadalupe Valley. Taste the experimental wine projects in the cellar of this small wine school to see who is up-and-coming in this region.

BAJA CALIFORNIA, MEXICO

143 Take bites between boutique wineries

Baja California is filled with excellent food trucks, and many of them are parked at the boutique wineries of Guadalupe Valley. Spend an afternoon sipping at the wineries and snacking at the food trucks, including Adobe, Finca Altozano, and Troika.

BAJA CALIFORNIA, MEXICO

144 Fine dine in Mexican wine country

The Guadalupe Valley isn't only home to the top wineries in the country—it is also home to some fantastic fine-dining restaurants. Combine culinary pleasures with wine tasting at some of the top restaurants in the region, including Laja, Deckman's, Malva, and Corazón de Tierra.

144 *Below:* Laja offers a four-course menu with wine pairings

BAJA CALIFORNIA, MEXICO

145 Combine glamping with wine and sunsets

Right on the water's edge, Cuatro Cuatros is a stunning wine estate near Ensenada, where glamping is much more comfortable than you can imagine—the views at the sunset wine bar are to die for! Spend the evening sipping on coastal Sauvignon Blanc as you watch the sun setting over Mexican wine country.

BAJA CALIFORNIA, MEXICO

146 Stay in a stunning wine hotel

Baja California is filled with chic wine lodges and hotels, and the contemporary design of Encuentro Guadalupe is one of the region's best. Sit outside under the stars by the outdoor fireplaces and lounge area with a warming glass of local red in your hand.

BAJA CALIFORNIA, MEXICO

147 Soak up sparkling wine and oysters

Hugo D'Acosta is one of Mexico's top winemakers, and just above his famed Casa de Piedra winery and vineyard in Guadalupe Valley is a fabulous oyster bar overlooking the vineyards. Take in the views and enjoy the oysters with a glass of his refreshing sparkling wine.

BAJA CALIFORNIA, MEXICO

148 Discover Ensenada's gastronomy and wine scene

Located on the coast of Mexico's top wine region, Ensenada isn't only known for its surf, but also for its excellent wine-and-food scene. Explore the restaurants and wine bars of this city and fall for the laid-back charm of Mexican wine country.

148 *Above:* The wine region of Ensenada in Mexico

149 Discover the oldest winery in the New World

It might surprise you that the oldest winery in the New World is actually in Mexico . . . Casa Madero, established in 1597 in Parras de la Fuente, was the first winery to open its doors—since the arrival of the Spanish—and the first vines on the continent. Taste New World wine history at this historic bodega.

150 Hunt out cellar delights in Mexico City

Mexico City (CDMX) is one of the biggest cities in the world, and so it is no surprise that it has its fair share of impressive wine cellars. Discover the underground gems of CDMX by visiting the top wine bars and restaurants in the capital. Loup Bar, Bar Romelia, and Le Tachinomi Desu should be high on your list.

151 Visit the tropics of Vale do São Francisco

Brazil's northernmost wine region is in the tropics of the state of Bahia, in the Vale do São Francisco. The region's proximity to the equator means you can harvest grapes all year round. Visit the banana plantations and vineyards of Vale do São Francisco and learn about the double-harvest technique.

152 "Brave" a winter harvest

The best time to visit the wine region of Serra da Mantiqueira is in the winter. Far from being greeted by brown earth and bare vines, you'll see the vineyards laden with purple grapes and resplendent in green leaves. The warm, dry, and sunny winter is ideal for grape growing, which is why producers have flipped the harvest on its head. Visit the wineries during their winter harvest and spend the afternoon indulging in the local cuisine and Slow Food Movement of the area.

SERRA DA MANTIQUEIRA, BRAZIL

153 Take a tour of altitude vineyards

Guaspari is a handsome estate known for its single-plot Syrah wines. Get to grips with the terroir by visiting the different vineyards on a tour with the agronomist and winemaker.

SÃO PAULO, BRAZIL

Unearth three areas of São Paulo's wine scene

154 Enoteca Saint VinSaint

São Paulo's wine scene is buzzing at the moment, and there's huge interest in natural-wine producers in South America and beyond. Visit the cozy wine cave of Enoteca Saint VinSaint, where the city's natural-wine movement started, and pencil in the next date for the massively popular wine fair, Naturebas.

155 Sede261

One of the hottest wine dates in São Paulo is the monthly boozy brunch at Sede261. Cram onto the streets of the bohemian Pinheiros neighborhood where this eclectic wine bar serves up a selection of artisanal wines from around Latin America. There's also a live dj and pop-up restaurant on the side.

156 Jundiaí and São Roque

São Paulo is one of the world's biggest cities, but before it became a capital of global dimensions, it was an agricultural region where fruit production (including grape vines) thrived. Visit some of the nearby wineries and step back in São Paulo history on the outskirts of Jundiaí and São Roque.

156

RIO GRANDE DO SUL, BRAZIL
157 Uncork Brazil's best bubbly

Brazilian sparkling wine is made in almost all the wine regions, but the mecca for top-quality bubbles is Pinto Bandeira, with famed names including Cave Geisse and Don Giovanni. Discover some of the nation's top bubbles while visiting the local wineries and learn why this terroir has a distinctive sparkle of its own.

RIO GRANDE DO SUL, BRAZIL
158 Indulge in wine therapy

Serra Gaúcha has a handful of luxury wine hotels, which attract weekenders from Rio and São Paulo year-round, but one of them is known for its X factor in relaxation. The five-star Hotel & Spa do Vinho sits perched above the vineyards. It has an indulgent wine spa that uses grape-derived products to help you unwind in wine country.

RIO GRANDE DO SUL, BRAZIL
159 Explore Brazilian wine country

Bento Gonçalves is in the heart of Brazilian wine country and is the top spot from which to explore the wine route. With dozens of wineries open for tourism and tasting, you can easily spend a couple of days here exploring the region sometimes known as "the Piedmont of Brazil."

RIO GRANDE DO SUL, BRAZIL
160 Enjoy a sparkling picnic at Miolo

One of Brazil's top wine producers, Miolo winery in Serra Gaúcha, is a popular winery in which to stop for a tasting and tour. Book yourself in for a lazy afternoon in the gardens and nibble on a picnic or pick from the food trucks while indulging in its renowned bubbly.

CINTI, BOLIVIA

161 Explore 250-year-old vines

Bolivia's Cinti Valley is one of the most historic wine regions in the country. Its old vines and artisanal winemaking traditions have remained remarkably unchanged over the past couple of centuries. With vineyards planted in the late sixteenth century, Cinti Valley boomed as a wine producer and restful resort, supplying the rich mining families of the great Potosí silver mine. By the seventeenth century, it had a population greater than London or Paris. Although the silver rush has since demised, Cinti remains one of the principal wine valleys of Bolivia and is steeped in tradition and heritage. Visit the boutique producers and wine families in Camargo and Villa Abecia, whose vines are often some 250 years old and grow around the wide trunks of pink peppercorn trees. Taste the artisanal wines and discover why Moscatel de Alejandría is not only the most exciting wine in Cinti, but also makes a toe-warming brandy known as Singani.

TARIJA, BOLIVIA

162 Take in high-altitude wineries

Tarija is home to the lion's share of Bolivian production, and there's no wine country quite as high altitude as Bolivia—where vineyards start at 5,250 ft (1,600 m) and run up to more than 9,840 ft (3,000 m) altitude. Follow the dizzying wine route of Tarija, otherwise known as the "smiling capital," and visit some of the country's top producers.

TARIJA, BOLIVIA

163 Make your own Singani

Singani is Bolivia's equivalent of Pisco. Although made exclusively from high-altitude Moscatel de Alejandría vines, it is even purer and more delicate to taste. Learn how to distill your own Singani at one of the many artisanal distilleries in Cinti and Tarija. Complete the master class by learning the art of a Bolivian Chuflay cocktail.

SANTA CRUZ, BOLIVIA

164 Visit a boho village and wine route

Samaipata, in the subtropical forests of the Santa Cruz valleys, is a wine region quite unlike any other, with its own distinctively bohemian charm. It attracts artisans and musicians from all over the world, and you'll have plenty of creative companions to enjoy drinking the local vino with. Try Uvairenda and Landsuá for starters.

165 Taste Bolivia's native ingredients

Owned by Noma's Claus Meyer, Gustu is Bolivia's leading fine-dining restaurant. Meyer made it his mission to bring Bolivia's weird and wonderful native ingredients to the table in a memorable tasting menu experience, paired with the nation's diverse wines. Try the vinous and earthly delights of this South American country in an unforgettable tasting experience.

RIVERA, URUGUAY

166 Visit a winery that straddles two countries

On one side of the marker post at Bodega Cerro Chapeu it says "Brazil," and on the other, "Uruguay"—with vineyards on either side. Uruguay's northernmost wine region shares a lot in common with Brazil's southernmost, including the city of Rivera. Look out over the vineyards from the terrace of this Uruguayan-owned winery with vineyards in both countries.

MALDONADO, URUGUAY

167 Fly into the vineyards of Garzón

Spread over a 1,730 acre (700 ha) olive grove-and-vineyard estate, Bodega Garzón is one of Uruguay's most impressive modern ventures, owned by Argentine billionaire Alejandro Bulgheroni. Explore the grandeur of the coastal estate from the sky in a helicopter before dining at the exquisite restaurant with your feet back on the ground.

MALDONADO, URUGUAY

168 Raise a glass at Uruguay's coastal wineries

In the past decade, Maldonado has boomed—not only as a beach destination, but as one of the coolest wine spots in Uruguay. You could easily spend a couple of days hopping between the coastal wineries, from the luxurious estate of Garzón winery to the petite olive grove and family vineyard of Oceánica José Ignacio. Don't miss visiting the original pioneer of Maldonado: Alto de la Ballena.

MALDONADO, URUGUAY

169 Sip coastal Albariño in trendy beach bars

José Ignacio is the chicest beach town in South America, and there's no cooler place to sip Uruguay's coastal Albariño wines than from the comfort of a beach lounger, surrounded by golden sand and crashing waves at Bodega Oceánica José Ignacio. When you get peckish, head to Parador La Huella for sublime seafood.

CANELONES, URUGUAY
170 Tour Tannat country

Uruguay is the world capital of Tannat, with more than 3,955 acres (1,600 ha) under vine of this feisty variety, originally from Madiran. Since arriving in Uruguay in 1870, Tannat has found its home in Canelones, where two-thirds of the country's winegrowers reside. Despite being the busiest of Uruguay's wine regions, the relaxed pace and informal attitude of Canelones make you feel very at home. Almost all the wineries are family owned and usually attended by the owner, who is normally the winemaker too. Spend the afternoon touring some of Uruguay's most legendary Tannat producers and sit down to taste with the family, talk about the history of the region, and glean their thoughts on the future. Reinado De Lucca, the Pisano brothers, the Pizzorno family, Juan Andrés Marichal, and Antigua Bodega Stagnari are just a few of the multigenerational family wineries that should be on your bucket list.

CANELONES, URUGUAY
171 Step into Uruguay's oldest cellar

When the Deicas family acquired its historic winery in 1979, it also acquired the oldest underground cellar in the country, built in stone in 1745 by the Jesuits. It has been used as a wine cellar since the property was converted into a winery in the mid-1800s. Take an atmospheric tour underground and stay for a tasting in the cellar or at the restaurant aboveground.

MONTEVIDEO, URUGUAY

172 Explore the wine route of Montevideo

With more than a third of the country's population, Montevideo is not only the capital city, but the heart of Uruguay. It is the best place to start your exploration of this small yet fascinating Latin American country. Fortunately, you don't need to venture farther than the city to reach your first winery, and although creeping urbanization is pushing vineyards farther out to the fringes, there are still a handful of wineries to visit in the city. Try Bodegas Carrau, a historic producer, and Bodega Bouza for a modern vision—and to explore its state-of-the-art winery, classic car museum, and excellent restaurant.

MONTEVIDEO, URUGUAY

173 Uncover Montevideo's offbeat wine scene

Montevideo is possibly the world's most laid-back capital city, and the wine scene is relatively underground, although ripe for discovery. Take in the backstreets of the old town and unlock what's exciting in Uruguayan wine. Start with a guided tasting with the owners and hip sommeliers at Montevideo Wine Experience, Nicolas and Liber; indulge in the upmarket bistro cuisine and Uruguayan wine pairings at Baco Vino Y Bistro wine bar in the Punta Carretas neighborhood; or enjoy the urban vibe of Madiran wine bar at Mercado Ferrando, where sommelier Lucas will guide you through some of the latest releases from the new generation of winemakers.

MONTEVIDEO, URUGUAY

174 Drink *Medio y Medio* in Uruguay

There are two times of the year when everyone in the country is drinking *Medio y Medio* (a merry blend of wine and sparkling wine)— Christmas and New Year. But if you arrive before or after that week, head down to the portside market of Mercado del Puerto, which is bustling every weekend with a busy lunch crowd and has the local delicacy on tap.

174 *Above: Mercado del Puerto is the place to be to drink Medio y Medio*

CARMELO AND COLONIA DEL SACRAMENTO, URUGUAY

175 Locate Uruguay's traditional wine regions

A quick boat ride over the river from Buenos Aires, Carmelo and Colonia del Sacramento offer the ideal weekend escape and one of the most traditional wine regions of Uruguay. The cobblestone streets of Colonia, with its picture-perfect houses, are well worth spending the evening exploring, and you can spend the days winery-hopping in Carmelo. Narbona Wine Lodge, Campotinto, and El Legado are top picks.

178   *Above:* Piattelli Vineyards sits at one of the highest-altitude winemaking regions in the world

JUJUY, ARGENTINA
176   Reach the extremes of high-altitude red wines

The northernmost wine region in Argentina also happens to be one of the world's highest—with vineyards scaling more than 10,922 ft (3,329 m) above sea level in the canyon of Quebrada de Humahuaca. Discover the boutique wine producers in this new, dizzying wine region and explore its high-altitude red wines and mesmerizing hiking trails.

SALTA, ARGENTINA
177   Enjoy a *peña* while sipping Malbec

Salta is not only known for its high-altitude wines, but also for its lively folkloric scene, and there's nowhere better to combine both than at a local *peña*. Loosely translating as "crowd," a *peña* is an informal get-together of musicians who play local folkloric music. Sit back with a local wine and enjoy the show through the evening and into the early hours of the morning.

176   *Left:* The canyon of Quebrada de Humahuaca is one of the world's highest wine regions

178 Combine spicy empanadas and Torrontés

Although empanadas are common throughout Argentina, they are distinctive in the north for their added spice. Learn how to make classic *salteña* empanadas at Piattelli Vineyards in Cafayate, where you can pair them fresh from the fire with the flamboyantly floral and refreshing native Torrontés wine.

SALTA, ARGENTINA

179 Stay at Argentina's highest vineyard

Colomé vineyard is not only one of the highest vineyards in Argentina, but in the world, reaching more than 9,840 ft (3,000 m) above sea level. Linger over the high-altitude wines for a little longer by staying overnight at Colomé's estancia and hotel.

SALTA, ARGENTINA

180 Step back in time at a wine museum

Enter Cafayate's Museum of the Vine and Wine for a look back at how this beautiful wine region in northern Argentina developed, despite its dizzying isolation high in the Andes Mountains.

SALTA, ARGENTINA

181 Take a road trip through Cafayate's wine region

Almost three hours from Salta, Cafayate is a wine region that is best explored by car. En route, there are plenty of memorable rock formations carved out by wind and rain—from The Toad to The Devil's Throat. Spot the purple, pink, and blue sierras around Cafayate that offer a picturesque backdrop to old pergola vines and charming wineries.

CÓRDOBA, ARGENTINA

182 Explore Jesuit ruins and wine traditions

There are few ruins in Argentina quite as prized as the seventeenth-century UNESCO heritage Jesuit Block of Córdoba. Winemaking traditions here are just as old, and although the university city is also Argentina's capital of the wine variety Fernet, it's worth hunting down the modern wine producers resurrecting the ruins of Córdoba's wine industry.

183 Wine bar hop in Buenos Aires

Buenos Aires drinks more wine than anywhere else in Argentina, and the wine bar scene reflects the capital's thirst for vino *Argentino*. Spend an evening or two hopping between the many wine bars and get a feel for what's driving the city's sommeliers wild. Vico, Bar du Marché, Pain et Vin, and Aldo's Wine Bar are top picks.

184 Visit Argentina's first coastal winery

Argentina's wine regions have always been defined by the mountains, but in recent years there is a new frontier being explored: the coast. Costa y Pampa in Buenos Aires province is the first maritime winery to open. You can visit for a taste of what's to come from the country's coastal regions.

185 Drink in the tango of Buenos Aires

You'll hear vino mentioned more than once in tango lyrics sung in Buenos Aires. Sit back with a glass of wine at one of the city's many milongas and discover why, in its wine and tango heyday, this city used to consume as much wine as Paris.

186 Get to grips with Bonarda in San Juan

Sunny San Juan is best known for two things: the zonda wind and its bright Bonarda wines. Discover one of Argentina's top red grape varieties along the wine route and wineries of San Juan, and while you are there, indulge in the Syrah, Malbec, and Viognier too.

TOP 4

UCO VALLEY, ARGENTINA

Don't miss these four wineries in Uco Valley

187 Zuccardi

Third-generation vigneron Sebastián Zuccardi hasn't only taken his love of concrete into the wine cellar of the family's new winery—he's brought it to the very foundations. Drop into the custom-built, state-of-the-art winery and admire the architectural masterpiece made of concrete, stone, and steel—a splendid space for winemaking.

188 SuperUco

Matias Michelini has been one of the most influential figures in modern Argentinian wine, and his whole family (four brothers, their wives, and children) today produces several different labels of wines—each a game changer in its own right. Visit SuperUco, the communal winery, where biodynamics, natural-wine production, and family values are at the fore.

189 Salentein

Salentein is one of the most remarkable wineries to visit for its stunning architecture—on both the inside and outside. Dubbed "the wine cathedral," the most atmospheric stopping point is the cellar—where a lone piano, bathed in sunlight, awaits to be played. So, what are you waiting for?

190 Clos de los Siete

It was no mean feat to convince several of Bordeaux's top châteaux owners to invest in the New World in the late 1990s, but Michel Rolland managed to bring some of the most revered names in Bordeaux to Mendoza to form Clos de los Siete. Explore the French connection and taste the wines in this petite enclave in Vista Florès, and don't miss the Monteviejo Lindaflor Malbec.

190

UCO VALLEY, ARGENTINA

191 Sit down to a "seven fires" show

Siete Fuegos is the fire show of famed Argentine chef Francis Mallmann in The Vines Resort & Spa. Here, you can try not just one but seven of his flame-grilled cooking techniques! Indulge in the regional dishes while the sommelier plies you with expertly paired wines.

UCO VALLEY, ARGENTINA

192 Behold spectacular winery architecture

When the Uco Valley's wine production boomed in 2000, so did its winery architecture. Today, the region is home to some of the most exquisite winery architecture in the New World. Take in the views with a tour of Salentein, O Fournier, Zuccardi, Bodega DiamAndes, and Atamisque, for starters.

MENDOZA, ARGENTINA

193 Paraglide over Mendoza's vineyards

Get a bird's-eye view of the lay of the land over the vineyards of Mendoza by setting off in a glider from Cerro Arco, just west of the city in the Andean foothills. There are few more adrenaline-inducing ways to see Argentina's wine capital than from above.

MENDOZA, ARGENTINA

194 Explore new Malbec terroirs

Santiago Achával is one of the best-known Malbec producers of this century, and his winery, Matervini (established with Roberto Cipresso in 2008), is an adventure into the unexplored terroirs for Malbec in Argentina. The duo has pioneered new vineyards in unthought-of regions with tremendous results, which you can taste at the Mendoza winery.

MENDOZA, ARGENTINA

195 Join the gauchos among the vines

Exploring Argentina's vineyards on horseback is a memorable experience with the Andean backdrop and local gauchos (Argentine horsemen) as your companions. Hop in the saddle at one of Mendoza's wineries (try Nieto Senetiner or Casa de Uco) and finish with a well-earned glass of red. If you get the bug, continue across the Andes on horseback from the Manzano Histórico, just as Argentina's famed liberator General San Martín did.

MENDOZA, ARGENTINA

196 Languor in luxury digs

Mendoza is not only the capital of wine in Argentina, but also the capital of luxury tourism. Spend an evening lingering in the luxury of this iconic Argentinian wine region at the five-star digs of Cavas Wine Lodge, Entre Cielos Luxury Wine Hotel & Spa, Casa de Uco, and The Vines of Mendoza.

196 *Above:* Cavas Wine Lodge is a boutique property with only eighteen guest rooms

MENDOZA, ARGENTINA

197 Master the art of Malbec and steak

There's no better wine-and-food pairing than juicy Argentinian steak with Malbec. The best way to master the art of the ultimate Argentinian pairing is with a cookery class in one of Mendoza's wineries. Book yourself in for an indulgent master class and wine tasting, and develop your own twist for classic chimichurri dressing.

MENDOZA, ARGENTINA

198 Party at a grape harvest festival

It's time to party! Fiesta de la Vendimia is the world's biggest and busiest grape harvest festival. Mendoza has been celebrating it since the seventeenth century and holding its annual parade since 1936. Join the two-week-long celebration for parades, wine tasting, and performances that take place in every town in Mendoza from mid-February to early March.

MENDOZA, ARGENTINA

199 Step back in time at a wine museum

Argentina's wine history stretches beyond the 1600s, and there's one museum in Mendoza that goes back almost as far. In 1885, La Rural, owned by the Rutini family, started making wine. Discover why it's a fascinating ode to all the historic technology and winemaking methods over the past couple of centuries.

MENDOZA, ARGENTINA

200 Visit the ghost of the world's biggest winery

In its heyday, Giol winery was the world's biggest winery at the turn of the twentieth century. The winery, known as La Colina de Oro, is today defunct, but walk through the cavernous halls and you can imagine the 400 employees, 350 carriages, 1,400 mules, and team of coopers busy at work in yesteryear.

MENDOZA, ARGENTINA

201 Dine in a winemaking legend's home

Known for being the frontman and winemaker at Catena Zapata, Alejandro Vigil is one of the most renowned winemakers in the New World today. You can visit his home and boutique winery in eastern Mendoza, where you can taste his acclaimed El Enemigo wines and stay for lunch in the busy home-style restaurant.

LUJÁN DE CUYO, ARGENTINA

202 Climb the Mayan pyramid of Catena Zapata

When Nicolás Catena Zapata wanted to build an iconic winery for his family in Mendoza, instead of looking to the architecture of the famous châteaux in Bordeaux, he looked to architectural icons a bit closer to home—the ancient Mayan culture. Visit this Argentinian wine dynasty and climb the stairs to reach the vineyard view from the top of the pyramid.

202 *Above:* Founded in 1902, Catena Zapata sits at 3,117 ft (950 m) above sea level

LUJÁN DE CUYO, ARGENTINA

203 Explore the cradle of Malbec

Luján de Cuyo is known as the cradle of Malbec with good reason. Malbec vines have been growing in this wine region since the mid-nineteenth century, and there is more Malbec planted there today than anywhere else in the world. As one of Argentina's most important wine regions, you'll need weeks of exploring to do justice to the complex history and wealth of producers in Luján. But if you are in a rush, focus a day or two on discovering the old vines and modern wineries that have made this region one of Argentina's most revered. Top Malbec magnates include the historic wineries of Luigi Bosca, Norton, and Benegas; modern visionaries such as Alta Vista, Pulenta Estate, and Casarena; and the wineries of legendary winemakers Walter Bressia, Santiago Achával, Roberto de la Mota, and Susana Balbo.

LUJÁN DE CUYO, ARGENTINA

204 Meet a top Argentinian *garagiste*

There are few experiences quite like walking through the artisanal winery of Carmelo Patti and listening to his tales of making Malbec and Cabernet his own way for decades. Find out why Patti is one of the most loved wine producers of Mendoza for his personal and traditional approach to winemaking and his charming charisma.

LUJÁN DE CUYO, ARGENTINA

205 Taste historic vintages

Argentina's winemaking used to be much like that of Rioja in terms of long, patient aging for years in the cellar. Today, everyone moves at a much faster pace. But Cavas Weinert stays true to tradition and often ages wines for a decade before release. Try some of its old vintages from the late 1970s.

LUJÁN DE CUYO, ARGENTINA

206 Sample South America's oldest white wine

When the winemaking team happened across an old barrel of Sémillon from 1942 in the cellars of Lagarde, it imagined the wine wouldn't be drinkable. But this wine relic, the oldest white wine in South America, is still very much alive and kicking. Be there when the winery releases minute quantities to share the experience of tasting Argentinian wine history.

MAIPÚ, ARGENTINA

207 Visit Argentina's most historic wineries

When Argentina's wine production exploded in the nineteenth century, the wine region of Maipú was right at the heart of it. With a train line running from the wineries to the city of Buenos Aires, Maipú became home to some of the world's biggest wineries at the time. Explore the town's history and old vines while touring today's top producers.

Above: Wine casks made from French oak at the historic Norton winery in Luján de Cuyo

CHUBUT, ARGENTINA

208 Fish for Pinot in Trevelin Valley

Chubut's growing wine scene is quickly becoming one of the most unique in Argentina. Spend the day fly-fishing by the lakes and rivers of Los Alerces National Park, and indulge in the new movement of cool-climate Pinot Noir in neighboring Trevelin Valley.

RÍO NEGRO, ARGENTINA

209 Explore Río Negro's old vines

Producing wine for more than a hundred years, and with vines just as old, Río Negro is a mecca for old vines and classic wines. Taste the old-vine Riesling, Pinot Noir, Malbec, and Sémillon at historic Humberto Canale winery, or through the wines of Noemia, Chacra, and Riccitelli.

NEUQUÉN, ARGENTINA

210 Combine Pinot and paleontology

When Pinot Noir specialist Familia Schroeder was digging the foundations of its cellar, it got more than it bargained for . . . the remains of a *Panamericansaurus*! Familia Schroeder isn't the only haunt for dinosaur fossils and Pinot Noir. Visit this Patagonian wine region to discover more dinosaur museums—and great wine.

LIMA, PERU

211 Learn the art of pisco sour

Peru's pisco sour is world-famous, and the spiritual home of the local brandy-based drink is in the coastal city of Lima, where the country's top bars know how to mix a mean sour. Discover how one of the city's top wine bars, La Niña, balances sweet with sour.

LIMA, PERU

212 Savor Peruvian cuisine and wine

Central has long been known as Peru's most exciting restaurant. Genius chef Virgilio Martínez and his team recreate ancient Peruvian cooking techniques and scout out exotic indigenous ingredients from the altiplano to the ocean. Enjoy the full tasting menu experience paired with wines from around South America, expertly selected by the sommelier team.

ICA, PERU
213 See a traditional horse dance in Peru

Peru's longest-running winery is also one of the most popular visits on the wine route of Ica. Tacama was established in the 1540s, and you can discover the history of this prestigious Peruvian producer while visiting for a wine tasting and lunch. Don't miss the traditional Peruvian horse dance and show.

ICA, PERU
214 Sleep among the vines

The first and best wine hotel in Peru is at the colonial-style estate of Santiago Queirolo winery. Here, rooms spill out into the vineyards, large gardens, and swimming pool. Spend the weekend at this popular wine hotel while winery-hopping in Ica.

ICA, PERU
215 Visit wineries amid desert valleys

Peru's main wine region is an oasis in the desert—quite literally. You'll pass dunes and dust bowls until you reach the wine lands of Ica, which are nestled between sand dunes close to the river's edge in the heart of Ica. It is here where the country's wine and pisco production has blossomed, and you can visit several wine producers to learn the 500-year-long history of Peru's wine production. When you've finished winery visits during the day, stay overnight in nearby Huacachina—a small village built around a lagoon between dunes.

ATACAMA, CHILE
216 Explore a vine oasis in the desert

San Pedro de Atacama is known for its Moon Valley, salt-crusted lagoons with pink flamingos, and steam-spitting geysers. But did you know there are vineyards in the Atacama Desert too? The vineyards and boutique wineries of Toconao village are truly an oasis in the world's driest desert and an obligatory stop-off for any wine lover exploring the Chilean altiplano.

ELQUI, CHILE

217 Experience winemaking under the stars

Famed for its clear skies, the Elqui Valley is home to several observatories and some of the world's best stargazing. It is also home to Chile's best pisco production and a handful of small wineries in this steep mountain valley. The modern wine pioneers of the valley are Falernia and Mayu wineries, which each have their own observatory among the vines. If you visit Viñedos de Alcohuaz during the vintage season, you can help crush grapes by foot in the stone *lagares* during the day and spend the evening drinking its rich red blends while gazing into the infinite starry skies.

ACONCAGUA, CHILE

218 Peer over the vineyards of an Aconcagua pioneer

Since 1870, the Errázuriz family, a pioneer in Aconcagua Valley, has been making wine. In 2010, the historic nineteenth-century estate was embellished with a new state-of-the-art winery designed by Chilean architect Samuel Claro. The spiral-shaped winery disappears several floors underground, and an architectural highlight is the glass tasting room suspended high above the vineyards.

219 Winery-hop in Casablanca

When Pablo Morandé planted in Casablanca in the 1980s, he had no idea if the vines would survive the cold, let alone that Casablanca would end up becoming one of the New World's most important coastal wine regions. Recognized as one of the ten Great Wine Capitals of the world, Casablanca has a lively wine scene, with more than a dozen wineries open for tourism, and all within a short drive of each other. Highlights include Montsecano, for its boutique Pinot production; Casas del Bosque with its cool coastal wines and top-notch restaurant; Bodegas RE, which is the new vision of Morandé and his son; Viña Indómita, for its restaurant on the *terraza* overlooking the valley; Matetic, for a deep dive into biodynamic wine production; Emiliana, which is another top organic and biodynamic estate; Kingston, for its precision-driven Pinot Noir and Sauvignon Blanc; and Villard, for the vision of another pioneering Casablanca family. Spend the day, or a couple, winery-hopping between them.

220 Toast to the colorful chaos of Valparaíso

On the edge of the Casablanca wine region lies one of South America's most colorful cities, Valparaíso. The view of the Pacific Ocean crashing onto the rocky beaches, and steep hillsides covered in multicolored houses and eye-catching street art, is one to behold. Even better is drinking in the view with a glass of wine in hand on the terrace of one of the city's wine bars and restaurants.

221 Dive into Chile's experimental wine scene

There are few families who have been quite as influential in Chilean wine as the Morandé family. Pablo Morandé pioneered Chile's first cool coastal region, Casablanca, in the 1980s, and now he and his son, Pablo Jr., are bringing exciting orange wines, wines under flor, and unconventional blends. Taste their latest rule breakers at Bodegas RE.

CASABLANCA AND SAN ANTONIO, CHILE

222 Cool down in a handsome *casona*

Viña Matetic isn't only one of Chile's leading biodynamic estates, but it is also one of Chile's leading coastal producers—straddling both Casablanca and San Antonio appellations with its impressive 39,537 acre (16,000 ha) estate. At the heart of the estate is the eco-friendly winery, charming restaurant, and colonial-style *casona*, where you can spend the afternoon basking in the sunshine, drinking Sauvignon Blanc by the pool, and then in the evening, warming up with a hearty Syrah and supper made by your private chef.

222 *Above:* Viña Matetic has a colonial house that offers ten spacious guest rooms

223 Hop among Santiago's wine bars

Santiago's wine bar scene is a relatively new phenomenon, but it is an exciting one, embracing the growing diversity of wines being produced in Chile today. Spend an evening hopping between some of the best wine bars in the country. Visit Bocanariz (pictured left) for the experience of Santiago's original wine bar in Lastarria with 400 wines in the cellar; try out the expert advice of top Chilean sommelier Ricardo Grellet at La Cava del Sommelier in Providencia; take in the bustle of Patio Bellavista with a flight at Barrica 94; or imbibe while having a full cinematic experience at Vinolio's tasting room in Vitacura.

SANTIAGO, CHILE

224 Tuck into the wine-paired menu at Boragó

Contemporary Chilean cuisine is beginning to step into the limelight, and it is largely because chef Rodolfo Guzman put it on the map with his upmarket restaurant, Boragó. Indulge in the twenty-course tasting menu of native-inspired cuisine, expertly paired with a flight of Chile's most eclectic wines.

MAIPO, CHILE

225 Follow an iconic Cabernet route

On every wine lover's bucket list should be a tasting of Chile's top Cabernet Sauvignons and Bordeaux-style blends. The top terroir for Chilean Cabernet is Maipo Alto, at the foothills of the Andes. Don't miss Almaviva, Viñedo Chadwick, Don Melchor, Luis Pereira, and Lazuli, which are Maipo classics and among the best in the country.

MAIPO, CHILE

226 Visit the oldest wineries in Chile

Although wine has been made on an artisanal scale in Chile for 500 years, the first commercial wineries were established in the 1800s, surrounding the capital of Santiago. Retrace Chilean wine history by visiting some of these historic estates in Maipo and Santiago. The oldest and still running include: Cousiño Macul (established 1856), Viña Santa Carolina (established 1875), and Viña Concha y Toro (established 1883). Viña Santa Rita (established 1880) is perhaps the most spectacular of all—set on a beautiful estate with handsome gardens and a stunning colonial-era mansion that doubles as a hotel and is named after their iconic wine, Casa Real.

TOP 3

MAIPO, CHILE

Learn the stories behind these three Chilean vineyards

227 Viña Antiyal

Alvaro Espinoza is the most influential figure in biodynamic viticulture in Latin America, and you can chew the cud with him and his wife, Marina, at their family estate, Viña Antiyal. Work your way through the biodynamic wines and get a taste for how Espinoza has helped transform Chile's viticulture and wine styles over the past three decades.

228 Viña Concha y Toro

Viña Concha y Toro is not only the largest winery in South America, but one of the biggest in the world, so it's no wonder it needed to make up a ghost story of a devil prowling the cellar to deter thirsty employees from pinching the burgeoning supply. Visit the diablo yourself with a tour of the cellar and a pour of Casillero del Diablo wine.

229 Viña Carmen

For more than a hundred years, one of Chile's most planted grape varieties was thought to be something entirely different. In 1994, Viña Carmen harvested what it thought was Merlot, but turned out to be Chilean Carménère, as discovered by a French wine expert walking through the vineyard. Taste Carmen's wines at its Doña Paula restaurant in Maipo.

SAN ANTONIO, CHILE

230 Muse over mosaics and wine in Lo Abarca

The Marín sisters are known for two reasons in the small coastal village of Lo Abarca. María Luz Marín is one of Chile's leading female winemakers and a wine pioneer in San Antonio (planting vineyards just 3 mi/5 km from the coast), where she established Casa Marín winery. Her sister, Patricia Marín, is known for her colorful mosaics, which adorn the winery, village, and local church. Enjoy a picturesque and mouthwatering visit.

CACHAPOAL, CHILE

231 Be wowed by VIK estate's striking architecture

VIK estate's winery and hotel have architecture par excellence, designed by architects Smiljan Radić and Marcelo Daglio, respectively. Both will vie for your attention between the spellbinding water garden and state-of-the-art cellar, and the swooping bronze titanium rooftop of the hotel with panoramic views of the valley from inside. The hotel appears like a golden crown rising from beyond the vines, whereas the winery nestles itself into the foothills with rolling stones on its rooftop. Spend the day exploring the wines and vines of VIK estate, and in the evening admiring the hotel's eclectic art collection and the masterful fine dining. Best of all is the glorious sunrise that awaits you with the vineyard view through your bedroom window.

234 *Opposite: Cono Sur Vineyards & Winery features bicycles on its wine labels*

COLCHAGUA, CHILE

232 Breathe polo and wine at Casa Silva

Polo has been one of Chile's favored horse sports ever since the British first arrived in the nineteenth century, and several of the oldest wine estates have players in the family. No wine families are quite as committed to the game, however, as the Silva family of Casa Silva. Next to the vineyard and winery is a full-size polo field and clubhouse, which happens to be one of Colchagua's best winery restaurants. Catch a game with a glass of wine in hand, ideally from the Patagonian estate "Lago Ranco," where polo horses are raised.

COLCHAGUA, CHILE

233 Ride with the *huasos*

Wine country is also horse country in Chile, and Colchagua is the heart of both. Several wine estates offer horseback riding between the Andes foothills and vineyards, guided by *huasos* (the local horsemen, Chile's equivalent of a cowboy). Explore the different faces of Colchagua wine country by horseback with Tumuñan Lodge, MontGras, and Hacienda Los Lingues.

COLCHAGUA, CHILE

234 Cycle through the vineyards of Cono Sur

Although Cono Sur Vineyards & Winery may well have been a sponsor of the Tour de France, the bicycles on its label move at a much slower pace. Visit the winery in the village of Chimbarongo, where each morning the workers arrive by bicycle to work the vineyards. Hop on!

COLCHAGUA, CHILE

235 Get the full *fuegos* experience of Montes

Fire is the essential ingredient of all traditional cuisine in the southern cone, but Fuegos de Apalta restaurant has taken it to another level. Discover all the ways in which local vegetables, fruits, and cuts of meat and fish can be grilled and flamed at Francis Mallmann's restaurant among the vineyards of Montes in Apalta.

COLCHAGUA, CHILE

236 Slip into an infinity pool amid the vines

One of the grande dames of Colchagua, Lapostolle Residence is Apalta's most luxurious estate. It has private wine villas that overlook the rolling hillsides down through the valley of the 939 acre (380 ha) biodynamic estate. Dive into its infinity pool, which drops off into the vineyards below, for a few laps in Apalta luxury.

COLCHAGUA, CHILE

237 Meet the Santa Ana winemaking crowd

Tucked into the hills of Santa Ana is a nucleus of small producers. A retired count from Italy, a Chilean marble merchant, and a real estate agent-turned-*garagiste* are among the converts who have all chosen to make boutique-production wines here. Visit Clos Santa Ana (pictured right and below), Caminomar, and La Despensa Boutique Winery to get the inside scoop.

ITATA, CHILE
238 Drink *pipeño* in Itata

Chile's oldest vines and oldest wine traditions can be found down south in Itata, where locals still make their own wine for the year. While touring the beautiful old vines and granitic hillsides of Itata, pull over where the handwritten signs are scrawled with *"pipeño"* and *"chicha"* to try a glass or two of the local wine. It's a Chilean wine tradition preserved for hundreds of years.

MAULE, CHILE
239 Soak in a wine tub

There are many reasons to visit Bouchon Family Wines: to view the old vines growing on the plains, to take in the wild País growing in the trees, and to gaze at the stars from the comfort of the enormous old wine barrel hot tub. Spend a night or two at Casa Bouchon to enjoy the laid-back pace of life down Maule way.

OSORNO, CHILE
240 Visit vineyards near Chilean lakes

Chile's wine frontier keeps growing, and the new limit is near the snowy slopes of Osorno Volcano in Chilean Patagonia. Spend a weekend by the lakes down south and try the mouthwatering Riesling, Pinot Noir, and Chardonnay of Trapi del Bueno, Lago Ranco, Coteaux de Trumao, and Ribera Pellín.

240 *Above: Coteaux de Trumao is the creation of two French brothers*

Western Europe

France and Germany are two of the world's greatest wine nations, so it's no surprise that both countries overflow with wine-related activities. There's a real thrill to connecting the famous wines of Puligny, Margaux, or Châteauneuf-du-Pape to the actual towns and villages of their namesakes. For Riesling or Pinot Noir lovers, following the course of Germany's Mosel River will keep you occupied for weeks! Don't forget that Berlin has one of the liveliest wine scenes in the whole country.

Switzerland tends to keep its outstanding wines closer to its chest—that's because they're made in tiny quantities. The country's jaw-dropping alpine scenery provides a perfect accompaniment to those precious sips. Winemaking might be more up-and-coming in the United Kingdom, the Netherlands, and Belgium, but all these nations now have very serious wine offerings—both homegrown and from farther afield.

ZÜRICH, SWITZERLAND

241   Relax with a wine—or a coffee

There are real synergies between the worlds of specialty coffee and artisanal wine, and wine bar 169 West aims to demonstrate that by specializing in both. Too early for wine? Explore its single-origin coffees instead. You can work your way through the natural-wine list later on.

ZÜRICH, SWITZERLAND

242   Walk through lakeside vineyards

One of Zürich's hidden gems is its 340 acres (138 ha) of vineyards situated directly on the lake. Enjoy the lakeside views by walking the short 1.2 mi (1.9 km) route between Wilen and Freienbach. Just follow the signs with informative displays and stop at Leutschenhaus restaurant along the way.

TICINO, SWITZERLAND

243   Harvest some grapes

Ticino is sometimes called Switzerland's little Italy due to its borders and the Italian-speaking population. Get involved in the harvest in the town of Mendrisiotto, where Merlot is the main grape and where they have a special program that allows visitors to join in. Simply contact the Mendrisiotto tourist office for more details of this event that happens every year in September and October.

TICINO, SWITZERLAND

244   Visit a prestigious hillside estate

It's well worth the trek up to Cantina Monti, nestled into the same steep terraces as its vineyards at 1,805 ft (550 m) to understand the hard work that goes on there. This estate is so remote that, until 1978, it had no electricity. Sergio Monti has really pushed high-quality red wines in this region; his sons, Delio and Ivo, continue the travails.

241 *Opposite:* 169 West—a haven for good coffee and artisanal wine

TOP 5

Admire the scenic settings of five Valais wine producers

245 Domaine Chappaz

Visit Marie-Thérèse Chappaz's handsome wood-framed winery and tasting room in the spring—this is the only time you can taste her entire range. It's also quite likely the only chance to try her rare and hugely in-demand sweet wines. Chappaz farms biodynamically and produces wines of crystalline beauty and precision.

245

245

246 Clos de la Couta

Jean-René Germanier's Clos de la Couta vineyard is one of the most beautiful in Valais. Have your camera ready when visiting this perfect natural amphitheater, which plummets steeply down from the nearby road. You'll taste exemplary Valais wines at the nearby winery in Balavaud.

247 Domaine Beudon

You can taste a real alpine freshness in the wines of Domaine Beudon. Visit the estate and you'll find out why. Some of the extraordinarily steep vineyards require a private cable car to gain access. The estate was the first in Switzerland to eschew chemicals and convert to biodynamics.

248 Albert Mathier & Fils

Visit the family-owned Albert Mathier & Fils winery and you will quickly discover Amédée Mathier's fascination with the Georgian amphorae known as *qvevri*. Arrange to have a special tour and tasting in the amphora cellar, which has been christened the Amphorium, and focus on the outstanding *qvevri* wines.

249 La Vigne à Farinet

It may consist of merely three vines, but La Vigne à Farinet has big ideas. It's a place for reflection and is festooned with flags and the names of film stars, politicians, and other luminaries who have helped harvest the grapes each year. To get to the vineyard, walk the short picturesque route—Le Sentier des vitraux—from the village of Saillon, following the beautiful stained-glass signs. The harvest is blended with additional wine contributed by a local winemaker, and the 1,000 or so bottles are auctioned each year.

249

VALAIS, SWITZERLAND

250 Explore the beauty of Valais

The problem with Swiss wine is getting your hands on it—the Swiss like it so much, they drink most of it themselves! Still, Valais is the country's largest region of production—and also one of its most beautiful. It is a continuation of the Rhône Valley and the dramatic scenery in Valais is difficult to put into words. Take the train from Geneva to the main towns of Martigny or Sierre and be prepared to ride most of the way openmouthed as you stare at the impossibly steep, terraced vineyards that line the hillsides. It's no walk in the park making wine in these conditions, but the results are so exceptional that it's worth it. Pinot Noir produces great results here, as do white varieties such as Heida, Fendant (a regional name for Chasselas), and Petite Arvine. Valais gets a huge amount of sun, but frequently succumbs to snow in the winter—which only increases its beauty. If you're into hiking, you're in the perfect place, as there are boundless trails, and it's highly likely you'll be walking past vineyards for at least some of the way. Most of Valais is French-speaking, but east of Leuk, the language changes to German, and there's a subtle cultural shift.

VALAIS, SWITZERLAND

251 Ascend to Europe's highest vineyards

The vineyards that cover the mountainous Visperterminen region stretch 2,133–3,773 ft (650–1,150 m) above sea level, creating a stunning patchwork landscape. Admire the quilt-like scenery during the 5 mi (8 km) hike from Visp train station up to the vineyards. There are hundreds of individually owned parcels, but the wine is made by the cooperative winery St. Jodern Kellerei, which you can also visit.

VALAIS, SWITZERLAND

252 Feast on cheese and wine in a castle

If you really want to understand raclette—a whole dish based around grilled cheese—then head to Château de Villa. The statuesque castle is situated in the old center of Sierre and boasts a restaurant specializing in fondue and raclette, plus an expansive wine bar and shop. You'll discover an encyclopedic selection of Valais wines. Pro tip: order the raclette option with five cheeses for your whole table, and you can eat as much as you like. Be warned: the successive courses of grilled cheese don't abate until you make it clear that you've had enough.

VAUD, SWITZERLAND

253 See how a rockfall created amazing wine

Check out the bizarre crater-shaped vineyards at Domaine de l'Ovaille winery. They were formed almost 450 years ago (1584) by a massive rockfall. *"L'Ovaille"* means "accident" or "catastrophe" in Old French. The wonderful grand cru Chasselas is, however, no accident at all!

253 *Above:* The land at L'Ovaille was shaped by a massive rockfall

254 Ride through a UNESCO Site

Take the train through Lavaux's gorgeous lakeside vineyards, which were designated in 2007 as a UNESCO World Heritage Site. During the two-hour trip on the Lavaux Express, you'll see multiple vineyards and stop at a cellar en route for a forty-five-minute wine tasting. Choose from four tourist train routes that depart from Lutry or Cully.

255 Sip Swiss wines with a lakeside view

Enjoy the lakeside views from the terrace of wine bar and restaurant Le Rouge et Le Blanc during summer. It enjoys a perfect setting on a pedestrianized street right by Lake Geneva. The wine list focuses on small-production, artisanal, and natural Swiss wines and is a real treasure trove.

256 Stroll through Geneva's open cellars

Make sure you're in Geneva toward the end of May, when around eighty of the area's independent vignerons open their cellars for tastings of both new and old vintages. Caves Ouvertes occurs on just one day a year and means a riot of people, food, and festivities. Travel between the wine villages by rented bicycles, free shuttles, or special train services.

BERLIN, GERMANY

257 Pair wine with Chinese cuisine

You might not expect a Chinese restaurant to excel in wine, but Jianhua Wu's chinese restaurant Hot Spot is the exception—the German Wine Institute has even honored Hot Spot with an Excellent Wine Gastronomy award. Wu is a serious German Riesling and Bordeaux fan, and his list is great by any standards, not just those of Chinese restaurants. Marvel at the harmony of the spicier dishes paired with dry Rieslings, or the tea-leaf-smoked duck with Spätburgunder. Book a table and enjoy the outstanding by-the-glass selections, and you'll discover why the restaurant is deservedly popular with wine fans everywhere.

BERLIN, GERMANY

258 Have fun at a wine fair

The lively atmosphere of Markthalle Neun provides the perfect location for the annual RAW WINE fair in Berlin. Every November or December, you can taste a cornucopia of Central and Eastern European wines (plus some from farther afield) or grab a bite from one of the many artisanal and street-food stalls at the fair.

258 *Above:* RAW WINE fair celebrates natural, organic, and biodynamic wines

BERLIN, GERMANY

259 Go natural at Cordo

Want to drink from a vast list of Germany's and
Austria's top natural winemakers, with many
offered in verticals (a tasting that looks at just
one wine through a range of different years)?
Cordo in Berlin awaits you. Visit this stylish and
popular wine bar and restaurant that also has a
serious gastronomic offering. You'll find wines
from all over Europe on the list.

BERLIN, GERMANY

260 Toast the fall of the Berlin Wall

Check out Mauerwinzer, an effortlessly cool but
cozy wine bar situated right where a section
of the Berlin Wall used to split the city in two.
There's a superb list of wines from every German
region from east to west. Situated on the edge of
the hip Prenzlauer Berg district, the terrace even
has its own grapevines.

259 *Above:* Patrons of Cordo wine bar can grab a glass at
the bar, or sit down for a fully fledged meal

260 *Above:* Mauerwinzer features more than 150 different wines

AHR, GERMANY

261 Stroll through German vineyards

Get up close and personal to the Ahr's dramatic vineyard landscapes and unspoiled countryside by walking some of Der Rotweinwanderweg (the Red Wine Hiking Trail). So-called because of the predominance of Pinot Noir, it consists of 22 mi (35 km) of signed hiking paths, virtually all through vineyards. Walking the full route will take multiple days, but you have the option to choose many attractive short segments.

AHR, GERMANY

262 Explore the pretty Ahr Valley

The Mosel tends to steal the limelight, but visit Maibach farm's organic vineyards and you'll see that the Ahr Valley can easily hold its own when it comes to incredible scenery and top wines. The steeply terraced vineyards require backbreaking manual work, but you'll find the results more than justify the effort.

AHR, GERMANY

263 Marvel at views with perfect Pinot

Love Pinot Noir? Then head to Weingut Meyer-Näkel, a family winery that has pioneered high-quality dry Pinots since the 1980s. The family has vineyards in several of the Ahr's top locations, and sisters Dörte and Meike Näkel are in charge of this high-performing estate.

TOP 4

MOSEL, GERMANY

Visit four of Mosel's best wineries

264 Dr. Loosen

A trip to this "doctor" will certainly cure jaded palates, if not necessarily your health. Mosel wine estates don't come much more iconic than Dr. Loosen—it has been turning out some of the best single-vineyard Rieslings for decades. Revered winemaker Ernst Loosen has spent more than thirty years pushing the estate to new heights.

265 Weingut Kloster Ebernach

Take a tour of Weingut Kloster Ebernach's cellars and its impossibly steep vineyards to really appreciate the hard work that goes into making wine in the valley. Based in Cochem, right where the slopes reach their steepest inclines, this winery offers a real insight into its production processes.

266 Clemens Busch

Meander through the picture-postcard village of Pünderich and you'll reach the dramatic, breathtakingly beautiful vineyards of Clemens Busch. This small winery produces some of Mosel's most exciting dry wines (a style Busch specializes in) and has also pioneered biodynamic viticulture in the region. It'll give you a totally different angle on the Mosel.

267 Weingut Selbach-Oster

Mosel Rieslings don't come much more classic than those produced by Weingut Selbach-Oster. Visit the winery in Zeltingen, right in the middle of Mosel, and you can not only taste the exceptional range of wines, but also a wider selection that the family distributes via its *négociant* business.

267

MOSEL, GERMANY

268 Hike across Europe's steepest vineyards

Have a head for heights? The Mosel Valley is known for its steep inclines, and they don't come any steeper than the vertigo-inducing section around Calmont. Embark on the well-signed walk that starts from Ediger-Eller station and takes you high into the vineyards. Although named the Calmont Klettersteig, the equipped sections with ladders and ropes are not especially challenging, provided you have solid shoes and are moderately fit. You'll finish up in Bremm, where a hut serves drinks and snacks—including wine—and you can enjoy a stupendous view out over one of the Moselle River's horseshoe bends.

MOSEL, GERMANY

269 Party in the backyard of a Mosel winery

Staffelter Hof has centuries of history in winemaking, but also a serious program of gigs. Attend the various music events throughout the year and indulge in Jan Matthias Klein's own line of natural wines, with irreverent names such as Little Bastard and Little Red Riding Wolf. Then sleep it all off in simple lodgings above the winery.

268 *Above:* The Moselle River in Bremm, as seen from the Calmont vineyards

MOSEL, GERMANY

270 Spice things up in Ürzig

Ever noticed the phrase "*Ürziger Würzgarten*" on the label of top Mosel Rieslings? It's a reference to the superior vineyard location above the medieval village of Ürzig, and the spicy character that the red slate soil lends to the wine. Follow the steep path up from the village to visit an actual herb and spice garden (The Gewürziger Würzgarten), with hundreds of different edible plants to see. It's a great way to understand this top Riesling terroir, and also gives you exceptional views out over the river and across to the Wehlener Sonnenuhr (sundial).

MOSEL, GERMANY

271 Be awed by Mosel views

There are many ways to traverse the Mosel Valley—by road, river, or rail. Choose to go by rail, and on the ride from Trier to Koblenz, you'll be rewarded with wonderful views out over many of the valley's top vineyards and the famous *sonnenuhren* (sundials). Just make sure you're sitting on the correct side!

270 *Above:* Ürzig and the Moselle River in Germany's Mosel Valley

NAHE, GERMANY

272 Encounter Roman remains at a winery

Weingut Poss is an artisanal winery where you can experience the intersection of two historic wine cultures. The prizewinning architecture of the modern tasting room dovetails effortlessly with the Roman remains of the Villa Rustica—it's also possible to view archaeological finds from this site. Don't forget to enjoy the wines, which focus on Burgundy varieties both white and red.

NAHE, GERMANY

273 Navigate the Nahe by the glass

Choose from nearly 200 of Nahe's best wines at Nahe-Vinothek, housed in an attractive old building named Dienheimer Hof in Bad Kreuznach. The by-the-glass selection is especially impressive and includes choices from big names such as Emrich-Schönleber, Gut Herrmannsberg, and Dönnhoff.

NAHE, GERMANY

274 Walk the rocky road to Friedensbrücke

It's well worth the exertion of a two-and-a-half-hour hike to reach Friedensbrücke and its stunning view of vineyards emerging out of a 3,937 ft long (1,200 m), 663 ft high (202 m) red rock massif. The distinctive formations are the result of ancient volcanic activity. The circular walk starts and finishes in Bad Münster am Stein.

272 *Above:* Roman remains can be found at Weingut Poss

RHEINGAU, GERMANY

Discover three of Rheingau's historic gems

275 Kloster Eberbach

Step back almost a millennium
when you visit Kloster
Eberbach (founded in 1136).
Wandering around the
atmospheric cellars conjures up
images of the monks who first
made wine here some 900 years
ago. Don't miss the world-
famous Steinberg vineyard,
which is also the site of this
Cistercian monastery's modern
winery building.

276 Weingut Peter Jakob Kühn

If you thought that Germany's greatest Rieslings were sweet, Weingut
Peter Jakob Kühn will make you think again. Discover the superbly
nuanced, precise single-vineyard bottlings at this biodynamic estate—
which has been in one family for some 230 years—as well as the
Pinot Noir.

277 Schloss Johannisberg

With more than a millennium of
winemaking history and origins
as a Benedictine monastery,
Schloss Johannisberg is one
of Germany's most important
wineries. Visit to taste the wine,
or better yet, stay for lunch and
enjoy the highly rated restaurant
and its dreamy terrace
overlooking the vines in
this 1,200-year-old winery.

276

RHEINGAU, GERMANY

278 Sail high over Rheingau's vineyards

Take an open cable car from Rüdesheim am Rhein up to the Niederwald monument to encounter stunning views over a typical Rheingau landscape of rolling hills, vineyards, and wineries. Various options allow you to extend the trip, including the recommended "ring ticket." This involves an hour's walk from the top station of the cable car to a chairlift that takes you farther to the winemaking village of Assmannshausen. There, you'll find many good options for lunch or refreshments before returning to Rüdesheim by ferry. The whole trip takes around two and a half hours, and the service operates year-round.

PFALZ, GERMANY

279 See the world's oldest bottle of wine

Feast your eyes upon the oldest-surviving bottle of still-liquid wine in the world—even though you'll never get to taste its contents. You'll find it in the Wine Museum Collection of the Historisches Museum der Pfalz in Speyer. No one knows how the wine—dating from around 325 AD—tastes, and the museum confirms that it will never be opened. Also worth seeking out is a huge wooden wine press from 1727, which has been installed in the museum since 1910, when its new building was created. Many other exhibits relate to wine production in the Pfalz (aka Palatinate) region.

PFALZ, GERMANY

280 Relax at a village wine festival

Sample the Pfalz's best wine and food at Deidesheimer Weinkerwe (the Deidesheim Wine Fair) in the pretty village of Deidesheim. It's one of Germany's larger wine festivals—it attracts upward of 100,000 people over a long weekend in mid-August—but you'll find it feels intimate and authentic.

PFALZ, GERMANY

281 Check out an up-and-coming wine estate

Get your hands on some of the freshest, liveliest wines in Pfalz, courtesy of Daniel and Jonas Brand. The two young brothers have a simple motto: "Just raw grape juice spontaneously fermented in a bottle. Without any additives." Farming is organic. Don't miss Weingut Brand's pét-nats and the superbly refreshing Wilder Satz.

PFALZ, GERMANY

282 Drive along Germany's oldest wine route

Ponder the eighty-five-year history of the Deutsche Weinstraße (German Wine Route), as you drive the 50 mi (80 km) from Schweigen-Rechtenbach on the French border to Bockenheim an der Weinstraße. This is a wonderful way to see and connect up all the important wine villages and towns of the Pfalz region. Despite its name, the route doesn't cover the whole country. You'll see the imposing Deutsches Weintor (German wine gate) at the start of the route. At the end is the Haus der Deutschen Weinstrasse (the House of the German Wine Route), where you can eat a well-earned meal.

281 *Above:* Daniel and Jonas Brand make wines under the label Weingut Brand

RHEINHESSEN, GERMANY

283 Spy some new family talent

Bianka and Daniel Schmitt are, on the one hand, just carrying on the family business of winemaking. But they've taken it to the next level, by stripping back interventions to ensure that the grapes do the talking. The result? Pure, natural wines that are building a cult following. Complete the experience by staying in the guesthouse and dining at the simple restaurant on the premises.

RHEINHESSEN, GERMANY

284 Escape from a wine cellar

Weingut Domhof is a family winery with a difference—the red wine cellar is also an escape room! You'll need your wits and some wine knowledge to puzzle your way out within the time limit. If it all gets too taxing, sleep it off in the family's hotel.

RHEINHESSEN, GERMANY

285 Party like there's no tomorrow

You have a whole eleven days to celebrate the harvest at Binger Winzerfest in Bingen. This huge September festival, right at the heart of the Rheinhessen region, offers you limitless tasting opportunities, a full live music program, and a fireworks display to round things off. Come, as they say, to "celebrate, dance, and laugh."

RHEINHESSEN, GERMANY

286 Hike through scenic vineyards

You're spoiled for choices when it comes to hiking through the Rheinhessen's beautiful vineyards, thanks to the Rheinhöhenweg, a 318 mi (512 km) long hiking path that runs along both sides of the Rhine. The section between Bodenheim and Alsheim takes in the Brudersberg vineyards, which offer stunning views that can stretch almost as far as Frankfurt on a clear day. The route, which is clearly signed with a large black *R* on a white background, also passes through Rüdesheim am Rhein and Assmannshausen. Trails with the marking *RV* connect the left and right sides of the Rheinhöhenweg.

BRABANT, THE NETHERLANDS

287 Harvest grapes in the Netherlands

Want to experience the harvest and life on a working farm? Wijngaard Dassemus is a small winery and farm, idyllically situated in the village of Chaam, that welcomes volunteers. Winemaker Ron Langeveld grows only modern disease-resistant grape varieties such as Solaris and Regent, as he is a staunch believer in organic viticulture. The immaculate vineyards are not sprayed at all, not even with copper and sulfur, which are permitted under organic certification. Dassemus also has goats and chickens, and produces cider and a Dutch version of grappa. Participate in the communal and festive harvest, which stretches between September and October, depending on the grape varieties.

ZEELAND, THE NETHERLANDS

288 Taste some Dutch-style refinement

You might think that Dutch wine is an anathema or just a hobbyist's pursuit. Prepare to have those assumptions challenged when you visit Wijnhoeve de Kleine Schorre, one of the Netherlands' most revered wineries that even has its wines served in KLM's business class. Taste its crisp, elegant white wines and you're sure to be convinced.

287 *Above and right:* Wijngaard Dassemus grows only disease-resistant grape varieties

ANTWERP, BELGIUM

289 Get to know Belgian wines

Antwerp's wine bar Belgian Wines has achieved what might sound almost impossible. This comfortable space, right opposite the busy Saturday market, serves wines from only Belgian wineries. You can enjoy a wide range by the bottle or glass, from tasty sparkling cuvées such as the Chant d'Eole's grand cru to delicious whites, reds, and rosés.

LIMBURG, BELGIUM

290 Discover good Pinot from Belgium

Wijndomein Aldeneyck started out as a fruit farm until the owners had the idea of making wine. The gravelly soils and relatively dry climate in Limburg turned out to be perfect for Pinot Noir. Be sure to taste the elegant, complex Pinot Noir Barrique.

THROUGHOUT FRANCE

291 Snap up a bargain bottle

If you're in France during September, you'll be able to restock or fill up a suitcase during the annual Foire aux Vins. For two weeks prices are slashed across the country. Major supermarket chains, such as Auchan, Carrefour, and Intermarché, usually have excellent wine selections yet often sell an even larger range of wines at this time—they also offer free in-store tastings. *Vive la France!*

REIMS, FRANCE

292 Enjoy some bubbles

The perfect bistro in Champagne's capital city needs to have an excellent selection of top Champagnes and a certain grandeur about it. You'll find Café du Palais ticks both boxes with its wonderful interior and Art-Deco stained-glass ceiling. Choose from a list focused on the classics and from the simple but well-executed menu.

REIMS, FRANCE

293 Wade through a multiple-page wine list

The choice of Champagnes at Le Wine Bar by Le Vintage is both exceptional and imaginative. Here, you'll come across wines dating back to the 1980s and many bottles from cult producers such as David Léclapart and Selosse. If you can get beyond the twenty-five pages of bubbles, the rest of the list (fifty pages) is a treasure trove of serious artisanal wines.

REIMS, FRANCE

294 Sample a range of smaller-house Champagnes

When you want to get beyond the big brands, Les Caves du Forum is the wine store to visit. The selection of Champagnes from smaller houses and independent growers is impressive. Some 4,000 wines are available in the huge sixteenth-century cellars, including many rare bottles from across the whole of France. Take a trip to the tasting room, where any bottle can be uncorked and enjoyed for a small additional fee. You can also join an impromptu wine-sharing event that takes place each Saturday at 5 p.m.— buy any bottle, and it is shared with everyone else in the store. It's a great way to taste many different wines—and to make new friends!

294 *Above: Around 4,000 wines are available at Les Caves du Forum*

CHAMPAGNE, FRANCE
295 Enjoy a personal Champagne tour

Embark on a tour at Lanson and you not only get to see every stage of Champagne's production process, but you also get to walk among the vineyards. It's a more personal and detailed tour than some of the rather touristy offerings from other major Champagne houses. Tasting is of course an integral part of the experience!

CHAMPAGNE, FRANCE
296 Go to the grower

Calling all Champagne geeks! For a truly essential experience, make for the pretty village of Œuilly, where grower-producer Champagne Tarlant makes some of the most fascinating and delicious bottles in the region. The boutique winery has been established for some 400 years, and its Brut Nature has been produced without added sugar to show maximum terroir expression—it has become a classic in natural-wine circles. When visiting the dynamic Benoît and Mélanie Tarlant, be sure to try the sumptuous Cuvée Louis and also the vintage cuvées made from rare varieties, such as Arbanne and Petit Meslier.

296 *Above:* Benoît of Champagne Tarlant says: "Barrels help give a different texture to the wine"

CHAMPAGNE, FRANCE

297 Find bubbly with no added sulfites

Head off the beaten track to visit Drappier in Urville. It's well worth stopping in to see how this small, quality-minded house is pushing the envelope. If you're a lover of bone-dry styles, you'll appreciate the zero-dosage cuvées (unlike most Champagnes, these are completely unsweetened), including a superb Blanc de Noir made with no added sulfites.

ÈPERNAY, FRANCE

298 Sleep on l'Avenue de Champagne

Champagne obsessed? Then try sleeping in a beautifully renovated gîte that's actually situated on l'Avenue de Champagne, in the middle of Èpernay. Managed by the neighboring B and B Parva Domus, Gîte de l'Avenue de Champagne is a comfortable lodging that can sleep up to twelve people in four separate bedrooms. So, will you dream of bubbles?

ALSACE, FRANCE

299 Amble around a gorgeous Alsatian village

Alsace is full of beautiful winemaking villages, but Eguisheim is a contender for the top spot. Admire its cobbled streets full of flowers and historic buildings. You'll also find that it is home to more than thirty wineries, including Bruno Sorg, Paul Zinck, and Léon Beyer. You'll find plenty of eating, drinking, and sleeping options.

ALSACE, FRANCE

300 Eat, drink, and be merry in a *winstub*

Check out one of Bergheim's warmest and most friendly bistros: Wistub du Sommelier is a traditional Alsatian "stube" with a dream wine list from top local producers. Despite the untimely death of the erstwhile patron, the restaurant continues to live up to its reputation.

ALSACE, FRANCE

301 Indulge in grand crus

Not only is Le Cercle des Arômes a convivial Colmar wine bar with great charcuterie into the bargain, but it also offers a massive 180 wines by the half or full glass. Want to taste all of Alsace's grand crus without leaving your chair? This is the place to do it.

TOP 4

ALSACE, FRANCE

Discover Alsace's top four vineyards

302 Maison Trimbach

Maison Trimbach makes what has sometimes been described as the world's top Riesling—the single-vineyard Clos Sainte Hune. Visit the tasting room and cellars in Ribeauvillé for the opportunity to try the full range, including Cuvée Frédéric Emile and the divine late-harvest sweet wines.

303 Domaine Barmès-Buecher

Visit the charming Barmès-Buecher family at its domaine between Colmar and Eguisheim, and you'll taste some of the most vibrant and precisely made grand cru wines from the region. The family farms its plots biodynamically, which really helps the wines express the unique character of their sites and soils.

303

304 Domaine Marcel Deiss

Domaine Marcel Deiss is one of the most respected winemaking families in Alsace. Visit the family's cellars in Bergheim to taste some exceptional wines. For something different, also request to try the wines of Jean-Michel Deiss's son, Mathieu, who produces a more eclectic range under his own brand, Le Vignoble du Rêveur.

303

305 Domaine Zind-Humbrecht

Passed down through generations since the seventeenth century, Domaine Zind-Humbrecht has become one of Alsace's top estates. The family now has vineyards at ten different sites, including the exalted Rangen-de-Thann grand cru, one of Alsace's steepest and most challenging vineyards. Venture into the impressive cellars to understand the passion and attention to detail at this domaine.

305

LOIRE VALLEY, FRANCE

306 Soak up Saumur's surroundings

Avoid Saumur's tourist traps and head to La Tonnelle, a buzzing, riverside wine bar focused on natural wines. You'll enjoy an outstanding selection of tipples from all over the Loire, plus some great picks from farther afield. Live music in the square adds to the ambiance, and the shop will keep you stocked up for takeouts.

TOP 3

LOIRE VALLEY, FRANCE

Drop in at three of the Loire Valley's best wineries

307 Domaine Bobinet

A visit to Saumur isn't complete without visiting the traditional cellar dug into the tuffeau limestone. Domaine Bobinet is an artisanal grower with a particularly fine and expansive barrel cellar. Sample its wines made with minimal intervention and often with no added sulfites—they are typical and delicious examples of the local Chenin and Cabernet Franc.

307

308 Maison Langlois-Chateau

The Loire Valley is justly famous for its excellent Crémant (sparkling wines made using the same method as Champagne, but for a fraction of the price), and Maison Langlois-Chateau is one of the top brands. Take a trip to the modern winemaking facility built into the tuffeau hillside based just outside Saumur to purchase your own bubblies.

309 Domaine Breton

Catherine and Pierre Breton are two of the best exponents of Loire Cabernet Franc and come from four generations of Breton family winemaking history in Bourgeil. Learn more about their low-intervention winemaking and organic viticulture at the cellars in Vernou-sur-Brenne and discover the secret to the refreshing, elegant wines.

310 Traverse through Burgundy's top vineyards

To the ordinary motorist, it's just the D974, but for wine amateurs, this is the entry point to the Route des Grands Crus—a 37 mi (60 km) stretch of road that takes you through Burgundy's most famous villages and vineyards. Bring Gevrey-Chambertin, Puligny-Montrachet, Vosne-Romanée, Meursault, and more to life as you visit the places that gave their names to such iconic wines. The route is clearly signed—brown road signs depict a bunch of grapes. It's possible to cycle the whole way via the dedicated Véloroute des Grands Crus—rent a bicycle in Beaune and follow the admirably clear cycling-route signs, or join a group tour if you don't fancy your own route-finding abilities. There are countless wineries, restaurants, and bars clustered around the various villages, but for the best experience, venture off the main road and explore some of the side streets. Many wineries offer ad hoc tastings, some for free, and some for a small charge. Most will expect you to buy a bottle or two. Don't expect to be able to get into big-name estates like Domaine de la Romanée-Conti or Anne-Claude Leflaive, though, since they're not open to the public. For the most beautiful vineyard vistas, visit around October and November when the colors are especially magical.

Route des Grands Crus

BURGUNDY, FRANCE

Call at these three Burgundy winemakers

311 Domaine Chevrot et Fils

A father and son work together at Domaine Chevrot et Fils, where, in 2006, they renounced all chemical vineyard treatments. Horses are now used to work some vineyards, to treat the soil as gently as possible. It's worth getting to know the wines, which include some lesser-known appellations, such as Maranges and Santenay.

313 Domaine Anne Gros

Tasting wines from the prestigious grand cru vineyards of Richebourg, Clos Vougeot, and Echézeaux is a very rare treat. Visit the highly reputed Domaine Anne Gros, based in the village of Vosne-Romanée, and you can try some of the very best examples from this winery's hallowed sites.

312 Maison Joseph Drouhin

Maison Joseph Drouhin is one of Beaune's great winemaking names. Taste from the family's impressive and labyrinthine cellars, which run directly under the streets of Beaune. Three different tasting options are available, depending on what quality/price level of wine you wish to sample.

312

312

BURGUNDY, FRANCE

314 Spectate at a top wine auction

For one Sunday in November, the wine world focuses on a former charitable almshouse in Beaune. The Hospices de Beaune's historic Hôtel-Dieu building is now a museum. The hospice owns many precious vineyard parcels in top premier and grand cru locations, and its entire annual wine production is sold by the barrel for high prices during the Hospices de Beaune Wine Auction. Beaune throbs with three days of festivities, tastings, and dinners. Join the crowds that gather outside the Halles de Beaune to watch the auction itself on a big screen.

ARBOIS, FRANCE

315 Visit an iconic Arbois estate

Taste the world-famous characterful Jura and Arbois wines from Domaine de la Tournelle, a tiny estate with less than 15 acres (6 ha) of vines. Try local red varieties such as the lightweight Ploussard and Trousseau, the exceptional Fleur de Savagnin, and of course the Vin Jaune. If you're there between June and August, make sure you visit the peaceful bistro in the garden.

JURA, FRANCE

316 Watch a wine being blessed

Every year at the beginning of February a different Jura village hosts La Percée du Vin Jaune. Join the procession of winemakers carrying a barrel of the mysterious Vin Jaune, which is ceremoniously opened for tasting after its six years and three months of aging. The festivities span two days and are extremely popular.

VINCELLES, FRANCE

317 Stock up in Chablis

If you're passing through Vincelles, close to Chablis, make a beeline for La Croisée des Vins—one of Burgundy's best addresses to shop for the region's wines. You'll stumble upon a warm welcome and experienced advice from Raoul, the proprietor. He will ensure that you'll leave well stocked, whether with wines from the region or from farther afield.

BEAUJOLAIS, FRANCE

318 Relax at a pretty family winery

Sample some very serious Fleurie wines at the
charming Château des Moriers, a small family
estate close to the appellation border with
Moulin-à-Vent. It has been in the family for 200
years. You might not want to leave the bucolic
surroundings, but that's fine, since you can stay
in the *petite maison*'s guest rooms. Try some of
daughter Anne-Victoire Monrozier's own line
of wines under the name Miss Vicky Wine.

BEAUJOLAIS, FRANCE

319 Celebrate the arrival of Le Beaujolais Nouveau

It's become a world-famous celebration: at
precisely 12.01 a.m. on the third Thursday
in November, the current year's Beaujolais
Nouveau wines are released. Party at the source,
with the oldest and best festival in Beaujolais!
The five-day Les Sarmentelles de Beaujeu will
ensure you stay lubricated with the young,
fresh-tasting Gamay.

BEAUJOLAIS, FRANCE

320 Try and then buy Moulin-à-Vent wines

There are more than forty great producers
making wine in the Moulin-à-Vent appellation,
but don't worry about getting around to them
all. Right opposite the windmill is Caveau du
Moulin-à-Vent, a shop and tasting room run by
the local winemakers association. There's always
something open to tempt your taste buds, before
you load up your shopping cart.

BEAUJOLAIS, FRANCE

321 Take in superb vineyard views

Survey the panorama of some of Beaujolais'
top vineyards from Moulin-à-Vent, one of
Beaujolais' top crus (or quality subregions).
It takes its name from the windmill that stands
close to the peak of the hill, above the village
of the same name.

321 *Above:* The picturesque windmill that stands amid the Moulin-à-Vent vineyards

BEAUJOLAIS, FRANCE

322 Sample Juliénas off the back of a van

The historic vaulted cellars of Château de Juliénas are just one reason to visit this estate in Juliénas. A quick tasting and tour are free, or you can spend more time for a fee. If the weather's good, join a special tour and tasting in the vineyards, served out of a vintage VW camper van.

BEAUJOLAIS, FRANCE

323 Experience the life of a vigneron

Take a special "winemaker for a day" tour organized by hotel l'Auberge de Clochemerle, in Vaux-en-Beaujolais. A morning drive to the vineyards and an introduction from a local winemaker is followed by a gourmet picnic among the vines. A visit and tasting in the cellar conclude the itinerary. Combine it with dinner at l'Auberge's Michelin-starred restaurant, which is affordable and has an excellent wine list.

322 *Above:* Tastings at Château de Juliénas take place out the back of a VW camper van

RHÔNE, FRANCE
324 Be thrilled by this winemaker

Taste some of northern Rhône's most thrilling wines at Domaine de Pergaud in Brézème. Winemaker Éric Texier used to be a nuclear engineer in Bordeaux before changing career to winemaking. His analytical mind and drive for minimal intervention has resulted in amazing wines.

RHÔNE, FRANCE
325 Kick back in a Caromb wine bar

It describes itself as a wine bar, but you'll find that Vin Ensèn (based in Caromb, close to Capentras) is much more than that. Dine on high-quality food and purchase bottles that are available to go. You'll find many Rhône wines on the wine list, along with excellent selections from farther afield.

RHÔNE, FRANCE
326 Learn how the cosmos influences wine

Domaine Viret is definitely one of the Rhône Valley's quirkier wineries. Utilizing a philosophy called "cosmoculture," which aims to channel energies and balance magnetic forces to the maximum benefit for vineyard health, the results (reds, white, and orange, some fermented in amphorae) are nonetheless characterful and delicious. Swing by to understand Philippe Viret's admittedly bonkers-sounding methods better.

LYON, FRANCE
327 Savor the wines of the angels

Shop or drink from some 800 different wine options at Ô Vins d'Anges, one of Lyon's best *enotecas*. The focus is on natural or minimal-intervention wines, and the exceptional list includes interesting artisanal wineries from across France. The selections from other parts of Europe are also worthy of note.

LYON, FRANCE
328 Splash out at a classic Lyon restaurant

Pierre Orsi is one of Lyon's true gastronomic temples—the food is classic and flawless, the service glides like a ballet, and the wine list has boundless variety and fair pricing. Ask to see the cellars, where some wines date back to the nineteenth century.

LYON, FRANCE
329 Relax in an easygoing wine bar

Want to see what all the fuss is about with France's cult artisanal vignerons? Le Vin des Vivants can furnish you with Breton, Puzelat, Métras, Clos Fantine, Ganevat, and many, many more. This unpretentious, friendly wine bar spills out onto a lovely terrace in the summer.

330 Visit one of Rhône's giants

Michel Chapoutier has become one of the most
respected winemakers in France, pioneering
biodynamic viticulture and rediscovering
forgotten terroirs. Maison Chapoutier now
makes wine all over the south of France, and
although the operation is sizable, quality
standards remain very high indeed. Drop into
Chapoutier HQ in Tain l'Hermitage for a tasting
and tour. You can also arrange a cycle ride on the
hill of Hermitage—the site of northern Rhône's
most prestigious vineyards.

TOP 4

PROVENCE, FRANCE

Indulge in the wines on offer at these four Provencal places

331 La Verrière

La Verrière is a beautifully restored medieval property, with some parts dating back to the ninth century. It houses a modern winery (Chêne Bleu) that makes ambitious reds, and boutique accommodation. Whet your appetite with a winery tour and tasting, but stay a night or two to fully enjoy the spectacular surroundings—including a pool and the on-site chef and restaurant. Don't fancy driving up the small mountain roads? Well, then, make use of the property's helipad!

331

333 Domaine Tempier

With a name synonymous with the dark, meaty red wines of Bandol, Domaine Tempier is one of Provence's truly iconic estates. Visit its tasting room to sample the whole range, including a little-known white wine. The rugged, Mediterranean scenery that surrounds the winery will blow you away.

332 Domaine Henri Milan

Take an engaging tour of the winery and beautiful vineyards of Domaine Henri Milan, one of the first Provençal wineries to work organically and to reduce the use of sulfites in its production. Many of the wines, which are pure and fruit-driven, are now made without the use of added sulfites.

334 Café Léoube

Provence may be famous for its rosé, but Château Léoube takes it one better. Saunter down to its Café Léoube, situated on the private Pellegrin beach, where you can enjoy a glass of the delicious, organic rosé, together with a view of the pine forests and the sea.

ROUSSILLON, FRANCE

335 Drink in dramatic mountain scenery

You can't help but be blown away by the views over the foothills of the Pyrenees when you visit Vignoble Réveille, a small organic winery established in 2007 near Perpignan. The wines are made by France Crispeels, a Belgian whose delicate touch has led her to be hailed as a rising star in the region.

LUBERON, FRANCE

336 Sip on a château's exceptional wines

Located in the jaw-droppingly beautiful Bonnieux village, high in the hills of the Luberon National Park, Château la Canorgue produces outstanding, elegant wines that are among the best in the region. Visit the tasting room and shop to stock up on these exceedingly well-priced gems. Note that you can't visit the château itself.

LUBERON, FRANCE

337 Taste top wines at a campsite

The Domaine Les Vadons sign may well tempt you off-road to stay at its comfortable gîte or on its large camping site situated in a peaceful corner of the Luberon Valley. But wait, there's more! This unassuming winery makes quite exceptional wines, so it's likely that a drop such as cuvée La Melchiorte—an exceptional and age-worthy red blend, frequently praised in *Le Guide Hachette des Vins*—will tempt you even more.

336 *Above:* Château la Canorgue is located in the picturesque village of Bonnieux

CHÂTEAUNEUF-DU-PAPE, FRANCE

338 Celebrate the coloring of grapes

For a taste of medieval France, join in Châteauneuf-du-Pape's Fête de la Véraison—an early-August festival dedicated to the magical moment when grapes change from hard green berries and start to color and ripen. More than 200 street performers in medieval costumes, wandering minstrels, and puppeteers provide the entertainment during the three-day festivities, which include knight tournaments, theater performances, music, and dancing. Your tasting glass (on sale all over the village) allows you to sample countless wines at the many cellar doors and wine merchants throughout the town.

CHÂTEAUNEUF-DU-PAPE, FRANCE

339 Wander these medieval streets

Walk around the medieval village of Châteauneuf-du-Pape and you'll be in no doubt that wine is the first order of business here. Wine merchants and producers' tasting rooms are crammed into the small cobbled streets. Head up to the castle ruin for a great view of the surrounding vineyards.

CHÂTEAUNEUF-DU-PAPE, FRANCE

340 Understand a unique winemaking landscape

Visit the vineyards of Domaine de Villeneuve to experience Châteauneuf's extreme terroir: the large stone galets that make up the topsoil reflect stored heat back onto the vines at night. This exceptional winemaker farms with maximum respect (and biodynamic certification) to create wines that retain regional character without being overblown.

338 *Above:* Châteauneuf-du-Pape's Fête de la Véraison

BANDOL, FRANCE

341 Wine and dine at this hidden gem

The quality of the wine service will draw you to De la Terre au Vin, but the food—a tapas-like concept—is also exceptional. The knowledgeable and friendly staff will help you choose from the sixty or so local wines on offer, and many wines can be tasted before you commit.

AVIGNON, FRANCE

342 Unwind in an intimate restaurant

The excellent seasonal cuisine and an inviting list of local wines are just two of the reasons why restaurant Fou de Fafa is so popular and should be on anyone's bucket list. Dishes focus on traditional Provençal flavors but often with a twist. It's a tiny restaurant, and this husband-and-wife-operated establishment feels intimate too. Reserve in advance!

AVIGNON, FRANCE

343 Try before you buy

Le Vin Devant Soi is a wine shop with a difference—you can taste many of the wines at your leisure from self-dispensing Enomatic machines. Simply buy a card preloaded with credits and then choose what to taste. Alternatively, relax on the terrace with a full glass from the excellent selection from across the Rhône, Languedoc, and south of France.

LANGUEDOC, FRANCE

344 Lap up great views and wines

Lunch with a view is on the agenda at La Cave
Saint-Martin, an easygoing wine bar and bistro
in the pretty village of Roquebrun. It offers
delicious food, including charcuterie, and a tasty
selection of local artisanal wines. Don't miss the
wines of Thierry Navarre, which are usually well
stocked here.

LANGUEDOC, FRANCE

345 Go back to the roots at Mas Zenitude

In 2006, Swede Erik Gabrielson and American
Frances Garcia created the Mas Zenitude
estate. The aim? To make wine with the
absolute minimum of intervention. Farming
is biodynamic, and no additives of any kind—
including sulfur—are used. The result? You'll
find earthy, lively wines with big personalities—
a bit like their guardians. Try the standout
Carignan-based Equinox and Vent d'Anges reds.

345 *Above:* Mas Zenitude avoids using additives of any kind in its wine

LANGUEDOC, FRANCE
346 Stumble upon a winery village

It's still formally known as Assignan, but this village in a forgotten corner of the Saint Chinian appellation is now almost wholly owned by winery Chateau Castigno. It has redeveloped the village as the Castigno resort in its own unique style: in colors of red, purple, and pink. Customized signs even rebrand the village as "Castigno." You can stay in super–high-end accommodations or more basic gîtes, and dine at a selection of restaurants and cafés, including the Michelin-starred La Table. Take selfies by the extraordinary tasting room, which is built in the shape of a giant bottle of wine laid on its side.

LANGUEDOC, FRANCE
347 Track down wine in Montpeyroux

Mas d'Amile based its winery (established in 2007) around some very old vines—chiefly Carignan and Terret Blanc, planted eighty years ago by Amélie and Sébastien d'Hurlaborde's grandfather. The wines are fruit-driven and extremely elegant. This estate has a bright future, so catch it on its way up!

CORBIÈRES, FRANCE

348 Discover fresh wine in a hot climate

Visit the wonderful region of Languedoc, where you'll find Domaine Sainte Croix tucked away in a rugged corner. The boutique English-owned winery focuses on fresh, lively styles of wine— no easy matter in the hot, dry climate. Explore the surrounding area, littered with Cathar castles and gnarled old bush vines.

LOT, FRANCE

349 Taste a Lot of Cahors

Southwest France is home to interesting lesser-known wine appellations such as Cahors and the Côtes-du-Lot. Get to know many of these wines and their makers a little better at the annual Fête du Vin in early August. It is organized by Les Vignerons Indépendants du Lot in Puy l'Évêque.

349 *Above:* The vineyards at Château de Chambert near Cahors are among the oldest in the region

SAINT-ÉMILION, FRANCE

350 Uncover Bordeaux's natural side

You might not immediately associate Bordeaux with the thriving organic and natural-wine movement, but the wine shop Les Caves Natures will change your thinking. The selection is exclusively organic, biodynamic, and natural, with wines from Bordeaux and southwest France. Discover many interesting young winemakers, and classics such as Château Le Puy and Château Meyney.

SAINT-ÉMILION, FRANCE

351 Snag your birth-year wine

The ridiculously pretty town of Saint-Émilion has a crazy concentration of fine wine shops clustered around its historic center. Many specialize in older vintages, and there's a good chance that you'll be able to locate that special birth-year wine—assuming price is no object!

SAINT-ÉMILION, FRANCE

352 Soak up Saint-Émilion scenery

Call at Château Fonroque and you're in for a real treat, for both the wines and the scenery! The sensational Saint-Émilion grand cru wines produced at the château completely outperform their price point. This is perhaps due to the careful and respectful work done in the vineyards, which are farmed biodynamically by winemaker Alain Moueix. Sit back and relax with a glass of red in your hand and admire the lovely landscape.

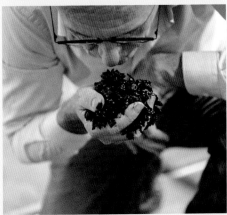

FRONSAC, FRANCE

353 Taste history in Fronsac

Spend a few days at Château de la Vielle Chapelle's comfortable Chambres d'hôtes (B and B) to get to know more about the pretty biodynamic domaine, which backs right onto the river Dordogne. Owner–winemaker Frédéric Mallier has a precious plot of one-hundred-year-old vines, still planted on their own roots (unlike 99 percent of modern vines, which are always grafted onto American rootstocks, to resist diseases). These grapes, including several now-rare varieties, go into the unique Bouchalès-Merlot, a Bordeaux wine that really offers a taste of history. Discover Mallier's other fascinating experiments—he has several on the go, including a wild nursery where he's breeding ancient varieties, and a new plot that will be flooded annually, as per a late-nineteenth-century tradition.

MÉDOC, FRANCE

354 Run a wine marathon

Join thousands of runners who, every September, compete in Le Marathon du Médoc, in full fancy dress! While there is a competitive element, you can also pause along the route for wine tastings and oysters. The fastest and the best dressed receive cases of Médoc wines as their prizes. If that sounds like too much effort, you can cheer the runners on instead.

MARGAUX, FRANCE

355 Stay in a top château

Ever dreamed of living in a castle? Château Giscours, one of Margaux's top estates, can make that dream come true. Choose from three luxuriously appointed guest rooms, with vineyard views, breakfast, and a free tasting of the grand vins included. The feeling of having the estate to yourself is priceless.

354 *Above:* Le Marathon du Médoc first took place in 1985

BORDEAUX, FRANCE

356 Taste your way across France

It might be famous for cocktails, but one look at the huge wine list at Point Rouge will show where the owner's passions lie. If you love classic French labels, this classy restaurant and wine bar has pretty much every region and style covered, often in multiple vintages and with some nice surprises among the big names.

BORDEAUX, FRANCE

357 Immerse yourself in the city of wine

It took years to build, but Bordeaux's La Cité du Vin was worth the wait. Allow a few hours to admire the architectural thrills and highly interactive wine exhibitions. Most are French-focused, but changing guest exhibitions also cover worldwide wines. Don't forget the complimentary glass of wine at the end.

BORDEAUX, FRANCE

358 Imbibe in a scenic setting

Wondering how Bar à Vin can offer such bargain prices? It's run by Bordeaux's wine promotional agency, the CIVB. Pop into this perfect wine bar situated in the handsome eighteenth-century Maison du Vin de Bordeaux building and settle on the great terrace for sensational summer sipping.

PESSAC-LÉOGNAN, FRANCE

359 Couple sculpture with wine

The warmth of owners Florence and Daniel
Cathiard radiates through Château Smith Haut
Lafitte, one of Pessac-Léognan's top estates, with
its enjoyably over-the-top faux-medieval pagodas
and towers. Admire the considerable sculpture
collection on an excellent vineyard walk. The
wines need no introduction.

MADIRAN, FRANCE

360 Get to grips with a
magnificent Madiran

Madiran's wines used to have a reputation for
being tough and tannic, but Domaine Capmartin
has helped change that with skilled winemaking
and organic viticulture. Visit to discover some of
France's most muscular but also approachable
wines, and you'll also enjoy views all the way to
the Pyrenees.

360 *Above and top:* Sheep roam among the vines at Domaine Capmartin

CORSICA, FRANCE

361 Frolic at a lively wine fair

If you find yourself in northern Corsica during July, be sure to attend Fiera di u Vinu (Festival of Corsican Wine). Producers come from all over the island to show their wines, so it's the perfect opportunity to sample their punchy whites, rosés, and reds, accompanied by great local food, music, and festivities.

CORSICA, FRANCE

Discover four of the best wine-related experiences in Corsica

362 Clos Signadore

Taste rare local varietals such as Bianco Gentile, Nielluccio, and Riminese at Clos Signadore, a boutique organic winery. Christophe Ferrandi works the vines in a rugged, mountainous landscape. Winemaking is done with the minimum of intervention, so that northern Corsica's unique terroir can speak louder than words.

363 Antoine Arena

Antoine Arena has been a force for change in Corsican wine, showing the world that the Patrimomio region is capable of producing very fine wines. Drop into the domaine to admire his old vines, situated high up in the mountains. The wines themselves are characterful and typical of this rocky, Mediterranean landscape.

364 Casa Vinu

For top seafood cooking, avoid the marina in Calvi and head a little farther to Casa Vinu. As befits its name (house of wine), this restaurant and bottle shop has an excellent selection of both Corsican wines and selections from mainland France. Follow the staff recommendations of wine pairings with different options for each course.

365 Domaine Saparale

If the luxurious accommodation at Le Hameau de Saparale in Figari isn't enough of a draw (and it should be), the winery (Domaine Saparale) also offers an option for you to blend your own wine. After two blending sessions on consecutive days, you'll receive three bottles of your personal blend to take home.

366 LONDON, ENGLAND
Salivate in a luxurious wine shop

Hedonism might just be the most over-the-top wine shop on the planet. Situated in Mayfair, it has an extraordinary selection of 6,500 bottles to choose from. Whether you're in the market for a bottle of Château d'Yquem Sauternes from 1847 ($125,000) or a complete vertical of Château Mouton-Rothschild from 1945, this store has it. Russian-owned, it nonetheless has attractions for all tastes and price levels. Six Enomatic machines allow you to sample everything from Georgian Tsolikouri to vintage ports and iconic Barolo. A kids' play area is provided, as you'll need more than twenty minutes to get around this temple to wine!

LONDON, ENGLAND
367 Treat a loved one to a romantic night out

An absolute gem of a restaurant, Andrew Edmunds is cozy and vibey, and offers high-class bistro fare, with a changing handwritten menu and an immaculately curated wine list. Choose from plenty of classics, including well-priced mature claret and Burgundy, or something quirkier, such as an Elisabetta Foradori wine or a Lebanese rosé.

KENT, ENGLAND
368 Fall into a Kent winery

There's a whole cluster of wineries around the town of Tenterden, of which Chapel Down is the most major. The visitor experience is excellent, as you'd expect. Either book a full winery and vineyard tour or turn up for ad hoc tastings. Feed your appetite at the winery's on-site restaurant, The Swan, which receives many plaudits.

368 *Above:* Chapel Down offers full winery and vineyard tours, and produces the Kits Coty single-vineyard range

LONDON, ENGLAND

369 Become a winemaker for a day

Why take a regular tour when you can have a more hands-on experience? In addition to its tours, London Cru also offers a Winemaker for a Day activity that gets you involved in tasting and blending. It's the capital's first urban winery (opened in 2013), and sources fruit exclusively from English vineyards. The winery has also won many awards for its output.

LONDON, ENGLAND

370 Quench your thirst at this London bar

When Terroirs wine bar opened in 2008, it was one of a kind—a large and informal bar bistro serving exclusively small-production natural wines, mainly from France, Spain, and Italy. It remains one of London's top alternative wine lists, and one of its liveliest wine venues. Grab a barstool for lunch or book ahead for dinner.

EAST SUSSEX, ENGLAND

371 Celebrate wine at Ridgefest

The chalky soils of the beautiful South Downs provide perfect conditions to make sparkling wine, and Ridgeview has cemented its position as one of the United Kingdom's top producers, since 1995, when the winery was created. Drop in year-round or come for Ridgefest, the winery's own mini-festival, which is held on the public holiday in late August.

WEST SUSSEX, ENGLAND

372 Discover an English sparkling wine

Nyetimber's exquisite sparkling wines, produced only from its own estate-grown grapes, can rival those of Champagne. Put its opening dates in your diary, as the estate opens its doors to the public for just five weekends a year. You can also book a luxurious tour-and-dining experience.

CORNWALL, ENGLAND

373 Check out a Cornish vineyard

Long-established Cornish winery Camel Valley now spans two generations of the Lindo family. Sparkling wines and the Bacchus dry are exceptional. Book a tour or simply drink a glass on the terrace. Stay in one of two holiday cottages if you'd like to wake up to the beautiful vineyard views.

373 *Above:* Guests in Camel Valley's holiday cottages wake up to stunning vineyard views

Italy

Where else does the thickness of a pizza crust or the variety of tomato spark such an impassioned debate? Regional identity and variation really drive Italy—and this includes wine. You'll find the most extraordinary diversity of wine styles, indigenous grape varieties, and wine terrains from north to south.

Northerly regions such as Alto Adige and Friuli-Venezia Giulia have fascinating cultural overlaps with their neighbors (Austria and Slovenia), and offer some of Italy's most elegant wines. The idyllic scenery unfolds as you head south—Lake Garda, the dramatic Prosecco road, and Piedmont's tumbling hills.

Some may get no farther than Tuscany, but there's a wealth of amazing wine and traditions farther south—such as Lazio, Marche, and right down to Puglia. Don't forget the islands of Sardinia and Sicily, which offer some of the country's most exciting wines and its most lip-smacking cuisine.

ALTO ADIGE, ITALY

374 Be wowed by these tasting rooms

Cantina Tramin's winery and tasting rooms are
housed in an architectural gem that will blow you
away. It boasts an impressive asymmetric lattice
design that frames outstanding views over the
valley. This major, quality-focused cooperative
produces stunning single-vineyard wines—be
sure to try the Gewürztraminer and Lagrein.

375 Time travel with Terlan

Ever tasted a forty-year-old Pinot Blanc? Kellerei Terlan keeps stocks of its best wines going back to 1979, and each year a small amount is bottled and made available for sale. Visit to see its impressive cellars, with bottles dating back to 1893, when the cooperative was formed. You might not taste anything quite that old, but the new vintages are also great.

376 Dine on a lakeside terrace

Set yourself in a delightful location overlooking Lake Caldaro at Seehof Keller's idyllic terrace. The charming restaurant's cooking doesn't disappoint, either—it boasts high-class dishes based on the region's traditional cuisine. Choose from a great selection of local wines, although by-the-glass options are relatively scarce.

377 Try some juicy reds

Kellerei St. Michael-Eppan cellar is a large, quality-minded cooperative, with 330 grower-members. Want to sample and buy juicy, lightweight reds such as the Santa Maddalena blend, the Edelvernatsch, or the satisfying complex Schulthauser Pinot Bianco? This tasting room is the place to go. Don't miss the huge three-dimensional map of the region—a great way to understand the different vineyards and terroirs.

378 Marvel at a multitude of amphorae

Drive to the edge of Trentino town and you'll find Agricola Foradori, dramatically framed by the Dolomites. Taste the Foradori family's delicious, refreshing, and now iconic wines from rare local varieties such as Teroldego and Nosiola, and arm your camera for the spectacular amphora cellars—the family has well over a hundred of them.

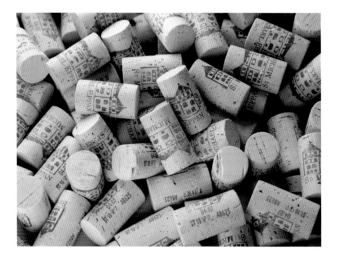

377 *Above:* Wine corks from the co-operative wine producers Kellerei St. Michael-Eppan

FRIULI-VENEZIA GIULIA, ITALY

379 Indulge at the Collio's top address

Looking for the best cuisine, wines, and hospitality in the Collio? This is what you'll find at La Subida, opened in 1960 by Joško Sirk. Situated close to the Slovenian border, the trattoria is now a Michelin-starred eatery and offers seasonal cuisine elevated to a high level. On top of that, the wine list is nothing short of a dream for any fan of Friulian and western Slovenian wines. Iconic local producers such as Gravner, Ronchi di Cialla, or Radikon are represented with huge verticals. There's also a flawlessly curated selection of artisanal wines from across Italy, and smaller selections from other European countries. La Subida also offers a more informal dining experience in its osteria, plus a number of accommodation options spread around the nearby forest.

FRIULI-VENEZIA GIULIA, ITALY

380 Wine and dine with one foot in Slovenia

Be sure to take a look in the cellar at Lokanda Devetak, which is stocked with around 14,000 top Italian and Slovenian bottles that you can select from. Although you're technically in Italy, this restaurant's heart and cuisine are firmly Slovenian. Tasting menus focus on what's been freshly harvested from the garden or caught in the woods.

FRIULI-VENEZIA GIULIA, ITALY

381 Stay in a converted farmhouse

Lis Neris winery is known for its elegant white wines, which evoke the terroir of Friuli Isonzo. Don't miss the opportunity to stay at Relais Lis Neris, a beautifully converted farm building with four spacious rooms arranged around a stately courtyard.

FRIULI-VENEZIA GIULIA, ITALY

382 Check out an enterprising winemaker

As you taste Mitja Miklus's range of orange wines, produced at the Draga Miklus winery, you'll be in no doubt that his star is rising. Enjoy wonderful views from his tasting room, which backs onto vineyards from the famous Gravner and Radikon families. You can also see the macabre collection of World War I weapons that were found on the estate.

FRIULI-VENEZIA GIULIA, ITALY

383 Take a historic drive through vineyards

Few roads are as steeped in history as the SP17 that winds up through the Collio hills from Nova Gorizia in western Slovenia, through Oslavia, to the peak of the hill at San Floriano del Collio. Not only will you drive past a near-continuous patchwork of vineyards and bucolic countryside, but you'll also see evidence of previous wars. Oslavia was the site of some of World War I's most brutal fighting—there's a large war memorial (ossuary) that contains the remains of 57,200 Italian soldiers. As you leave Oslavia proper, look out for a series of iconic wineries on the ascent to San Floriano; Gravner, La Castellada, and Il Carpino are among them. Radikon and Dario Prinčič are also in the area, but are not signposted.

FRIULI-VENEZIA GIULIA, ITALY

384 Feast on the view and the cuisine

Head to the northerly reaches of Friuli and you'll hit Ramandolo; a subregion dedicated to sweet wines. Perched high on the hills just outside Torlano, Osteria di Ramandolo offers not only commanding views down to the valley, but also superior local cuisine and a wine list full of buried treasure. Little-known, rare bottlings from local winemakers are something of a specialty here.

385 Visit a famous Oslavian winemaker

Josko Gravner is one of the region's true iconoclasts—a winemaker who redefined everything for Oslavia, choosing to shun technology and imported grape varieties. His focus is purely on the native Ribolla Gialla, which he ferments in Georgian amphorae (*qvevri*), with its skins. Visit the Gravner winery and tour the tranquil amphora cellar, and finish with a tasting of these exceptional and complex wines.

386 Taste back through the years

Discover the perfectionist family winery of Ronchi di Cialla—it sits in its own valley (the Cialla), which gives its vineyards such a special character that they have their own protected denomination. Here, the focus is on only Friuli Colli Orientali's indigenous grape varieties, and on making wines that can be aged for decades. Try the peppery, fifteen-year-old Schioppettino, and marvel at its youthfulness!

FRIULI-VENEZIA GIULIA, ITALY

387 Fulfill your hunger and thirst

Need lunch in the village of Schioppettino (Colli Orientali)? There's nowhere better than Trattoria da Mario, also known as the Enoteca dello Schioppettino. As you'd expect from the name, this homey but decidedly excellent trattoria offers a large selection of local wines made from the delightful Schioppettino grape variety.

FRIULI-VENEZIA GIULIA, ITALY

388 Celebrate wine in a ski resort

Tarvisio isn't known for wine. In the winter it's a ski resort that's so far north in Friuli that it's practically in Austria (and some of the residents are German speaking). But go there during October and you'll discover that for one week the town is taken over by the Ein Prosit festival—a celebration of Friuli's wine. Around fifteen producers show their wines, and there are a number of exclusive dinners with famed Italian chefs and carefully considered wine pairings.

FRIULI-VENEZIA GIULIA, ITALY

389 Wine, dine, and stay at a homey tavern

Overnighting at restaurant, winery, and guesthouse Klanjscek feels like heading to your own country retreat. Enjoy the open fireplaces, the comfortable rooms, and the house specialty: *peka* dishes—made from the Croatian method of slow-cooking meat or fish on embers under a bell-shaped lid.

389 *Above:* At Klanjscek you can dine on *peka*—the house specialty

FRIULI-VENEZIA GIULIA, ITALY
390 Taste amazing orange wines

It's hard to say which is the more magical: Sandi Skerk's beautifully elegant orange wines or his dramatic cellar, carved deep into the raw Carso limestone. Call into Azienda Agricola Skerk in Prepotto to experience both, and to also admire the organic vineyards, with views stretching to the Adriatic coast—on a clear day, you can make out the nineteenth-century Castello di Miramere.

FRIULI-VENEZIA GIULIA, ITALY
391 Visit an artsy cellar

Don't miss one of the most impressive cellars in Friuli Carso. At Kante, in Prepotto, three circular levels descend deep into the ground, and every floor is adorned with winemaker Edi Kante's abstract paintings. The wines have an impressive precision and purity about them—don't miss the Vitovska, which is a specialty in this region.

FRIULI-VENEZIA GIULIA, ITALY
392 Enjoy Felluga's wines in comfort

Spend an evening at Terra e Vini, an osteria (bistro) and guesthouse owned by the world-famous Livio Felluga winery. Located just across the road from the winery, there's a short and seasonal menu focused on hearty local cuisine. It doesn't disappoint! Wines by the glass are from Felluga, while the bottle list has a great selection from a wide range of Friulian producers.

VENETO, ITALY
393 Drive the Prosecco road

As you circumnavigate the winding road between Prosecco's two most important towns, Valdobbiadene and Conegliano, you'll be in no doubt why this subregion is UNESCO listed. Not only is this the home of the highest-quality Prosecco styles (Prosecco superiore DOCG, Rivé, and Cartizze), it's also jaw-droppingly beautiful, with tumbling hills and vineyards as far as the eye can see.

393 *Above:* Green vineyards on the hills near Valdobbiadene

VENETO, ITALY

Seek out these five fab, wine-related Veneto attractions

394 Malibran Vini

Not far from Conegliano is a small artisanal winery named Malibran Vini, which will redefine how you view Prosecco. Malibran's specialty is its col fondo wine, Sottoriva, made the ancient way with a natural second fermentation in the bottle. It's unfiltered and bottled with the yeasty sediment—gently shake it up and enjoy a superdry, flavorsome beverage.

395 Ruggeri

Ruggeri is one of Valdobbiadene's top Prosecco producers, showing that the DOCG version (made only in a small subregion between Conegliano and Valdobbiadene) can be very fine indeed. Try its exceptional zero-dosage Vecchie Viti, made from one-hundred-year-old vineyards on the hill of Cartizze.

396 Garbara

Prosecco isn't just about industrial-scale production. Garbara is a boutique winery working organically on the hill of Cartizze. Its handmade wines include a drier style of Cartizze and a savory, yeasty col fondo. Visit its welcoming tasting room and chat with owner-winemaker Mirco Grotto.

397 Osteria senz'Oste

Help yourself to Prosecco, halfway up the hill of Cartizze. From the Prosecco road, go to Osteria senz'Oste (the osteria without host), which is an honesty deli where you can pick up cheese, cured meats, olives, and bread. You may spot a goat standing guard next door. Follow the signs up the hill and you'll find what might seem like a mirage: a vending machine where you can buy a range of Prosecco, and even some paper cups if you didn't come prepared. You can picnic with a backdrop of Valdobbiadene's most gorgeous views—walk yet farther up the hill, and there are even foldout chairs and a table.

398 Agriturismo Lemire

Just off the Prosecco road near Conegliano, you'll find Agriturismo Lemire, a real hidden gem. Kick back in this blissfully quiet bed-and-breakfast's comfortable rooms in a restored country house, and enjoy an outstanding breakfast that you can take on the terrace with a view of Lemire's vines. The eggs are from the property's own hens, and fruit is also freshly harvested.

399 Visit the winery that put Amarone on the map

Named the godfather of Amarone by some, Giuseppe Quintarelli defined one of Veneto's most iconic wine styles. Quintarelli passed away in 2012, but his family continues to produce the exceptional wines that the estate is known for—even if the handwritten labels have to be facsimiles these days! You'll need to plan ahead, and bear in mind that the winery has no website, but the effort of seeking out its wines is well worth it.

400 Get merry at Lake Garda

Join around 100,000 visitors at Lake Garda for the Festa dell'Uva e del Vino (Grape and Wine Festival), spread over the first five days of October each year. There is plenty of wine tasting, drinking, and eating. The focus is on the latest vintage of Bardolino—Amarone's lighter, fresher red cousin. Wineries set up their tents directly around the lake, and you can taste a wide variety for a very nominal amount. The festival ends with a spectacular fireworks display over the lake on the final evening.

401 Taste small-production Amarone wines

Valpolicella and Amarone are popular styles of wine that are often mass-produced to fit a budget price, but head to the small Corte Sant'Alda winery and you'll see that winemaking here is a labor of love. You'll discover a different level of freshness and focus in these wines. The vines are farmed organically, wines are fermented with wild yeasts, and you'll taste fruit in the Amarone—not just caramel and oak flavors. A visit will take in a tour of vineyards and cellar, and you can also stay on the farm itself, at Podere di Castagnè.

GAMBELLARA, ITALY

402 Observe traditional winemaking methods

It's time for Soave to move over—head to lesser-known Gambellara instead and be amazed at the output of young winemaker Sauro Maule. His winery is modern and squeaky clean, but the methods used are ultratraditional. You'll taste wonderfully pure wines, since Maule uses no chemicals in the vineyards and very minimal intervention in the cellar.

GAMBELLARA, ITALY

403 "Marble" at the world of natural wines

The location—in a marble warehouse—might seem odd, but the annual VinNatur Tasting offers a riot of fascinating wines from France, Greece, Italy, Portugal, Slovakia, Slovenia, and Spain. Don't miss this three-day event that is attended by more than 180 of VinNatur's member-winemakers.

403 *Above:* Learn more about natural wines at VinNatur Tasting

404 Seek out this small artisanal winery

It's well worth hunting down Cantina Filippi, a small artisanal winery on the edge of the Soave Classico zone, in località Castelcerino. You'll taste Soave wines with greater individuality and nuance than those that are typically found on some supermarket shelves. The family's house and winery are themselves historically interesting buildings.

405 Explore beautiful Soave

Hit the Strada del Vino Soave (Soave Wine Route) that stretches for more than 30 mi (48 km), winding its way through the Soave region's rolling hills. You'll find the area littered with historic castles, churches, and, of course, vineyards. Clear signage allows you to follow various itineraries, and you're never far away from a cellar door or a restaurant to sample the local wines.

406 Visit a top Soave producer

Gini is justifiably one of Soave's biggest names. Sandro and Claudio Gini never stopped pushing for quality in a region that was resting on its laurels a few decades ago. Their entire vineyards are now certified organic, and the wines express their origin beautifully. Visit the impressive stone cellar carved into the volcanic rock, and be sure to taste the Amarone.

PIEDMONT, ITALY

407 Head for the hills for Nebbiolo

Go to Alto Piemonte, in northern Piedmont, at the end of May for the three-day Taste Alto Piemonte festival. An up-and-coming region, Alto Piemonte offers deliciously fresh Nebbiolo without the big names or the price tag of Barolo. The festival gathers fifty producers from the ten different appellations (including Gattinara DOCG, Ghemme DOCG, and Boca DOC). The tasting takes place in the stately Castello di Novara, surrounded by markets and food stalls.

PIEDMONT, ITALY

408 Find out why people love this *enoteca*

It's worth visiting the small town of Nieve, just north of Barolo, solely to spend a few hours at the cozy Enoteca al Nido della Cinciallegra di Michela Gallo. This small, superfriendly wine bar and shop welcomes you with the opportunity to taste a huge number of local wines. You'll get expert advice and information into the bargain. Situated on a pretty cobbled street, the *enoteca*'s terrace also gives you great views over the valley.

PIEDMONT, ITALY

409 Dine in the heart of Asti country

What's not to like about a low-alcohol sparkling wine with natural sweetness? Moscato d'Asti production is centered on the town of Canelli, which lends its name to an Asti grand cru. To appreciate this wine at its best, have dinner at Ristorante Enoteca di Canelli. Not only does this restaurant-cum-*enoteca* serve exquisite pasta and other local dishes, it also has an excellent selection of local wines. Enjoy the Moscato either as an *aperitivo* or with your dessert. You'll find on offer many of the region's other red and white wines to pair with the rest of your meal.

PIEDMONT, ITALY

410 Experience truly great Barolo

Find out why wine lovers go gaga over top Barolo by visiting GD Vajra, one of the region's top estates. Francesca and family are great hosts, the winery buildings are beautiful, and the wines are divine. Vajra also makes an excellent Freisa and a delicious Moscato d'Asti, so don't forget to try those too.

PIEDMONT, ITALY

411 Spend the night at a Barolo estate

Stay in one of Azienda Agricola Guido Porro's comfortable, traditionally furnished rooms, and you'll wake up to the dreamy vineyard views around Serralunga d'Alba. When you've finished enjoying this beautiful corner of the world, head to the cellar to taste Guido Porro's outstanding and very well-priced wines.

412 Visit a boutique producer in Morra

Discover the passion of the family at Azienda Agricola Curto Marco, a small winery producing exceptional-quality Barolo. The family works organically in the vineyards, and the wines have minimal intervention in the cellar and are expressive and typical of the region. A visit to this estate is an intimate and joyful experience.

413 Discover the joys of Timorasso

White wine rather than red is the specialty in Piedmont's Colli Tortonesi area—local grape variety Timorasso has had an extraordinary rebirth since Walter Massa started championing it in the late 1980s. Taste this delicious, age-worthy white wine at the annual Quatar Pass per Timurass in June—an open-cellar-door festival involving all the producers in the region.

412 *Above:* All grapes are harvested manually at Azienda Agricola Curto Marco

ALBA, ITALY

414 Pair truffles with a top Barolo

Enoclub is a wine-themed restaurant with a small but delicious à la carte menu. Your white truffle lust can be satisfied here—just be sure to visit in season! The wine list focuses mainly on Piedmont, with a huge choice of top Barolos, plus lesser-known but equally exciting wines from around Alba and Monferrato—try a Freisa or a Grignolino.

ALBA, ITALY

415 Indulge your truffle cravings

Alba is a winemaking town, but it has another even bigger claim to fame: it's in the middle of the world's best truffle-hunting countryside. Visit during autumn's white truffle season, and you'll find restaurants all over town offering shavings of the heavenly fungus. Freshly grated or sliced truffles are available everywhere from pizzerias to serious eateries such as Osteria dell'Arco, which has a special white truffle menu. It comes as no surprise that local wines such as aged Dolcetto d'Alba or Barbera are the perfect match.

414 *Above:* Order white truffles at wine-themed restaurant Enoclub on Alba's Piazza Michele Ferrero

EMILIA-ROMAGNA, ITALY

416　Feast on Modena's bounty

The rolling hills around Modena and Bologna are famous for the frothy delight that is Lambrusco; the rich, luxurious cuisine; and the extraordinary complexity of decades-aged balsamic vinegar. Enjoy all three when you stay at the winery and hotel Opera 02. Rooms are accessed alongside the vinegar cellar, and the spacious terrace restaurant serves upscale, traditional menus.

EMILIA-ROMAGNA, ITALY

417　Savor a glass of red bubbly

The handsome Roman city of Modena sits at the very heart of Lambrusco country and is the perfect place to get to know this quintessential *frizzante* beverage. If you thought Lambrusco was cheap, sweet, and nasty, think again. Traditionally, it is always dry, and often of very high quality. Emilia-Romagna's answer to Prosecco, it is usually made from red grapes. Modena's Old Town is full of convivial bars and restaurants ready to serve you a glass—there's no better *aperitivo*, and no better accompaniment to the region's rich, pork-based cuisine.

EMILIA-ROMAGNA, ITALY

418　Combine wonderful wine with great cooking

Andrea Cervini makes big, bold natural wines at this boutique wine estate, but he's also an expert in the kitchen. Stay at his Il Poggio Agriturismo (farm stay) for a rootsy experience in northern Emilia-Romagna—or just visit for a wine tasting and lunch or dinner.

EMILIA-ROMAGNA, ITALY

419 Drop in on a natural-wine giant

Visit the impressive cellars of La Stoppa, a cult winery based in the Trebbiola Valley in Piacenza province. Much loved in the natural-wine community for its highly aromatic Ageno orange wine, it also produces complex red blends that are aged for a decade or more before release. You may recognize owner Elena Pantaleoni, who is featured extensively in the 2014 documentary *Natural Resistance*. Don't miss the stately tower, as seen on the bottle labels.

TUSCANY, ITALY

Discover these four fantastic Tuscan winery experiences

420 Castello di Ama

Tasting top-quality Chianti Classico wines takes on a new dimension at Castello di Ama, due to the winery's impressive collection of specially commissioned, site-specific modern art. Names include Louise Bourgeois, Anish Kapoor, and Chen Zhen. While you're there, also check out the upscale restaurant and hotel suites.

421 Fattoria di Sammontana

Visit the historic boutique estate Fattoria di Sammontana, where the Dzieduszycki family, originally from Poland, have been making wine for four generations. Big fans of amphorae and cement tanks, the family wants its wines (from biodynamically farmed grapes) to be pure-fruited rather than oaky.

422 Salcheto

Enjoy wonderful views and great wines at Salcheto in Montepulciano. The winery generates all of its own energy and focuses on having the smallest possible environmental footprint. You might get tempted to stay for lunch—or overnight in one of the nine ecosuites.

423 Podere Anima Mundi

With wine names such as "Kiss Kiss Bang Bang" or "Ironista," you'll soon realize that this isn't your average Tuscan winery! Drop in to hear more about Marta Sierota's raw/natural winemaking philosophy. A wine tasting includes 20 percent off a visit to the nearby spa of Terme di Casciana.

423

TUSCANY, ITALY

424 Get festive in the heart of Chianti

Make sure you're in Tuscany during the second week of September, when the main square of Greve in Chianti turns into a massive wine tasting for three days. The event? The Expo Chianti Classico, which brings together more than a hundred Chianti producers offering their wines for tasting—you can buy them too. There are also various concerts, exhibitions, dances, and a photo contest during the festival.

TUSCANY, ITALY

425 Drive Tuscany's most famous wine route

Set out on the Strada del Vino, a set of twenty wine routes that take you to every corner of beautiful Tuscany. The most famous is SR 222, also known as the Chiantigiana. It runs from Florence to Siena, so you can explore many of Chianti's most famous wine towns, Greve, Radda, and Castellina among them. It will be slowgoing, since you'll want to stop often to take photos of the vine-covered hills, historic winery buildings, and stone castles in this fairy-tale landscape.

TUSCANY, ITALY

426 Explore peaceful Lucca

If you're suffering from Tuscan tourist overload, the gentile walled town of Lucca is a real haven. Head to Enoteca StraVinSky for a warm and enjoyably offbeat restaurant experience. There, you'll find a great selection of handpicked wines from north to south.

TUSCANY, ITALY

427 Turn back time at this island festival

Just off the Tuscan coast, you'll find Napoleon's old retreat—the island of Elba. Visit during September or October, and you might think you've entered a time warp. Around 5,000 locals dress up and act out historical winemaking activities for the annual three-day Festa dell'Uva (Grape Festival) in the town of Capoliveri. It's a colorful and lively pageant!

425 *Above:* The Strada del Vino takes you through the scenic landscapes of Tuscany

MARCHE, ITALY

428 Meet, greet, and taste Marche's top artisans

November is the perfect time to head to Ancona, where you can enjoy the Terroir Marche Festival and taste the wines from Terroir Marche's twenty or so winery members (all organic). You'll get a wonderful overview of the best that Marche offers—don't miss the full program of seminars and evening events, all of which need to be reserved in advance.

MARCHE, ITALY

429 Stay at an organic winery

Wake up to a dreamy vineyard panorama when you stay at the farmhouse of winery Fiorano, one of the founding members of Terroir Marche and a producer of very fine Pecorino and red blends. This is a charming property, run by the affable Paola and Paolo, and with easy access to the town of Macerata.

428 *Above:* Discover more than 180 wines at Terroir Marche Festival

MARCHE, ITALY

430 Sip delicious local wines

Enjoy a stroll through the charming, walled town of Macerata and finish up at Koinè Vineria. This cozy restaurant and wine bar has a real passion for handmade wines, and its selection of both local producers and some from farther afield is peerless. Ask Emanuele or Marta for a recommendation and you'll be in good hands.

MARCHE, ITALY

431 Taste Marche's top red wine

You won't find any 1970s disco classics at Cantine Moroder winery, but don't miss its outstanding red wines—Rosso Conero is the specialty in this part of Marche. The must-try is Dorico. The on-site restaurant and pizzeria (known collectively as Agriturismo Aión) is justly popular.

430 *Above:* Koinè Vineria has a passion for handmade wines

UMBRIA, ITALY

432   Retrace the steps of winemaking Romans

Take a drive through the oldest wine-growing areas of Umbria—the Strada dei Vini Etrusco Romana (Etrusco-Roman Wine Trail) transports you through 2,500 years of winemaking history, via Roman towns such as Orvieto, Amelia, and Terni. You'll encounter the white Orvieto DOC wines and the surprising Lago di Corbara DOC red blends, which are usually made from non-native varieties such as Cabernet Sauvignon and Merlot. There are many attractions along the way, including Lake Corbara and the arid sandstone Calanchi mountains. Palazzo del Gusto in Orvieto is a good starting point, since it houses the Enoteca Regionale, which acts as an information point.

UMBRIA, ITALY

433   Venture into a villa among vineyards

It's hard to imagine a more idyllic spot than the 70 acres (28 ha) of cherry tree groves and vineyards at Agri Segretum. Enjoy the organic wines to the max when you stay at one of the three beautifully restored farmhouses and villas.

ABRUZZO, ITALY

434 Meet an Abruzzo legend

Trebbiano is generally thought of as a humble grape—but not when you're drinking Emidio Pepe's version, which is a real head turner. Call upon this iconic estate, where you can eat in the upscale farm-to-table restaurant or stay the night in the converted house where Pepe himself was born and raised.

ABRUZZO, ITALY

435 Drink from a wine fountain—for free!

Recreating an old tradition, Dora Sarchese winery has created a wine fountain just outside its property—which happens to be on the pilgrims' route of il Cammino di San Tommaso, from Rome to Ortona. It is free to all pilgrims—and thirsty travelers who find it— so if you fancy some tasty Montepulciano d'Abruzzo, the fountain awaits.

ABRUZZO, ITALY

436 Visit a self-sufficient farm

You will see why Francesco Cirelli abandoned city life in 2003, when you visit his tranquil Agricola Cirelli estate. Taste his passion—wine fermented and aged in Tuscan amphorae—and admire the geese, olive groves, and sunflower fields.

436 *Above:* Agricola Cirelli's wine is fermented and aged in Tuscan amphorae

LAZIO, ITALY

437 Try traditional wines from Rome's closest vineyards

You're not far from Rome, Florence, or Siena when you stand in Sergio Mottura's atmospheric medieval cellar—but you'd never know it. His winery nestles in the Lazio countryside. Taste wines from traditional varieties such as Grechetto and Procanico and admire the family's erstwhile home, La Tana dell'Istrice (the porcupine's tail depicted on the labels), which also offers comfortable guest rooms.

LAZIO, ITALY

438 Visit a world-famous boutique winery

The accessible, natural wines of Piana dei Castelli have become favorites on tables from New York to London and beyond. Drop by this cult winery and try the wines for yourself—Pinot Grigio will never seem the same again!

437 *Above:* The Sergio Mottura estate has been in the Mottura family since 1933

ROME, ITALY

439 Linger over long wine lists

Head to Enoteca Ferrara for one of Rome's
biggest and most varied wine lists, combined
with typical Roman cuisine. Ferrara comprises of
a restaurant space, a more informal osteria, and
a wine bar where you can take your time to
peruse the encyclopedic wine lists. By-the-glass
selections are wide-ranging.

ROME, ITALY

440 Escape the tourist areas

Stray way off the tourist trail to Monteverde
and enter Litro, one of the city's best and most
established natural-wine bars. It is a cozy space,
with a simple but high-quality food offering
and a great list of orange, natural, and
biodynamic wines.

ROME, ITALY

441 Drink with the pros

Eat at Epiro (the food is a sharing-plates concept) and you might rub shoulders with some of Rome's
sommeliers or other wine professionals—such is the repute of the wine list here. You won't find big-name
wineries; instead, the list pulls together an eclectic mix of small-production gems from both Italy and
France. You can also sometimes find other treats, such as Cantillon beers.

442 Get to grips with wild Aglianico

Set in a wild, mountainous part of Italy, the Basilicata region is home to the Aglianico grape variety, which produces big, spicy red wines. It's the south's answer to Barolo, and these are serious, age-worthy wines. Visit the family-owned-and-run Donato D'Angelo winery to taste excellent, typical examples.

443 Experience a womb-like cellar

Valentina Passalacqua gave up her career as a lawyer to make wine in a wild, arid corner of northern Puglia. She's created an ever-expanding playful range of natural wines, produced from biodynamically farmed vineyards. The winery building has a huge cellar designed around the concept of a womb for the wine. It's well worth a visit!

444 Try the roots of the south

Take the fantastic opportunity to try the wine of producers from all over the south: from Campania, Puglia, Calabria, and across the water to Sicily. All you have to do is go to the Radici del Sud, a competition and wine fair in and around Bari in June. After two days of wine judging, there's a large tasting event on the Monday, culminating in the announcement of the winning wines. Who will you put your money on?

444 *Above:* Radici del Sud celebrates the wines of southern Italy

445 Observe a different way of farming

Visit L'Archetipo winery and farm, and it's easy to be impressed by the range of delicious sparkling wines, the skin-contact Fiano, and the light, fresh touch with everything. But it's the vineyards that tell the full story. Valentino Dibenedetto has developed his own variant of organic/biodynamic/no-till farming, which he calls "synergistic agriculture." Whatever he's doing, it seems to be working!

446 Taste the fruits of Fatalone

Ever heard of wine audio therapy? The Gioia del Colle subregion of Puglia is the home of Primitivo—a sweet, concentrated, high-alcohol grape variety. Fatalone takes this raw material and coaxes it into complex, elegant wines that can age effortlessly. The winery is completely carbon-neutral, and the barrel cellar is the site of an experiment where the maturing wine is played a range of carefully selected audio frequencies to aid its development.

447 Visit the master of Nero di Troia

When you take a walk in the vineyards of Cantine Carpentiere, there are great views of the commanding Castel del Monte fortress. These are some of the highest-altitude vines in Puglia. Taste the freshness and elegance of its Nero di Troia wines—some of the very best in the region.

BARI, ITALY

448 **Consume fresh seafood and top wine**

The list at restaurant Biancofiore is a dream for artisanal wine lovers—just about every important Italian winery from north to south is represented. Whether you're after a bottle of Gravner, Frank Cornelissen, or Elisabetta Foradori, it'll be on the list somewhere. Feast on the freshness and precision of the seafood cookery, which is to die for.

CALABRIA, ITALY

449 **Get to grips with Gaglioppo**

Love structured, spicy red wines? Then you'll relish the discovery of the Ciro subregion and its native grape, Gaglioppo. Cataldo Calabretta is the winery that has done more than any other to bring this beauty back to prominence. Its vines are bush-trained (freestanding) in the traditional manner, and the winemaking also harks back to a pretechnology age. You'll find the wines are quite simply delicious.

CALABRIA, ITALY

450 **Enjoy the rural idyll of Nasciri**

Head out into the mountainous wilds of Calabria to visit Nasciri, a small family producer of organic olive oils and natural wines, based near the village of Gerace. The year-round warm climate and views out over the Ionian Sea on one side, and the mountains on the other, may well tempt you to stay in the family's farmhouse.

450 *Above:* Enjoy a farm vacation surrounded by nature in Nasciri's apartments

ETNA, ITALY

451 Visit the source of volcanic wines

You can't miss the distinctively shaped peak of Mount Etna, which dominates the skyline of northern Sicily. It is visible from pretty much anywhere in the Etna wine region, just under an hour north of the town of Catania by car. Mount Etna is one of the world's most active volcanoes—there's always a plume of smoke drifting out of its belly, and fresh dustings of volcanic ash can appear at any time. Etna's wines have become seriously hyped in recent years, and their characterful mineral flavors are due to the volcanic soils that cover the region. The soil composition is constantly changing, which certainly keeps viticulturalists here busy, but the constant activity doesn't pose any safety threats. Drive to the Funivia cable car station in the national park area, and from here you can either hike up to Etna's summit (10,827 ft/3,300 m) or take the cable car. Join a guided hike to the summit or take a 4x4 tour—you can organize both at the cable car station.

ETNA, ITALY

452 Hang out with the local winemakers

It's well worth the trek to the winemaking village of Solicchiata, on Etna's north face, to visit Cave Ox. This might just be Sicily's best pizza—where else can you have pizza toppings that have been created by the local winemakers? Try the lemon-zested Pizza Graci! Sandro Dibella presides over an extraordinary wine list—if there's an Etna wine missing from his list, it isn't worth drinking. The selection of artisanal wines from across Italy and France is similarly impressive. You'll find that your Cave Ox companions will likely be the local winemakers.

ETNA, ITALY

453   Meet modern Etna wine pioneers

The world might not be turned on to Etna's wine today if it wasn't for the Benanti family—their pioneering efforts in the late 1990s really paid off. The Benantis continue to make some of the most classic and understated Etna wines. Visit the winery in Viagrande to hear the full story.

ETNA, ITALY

454   Encounter a wall of black lava

Take in the dramatic vineyards at Fattorie Romeo del Castello. At the back, a huge wall of black lava towers above them. This lava flow from the 1981 eruption threatened to engulf the entire property, including the historic eighteenth-century house. Thankfully, they were spared, allowing Chiara Vigo to produce wonderfully elegant wines. Don't miss the thousand-year-old olive tree on the property.

SICILY, ITALY

455   Taste wines from clay

Head about as far south as you can in Sicily and you'll wind up in hot, sultry Vittoria. The must-see is COS winery, whose cult wines, such as Pithos Rosso and Ramí, have gained it worldwide renown. Hear the story of how three friends started this enterprise almost by accident and then innovated by replacing barrels with amphorae.

SICILY, ITALY

456   Visit an independent spirit

You can visit major corporate wineries in western Sicily, or you can spend time with Marilena Barbera. Her Cantine Barbera is practically a one-woman show, with impressive organic vineyards and three delicious orange wines to taste. Be sure to sample her Perricone—a light-bodied red variety you'll be hard-pressed to find anywhere else.

456 *Right:* Cantine Barbera's Arèmi is a natural organic wine

SICILY, ITALY

457 Discover the origins of Marsala

Western Sicily is home to Marsala wine—
a fortified delight that these days is usually
produced as a sweet wine. Drop by Marco
de Bartoli, one of the region's most iconic
producers, to taste and learn about the original
Marsala Vergine style that was unfortified and
much drier. De Bartoli's cellars include some
barrels of Marsala that are more than a century
old—and still waiting for their moment of glory!

AEOLIAN ISLANDS, ITALY

458 Drink Lipari's distinctive white wine

Lipari is the largest of the seven Aeolian Islands,
which can be reached by ferry from Messina.
This lively Mediterranean getaway gives its name
to the grape variety Malvasia di Lipari, which
produces a textured, fresh-tasting wine. Take a
stroll through Lipari's town center, find a good
terrace, and enjoy a glass with your *aperitivo* for
the perfect Lipari experience.

457 *Above:* The de Bartoli family are fans of classic cars as well as classic wines

Central and Eastern Europe

The vast swathe of Central Europe, which was once the Austro-Hungarian Empire, is one of the most exciting parts of the wine world. Austria's nuanced white and red wines make a divine pairing with its bucolic landscapes—Slovenia offers similar beauty and many charming family wine estates. Both countries will feed you exceptionally well!

The Czech Republic and Slovakia are brimming with younger winemakers and their own characteristic wine styles. Poland is also starting to join the party.

As you head farther into the Balkans and down to the southern Mediterranean, the tempo slows and the focus shifts more to full-bodied red wines. Both Croatia and Greece boast sizable archipelagos: each island has its own wine story to tell, and often its own indigenous grape variety too.

Wine culture is long-established in most of the Balkans—for the more intrepid, it is still developing in Bosnia and Herzegovina.

LOWER SILESIA, POLAND
459 Taste amphora-fermented wines

Winnica de Sas was one of the first wineries in Poland to start using amphorae. Visit the family's winery in the picturesque Barycz Valley and try their *qvevri* Gewürztraminer—it's superb! Make the most of your visit and stay in comfortable guest accommodation.

LOWER SILESIA, POLAND
460 Meet an innovative winemaker

Winnice Wzgórz Trzebnickich is leading the charge to show that Lower Silesia can produce great wine—and particularly great Chardonnay and Pinot Noir. Don't miss the orange Pinot Gris, which is also seriously tasty.

POZNAŃ, POLAND
461 Drink globally but eat locally

Indulge in a tipple or two at WinoBramie, a stylish and well-stocked wine bar in one of Poland's prettiest towns. Choose from plenty of Polish wines and also an outstanding selection from across Europe. Snack on food that is based around "Polish tapas." Knowledgeable staff can help you select that perfect bottle.

WARSAW, POLAND
462 Choose from a long by-the-glass list

Spend an evening at Kieliszki na Hożej, a nice restaurant that serves a modern take on traditional Polish cuisine. The big draw here is its huge and eclectic wine list—choose from a massive selection available by the glass. Alongside a solid selection of Polish wines, there are great choices from classic and cult producers, such as Yves Cuilleron, Gut Oggau, or Ostertag.

462 *Above:* The staff at Kieliszki na Hożej can suggest a wine to pair with your meal

463 Check out an independent wine shop

Wine culture is still building in Poland, but check out Wrocław's first independent wine shop, Powinno, to see what's on offer. Run by a group of wine-loving friends, it sells an eclectic selection of European wines (including some homegrown Polish examples) in a relaxed, arty, and dog-friendly atmosphere.

463 *Above:* Find Polish and other European wines at Powinno

MORAVIA, CZECH REPUBLIC
464 Pedal through the vines

An impressive 750 mi (1,207 km) of signposted cycle routes wind their way through Moravia—these are divided into eleven separate circuits. Cycling is a wonderful way to experience the charming, hilly, countryside landscapes dotted with castles and other historical points of interest. The routes vary, from the challenging Kyjovská Wine Trail, which rewards you with fine Muscat and Pinot Gris wines, to the more leisurely Strážnická Trail, which ambles through the orchid-studded meadows of the White Carpathians. If your preference is red wines, you should cycle the Brno route. Otherwise, the Znojmo Wine Route is a white wine lover's paradise.

MORAVIA, CZECH REPUBLIC
465 Taste some quirky natural wines

Don't head to Milan Nestarec's cellar in Velké Bílovice expecting anything conventional. You're about to spend time with one of the region's top producers of natural wine. Taste his ever-evolving range of wines, including staples like the delicious G&T (a lively Gewürztraminer) or the curiously named Podfuck.

MORAVIA, CZECH REPUBLIC
466 Visit a respected winemaker

If you're a white wine lover, Jaroslav Osička's tiny estate might just be your piece of heaven. Visit other local producers and you'll discover that his influence has been considerable, since he's mentored many young winemakers. His wines are pure and made with minimal intervention, and the vineyard work follows organic principles.

PRAGUE, CZECH REPUBLIC
467 Investigate Central European wines

Every year in early May, Praha pije víno (Prague Drinks Wine) brings together about seventy winemakers from the Central European countries that were once combined as the mighty Austro-Hungarian Empire. Join the riot of artisanal and natural wine and try the wines of many small and up-and-coming producers.

465 *Left:* Milan Nestarec's White and Red Forks and Knives wines

468 Check out an "authentic" wine bar

The cozy wine bar Veltlin has become a must-visit address in Prague for fans of "authentic wines" (as the bar terms them). Founder Bogdan Trojak is himself a winemaker and created the Autentiste Czech, a winemakers group. Expect small-production wines, an ever-changing selection, and a personal and characterful experience.

BRATISLAVA, SLOVAKIA

469 Get a crash course in Slovak and Czech wines

If you want to try to enjoy a wide selection of both Slovak and Czech wines, Grand Cru Wine Gallery in Bratislava is your go-to. The atmosphere is warm and pretension-free, and staff can provide a wealth of information about what you're drinking and where it came from.

LITTLE CARPATHIANS, SLOVAKIA

470 Lap up some lip-smacking Slovak reds

Winemaking runs in the Magula family, but it was interrupted by communism for a couple of generations. From 2011, Vlad Magula once again produced some delicious and individual wines that take their cue from the pioneering efforts of neighboring natural-wine producers. Make sure you try Magula's light, refreshing reds.

LITTLE CARPATHIANS, SLOVAKIA

471 Follow the Little Carpathians wine route

Taking place along the Little Carpathians wine route, which stretches from Bratislava to Trnava, the Wine Cellar Open Day is the perfect opportunity to tour many of the area's small cellars. Taste the new vintages from up to 200 of the participating producers and enjoy the festive atmosphere!

LITTLE CARPATHIANS, SLOVAKIA

472 Enjoy deliciously different Devin

Distinguished by its surreal rooster-headed-man logo, Slobodné Vinárstvo is a winery formed by four young friends in 2011, who breathed new life into an old family estate. Working with minimal intervention, the winery produces an idiosyncratic lineup, with several orange wines and some cuvées aged in Georgian amphorae (*qvevri*). Definitely don't miss the Devin!

472 *Above: Slobodné Vinárstvo ages some of its wines in Georgian amphorae (*qvevri*)*

473 STREKOV, SLOVAKIA
Toast the natural wines of Slovakia

Zsolt Sütő makes natural wines in the village of Strekov—which he's also adopted as the name of his winery (Strekov 1075). Pop in to see how Sütő focuses on tradition, ancestral methods, and local grape varieties. He's inspired many other local winemakers and continues to make some of the best wines in the region.

474 Party on the banks of the Danube

Organized by the Österreichische Traditionsweingüter (ÖTW), the Tour de Vin during the first weekend in May is a wonderful opportunity to immerse yourself in the stellar wines produced along the banks of the Danube—and specially in the Kremstal, Kamptal, Traisental, and Wagram regions. Almost forty of the ÖTW members open their cellar doors for tastings, with many offering additional food-and-wine pairing options. You'll also be able to taste the wares of guest winemakers who visit the region at this time, and then indulge at the magnum party, where winemakers bring their favorite large-format bottles. The modest entrance fee is a bargain. Go for guaranteed good vibes!

475 Hang out in Kamptal's best vineyards

Embark on the Weinweg Langenlois, a walking trail that connects many of Kamptal's top vineyards via imaginative sculptures that all have a wine theme. Don't miss the giant bunch of grapes at the top of Bründlmayer's vineyards. The entire trail is a little more than 3.5 mi (5.6 km) and can be walked in two hours. Starting points are either Loisium WeinWelt or Ursin Haus, both in Langenlois. Reward yourself with a glass of something local when you finish!

476 Check into a wine and spa hotel

Book the Loisium Wine & Spa Hotel Langenlois for a self-indulgent weekend away. The imposing Loisium complex looks like cutting-edge architecture aboveground—it was designed by New York architect Steven Holl and has been likened to a giant concrete Rubik's cube—but the cellars underneath date back as far as 900 years. Check out various wine exhibits, a wine shop, and a bar on-site—not to mention a fully functioning winery and vineyards all around, while staying at this luxury spa hotel.

LOWER AUSTRIA, AUSTRIA

477 Explore Austria's oldest winery

The twin turrets of Klosterneuburg Monastery
have presided over 900 years of history. Among
many other treasures, the complex houses
Austria's oldest winery, Stift Klosterneuburg,
which is still very much in operation. Visit the
cellars in November, when they host the
Fasslrutschen celebrations, where wine is tasted
from a huge 300-year-old barrel that holds
12,318 gal (46,629 L). Don't miss out!

LOWER AUSTRIA, AUSTRIA

478 Get lost in mazelike cellars

The winemaking town of Retz boasts an
underground secret: its 12 mi (19 km) of tunnels,
dug 65 ft (20 m) into the sandy soils under the
streets, form Austria's largest wine cellars: Retzer
Erlebniskeller. Book a guided tour of the cellars
that are used as a labyrinthine wine-storage
facility. Bring your jacket, since temperatures
never rise above about 55°F (13°C), and you'll be
down there for around ninety minutes. *Brr!*

477 *Above:* Klosterneuburg Monastery is the location of the annual Fasslrutschen celebrations

479 Stroll, hike, or drive the Wachau

It's Austria's most famous wine region, and also
a UNESCO World Heritage Site; the Wachau
region stretches along the banks of the Danube
between the medieval towns of Melk and Krems.
It's a beautiful landscape, strewn with vineyards,
monasteries, and castles in various states of ruin
and repair. Wine has taken center stage here for
many centuries, and it's where you'll find some
of Austria's top Grüner Veltliner and Riesling.
Feeling energetic? Then tackle the World
Heritage trail, a 112 mi (180 km) long hiking
route that takes in some of the most enchanting
scenery in all thirteen village areas and includes
Jauerling, the region's highest mountain.
Highlights include the stone-terraced vineyards;
twenty different fortresses, ruins, and castles; and
three ferry routes to cross back and forth over
the Danube. The hike can be split into any of
fourteen different legs for those who just want to
sample the walking, but why stop there when
there's wine to taste? As you would expect,
there's no shortage of accommodation across the
region, from serious luxury to basic pensions,
plus many *heurigen*—simple taverns where
wineries serve their own young wines and
simple food.

WACHAU, AUSTRIA

480 Sip wine in an idyllic courtyard

It's an estate that was built on the site of a medieval monastery, and the stellar quality of the wines is enough to warrant a visit to biodynamic pioneer Nikolaihof. However, you'll also want to check out the historic cellar and the tranquil courtyard where the *heuriger* has its tables. There are few greater pleasures in life than enjoying Christine Saah's upmarket traditional cuisine under the spreading linden tree as the sunset dapples the courtyard. The wines, focused on Riesling and Grüner Veltliner, are often aged for many years in large oak barrels before release. Nikolaihof offers its entire range by the glass at the *heuriger*—unusual for a winery operating at such a high level.

VIENNA, AUSTRIA

481 Roam through urban vineyards

Vienna is one of the only cities in the world with a substantial amount of vineyards within the city limits—there are some 1,700 acres (688 ha) in total. North of the city, Nussberg is one of its greatest sites, both in terms of wine quality and also for the dramatic hilltop views over Vienna. The combination of vines and skyscrapers in a single vista is quite surreal. Take the tram to Nußdorf station and then enjoy a leisurely walk up to the top of the vineyards at around 1,150 ft (350 m) above sea level.

VIENNA, AUSTRIA

482 Have a stab at riddling

Schlumberger Sektkellerei is one of the most renowned Austrian producers of sparkling wine. Visit its historic cellars to learn about the whole process and try your hand at riddling the bottles—gently rotating them in wooden racks, to allow dead yeasts to sink to the bottom of the bottles.

VIENNA, AUSTRIA

483 Fill your glass—again and again . . .

The cellars at Villon span three levels and date back to at least 1701, with the cellar walls perhaps being 200 years older. Villon operates as a wine bar where you can taste some forty Austrian wines by the glass, thanks to the modern Enomatic machines. Insert a prepaid tasting card and the machine will dispense wine into your glass. It's that simple!

VIENNA, AUSTRIA

484 Shop for your favorite drop

WEIN & CO is one of Austria's largest wine-shop chains. Pop into its flagship Naschmarkt branch, right next to the Naschmarkt supermarket, to find a quality drop. The shop incorporates a wine bar, where any bottle can be enjoyed for a very modest fee. The selection is excellent, with not only mainstream offerings, but also top bottles from many artisanal and natural producers.

VIENNA, AUSTRIA

485 Attend Austria's largest wine festival

VieVinum takes place only once every two years (during the first week of June), but it's well worth clearing your diary for this festival. Just about every serious Austrian winemaker attends this massive three-day fair, which takes place in the impressive Hofburg building in the center of Vienna. There is no better opportunity to meet, greet, and taste with Austria's top producers. You can also get involved in numerous side events, guided tastings, dinners, and parties that also take place over the three days.

485 *Above:* Vienna's Hofburg building is the venue for the VieVinum festival

TOP 3

VIENNA, AUSTRIA

Raise a glass at these three Vienna wine locations

486 Pub Klemo

Pub Klemo is a cozy wine bar and shop that boasts an eclectic selection of Austrian and other European wines. There's a strong orange and natural wine section among other goodies. This is the place to go if you want to get beyond the big names and explore up-and-coming producers. You can also satisfy your appetite on its easygoing food.

487 Wieninger Heuriger

Wander to the top of the Nussberg vineyards to Wieninger Heuriger, where cold cuts and wonderful Gemischter Satz (Vienna's traditional white field blend) can be enjoyed together with an unparalleled panorama of the city. Franz Wieninger has worked tirelessly to raise the quality bar of Vienna's wines, so don't miss his white blends, which are some of the greatest from this unique region.

488 Mayer am Pfarrplatz

The winery Mayer am Pfarrplatz has its restaurant and *heuriger* located in the house where Ludwig van Beethoven once lived, which means that you can have a meal where the musical genius reputedly conceived some parts of his Ninth Symphony. The historic building is in one of Vienna's most beautiful and romantic tree-lined enclaves, a suburb that was outside the city in the eighteenth century.

488

THERMENREGION, AUSTRIA

489 Imbibe at a traditional *heuriger*

Winzerhof Landauer Gisperg is one of the quirkier wineries in the Thermenregion. Be sure to try the very fine Pinot Noir, as well as two wines fermented and aged in Georgian amphorae (*qvevri*). The wines are far superior to those offered in most *heurigen*, and the food doesn't disappoint.

THERMENREGION, AUSTRIA

490 Hike a culinary mile

For most of the year, the Genussmeile (pleasure mile) is a charming hike through the vineyards of the Wienerwald. Walk it in September, when for one week it is transformed into a culinary mile. You'll stumble upon food and wine stands positioned along the whole length, offering tasty treats. *Guten Appetit!*

THERMENREGION, AUSTRIA

491 Let your hair down at a major wine fest

Get your party hat on for Thermenregion's biggest wine festival, which happens each spring in the town of Baden. The Weinfestival Thermenregion hosts around fifty-five wineries from across the region, numerous tastings, and other side events during its five days. If you want to get to grips with Zierfandler and Rotgipfler, there's no better place to do it.

BURGENLAND, AUSTRIA

492 Stroll around a village called Rust

It may be a small village, but Rust is hugely important for wine. It sits at the center of the Neusiedlersee wine region and is particularly famous for its sweet wines. There's no better time to visit than during the first weekend in November, when all the cellars are open for the Herbstzeitlos tasting. Purchase a bracelet/token at one of the information points, and then you're good to go and taste as much as you like! Don't forget to admire the storks' nests on top of many of the village chimneys. If you need a break from tasting, take a walk out to the lake itself.

BURGENLAND, AUSTRIA

493 Party with the winemakers

The winemaking village of Kleinhöflein (which these days merges almost seamlessly into the town of Eisenstadt) becomes one big street party for ten days in July as locals celebrate Winzerkirtag Kleinhöflein. Local winemakers set up their stands in the street, and there's traditional food and music too. So party with the locals and enjoy a glass or three of local Welchriesling, Leithaberg Weiß, or Rot.

492 *Above:* The picturesque village of Rust is famous for its sweet wines

BURGENLAND, AUSTRIA

494 Work your way through a wine flight

Right opposite the impressive Eisenstadt's Esterhazy Palace is Selektion Burgenland, a wine bar and shop run by the local winemakers association. Choose from a huge selection of the region's wines in this lively spot. Twenty or more options are always open by the glass, or available within suggested wine flights. If that's not enough, anything in the spacious shop can be enjoyed on the premises for a small fee. Just ask the knowledgeable staff for help and recommendations.

BURGENLAND, AUSTRIA

495 Wander through a wine village

Purbach must be one of the prettiest villages in Burgenland—head for its short Kellergasse (cellar alley) right in its center for a tipple. Better still, be there on a Saturday during summer, when the cellar doors are open for tastings and visits. Sample from wineries such as Birgit Braunstein and Kloster am Spitz, which are headquartered here.

BURGENLAND, AUSTRIA

496 Consume top lakeside food and wine

Indulge in quality traditional cooking and an excellent selection of local artisanal wines at Zur Dankbarkeit, a high-class tavern, wine bar, and guesthouse. Situated in Podersdorf, on the banks of the Neusiedler lake, the establishment is run by the Josef Lentsch winery, whose wines are available by the glass.

495 *Above:* Purbach winemakers built their cellars here in around 1850

BURGENLAND, AUSTRIA

497 Taste cult wines at their source

Gut Oggau is a *heuriger* with a difference—this high-flying winery serves all of its liquid jewels by the glass. The inner courtyard is spacious and atmospheric, and the cold cuts are outstanding. Gut Oggau's minimal-intervention wines, famous for their "imaginary family" labels and produced from biodynamically farmed vineyards, are revered around the world, but never taste better than here at their source. Don't get caught out by the opening times—most rural *heurigen* are seasonal; in this case, visit during weekends between April and September.

BURGENLAND, AUSTRIA

498 Taste playful cuvées from two young winemakers

Sisters Susanne and Stefanie Renner make some of the most delightful, fresh-tasting wines from the town of Gols, close to the Neusiedlersee—one of Central Europe's largest lakes. Visit their cellar to hear how they've shaken things up since they took over the winery (now named Renner & Rennersistas) from their parents in 2016. You'll love the adorable wine labels, the juicy thirst-quenching reds, and the textured whites.

BURGENLAND, AUSTRIA

499 Visit a producer who respects nature

Discover how Gernot and Heike Heinrich have developed one of Burgenland's most impressive wineries, all the while retaining utmost respect for the land. The entire 250 acres (101 ha) are farmed biodynamically, and wines are made with a very light hand in the cellar. Weingut Heinrich is fascinated with the potential of Georgian amphorae (*qvevri*), which now dominate one of the cellars. Visit to experience the elegant and precise wines.

499 *Above:* Georgian amphorae (*qvevri*) line the cellars of Weingut Heinrich

BURGENLAND, AUSTRIA

500 Take in panoramic vineyard views

Walk out onto the Weinblick viewing platform, near the village of Deutsch Schützen, and get a commanding view of the Eisenberg vineyards. This grand cru subregion for the red grape Blaufränkisch is responsible for some of Austria's finest red wines, made by producers such as Uwe Schiefer, Wachter-Wiesler, and Grozser Wein.

BURGENLAND, AUSTRIA

501 Do your best Buster Keaton imitation

Pedal a *draisine* (handcar) along 14 mi (23 km) of an old railway track as it snakes through the vineyards and landscapes of Mittelburgenland. If those vineyards make you thirsty, fear not. There are three gastronomic "stations" along the way where you can refuel. Start your Draisinentour at either Neckenmarkt or Oberpullendorf stations.

500 *Above:* The Weinblick viewing platform overlooks Eisenberg vineyards

BURGENLAND, AUSTRIA

502 Grasp biodynamics

If you want to get deep into the theory and practice of biodynamics, Meinklang winery and farm is the place to do it. Nestled right up against Austria's Hungarian border, it's one of Europe's largest biodynamic estates. You'll see cows mixed in with the vines, and you can sample the estate's beer as well as its delicious natural wines. The Meinklang estate also runs a Waldorf (Steiner) school, if you needed any more proof of its ethical qualifications.

BURGENLAND, AUSTRIA

503 Cycle among cherry blossoms

Are you a keen cyclist? Then pedal your way across the Kirschblütenradweg (B12 Cherry Blossom Cycle Path)! Starting in the village of Jois, you'll pass through 27 mi (43 km) of Lake Neusiedl's bucolic landscapes. Most of Burgenland is rather flat, but this trail takes you up and down the rolling foothills of the Leithaberg. When you need a rest, be sure to stop at one of the area's many wine taverns to quench your thirst. Note that the cherry trees come into blossom during April.

STYRIA, AUSTRIA

504 Steam through Schilcherland

All aboard the Stainzer Flascherlzug! This delightful vintage steam train takes its passengers on a two-hour ride through the western Styrian countryside. It's a rolling landscape of vineyards and farmland, with two stops along the route where you disembark for refreshments. Keep an ear out for an accordionist who sometimes plays on board the train. Start the journey at Stainz station.

503 *Above:* The Kirschblütenradweg passes through thousands of cherry trees

STYRIA, AUSTRIA

505 Go back to school, with wines and a hike

As with many serious wine regions, Styria has its own winemaker school at Silberberg. Drop into the tasting room to try the school's excellent wines. Also check out the Weinlehrpfad Silberberg, a 1 mi (1.6 km) hiking route through the school's vineyards. It's illustrated with informative display boards, and there are great views of the surrounding countryside. Many Styrian winemakers learned their craft here—it's the source of Styria's talent.

506 *Above:* Weingut Tauss offers relaxing and classy bed-and-breakfast accommodation

STYRIA, AUSTRIA

506 Enjoy Zen moments and beautiful wines

Weingut Tauss is the perfect place for a romantic weekend away. The small boutique winery also operates as a high-class bed-and-breakfast. The luxurious rooms are furnished with natural, ecological materials, in line with the winery's biodynamic ethics. Practice yoga or meditate in the House of Silence space, or simply relax by the pool. The exceptional breakfast features many homemade delicacies, and your stay will be topped off by the estate's magnificent wines.

STYRIA, AUSTRIA

507 Discover Styria's top Sauvignon Blanc

Situated in the heart of southern Styria, family-run Weingut Sattlerhof is known for its Sauvignon Blanc. Drop into the modern tasting room to sample the family's output, where the top wines age gracefully for a decade or more. Better yet, dine in the upmarket restaurant— but be sure to reserve a table in advance.

STYRIA, AUSTRIA

508 Ask for only wine at this tavern

If you want to drink wine—and only wine—in southern Styria, then Tamara Kögl's traditional Buschenschank is the place to be. Winemaker Kögl is an up-and-coming talent in the area, and her basic wine tavern (with cold cuts and her wine) proudly advertises "No cola, no beer, no coffee, no hot food, no hurry." So, enjoy a glass or three in the stunning Styrian countryside.

STYRIA, AUSTRIA

509 Order from a magnum

Right next to Tement winery is its restaurant and wine bar, Magnothek, with a gorgeous terrace cantilevered above steeply sloping vineyards. The twist here is that virtually all wines are served from magnums, and the selection spans many styles from across Styria. Pair your *wein* with traditional, high-level cuisine.

STYRIA, AUSTRIA

510 Admire jaw-droppingly steep vineyards

Explore southern Styria, one of the world's most dramatic wine regions, along the South Styrian Wine Road. The landscape is punctuated by the traditional *klapotetz* (windmill-like constructions to scare birds away from the vineyards), and you'll spot almost gravity-defying vineyards that plunge down the slopes. Driving the small roads is fun, but for a better view, take one of the many walking routes. Don't miss the two gorges of Altenbachklamm and Heiligengeistklamm, which offer views into neighboring Slovenia. Avoid autumn weekends, when it gets seriously busy.

STYRIA, AUSTRIA

511 Ponder history at a table bridging two countries

Straddling the border of Austria and Slovenia, the Südsteirischer Grenztisch (southern Styria border table) is a modern-day stone monument to a new age of peace. Brutally fought over during World War I, this border didn't even exist before 1918. Now it's a tranquil area with vineyards on all sides, and a great place to sit and contemplate.

STYRIA, AUSTRIA

512 Take a hike through picturesque vineyards

Take the Weinwanderweg Ratsch-Ottenberg, which begins right outside Maitz winery, to enjoy a two-hour stroll through some of southern Styria's most beautiful vineyards. This three-and-a-half-hour walk isn't taxing, but it'll help you build up an appetite, which can be satiated by any one of the many local taverns.

STYRIA, AUSTRIA

513 Taste exquisite single-vineyard wines

Wolfgang Maitz is one of the region's most talented younger winemakers, producing quite exceptional beverages from the area's village and single-vineyard sites. Don't miss the Morillon Ratsch, which is always a highlight. While you're there, dine at the excellent on-site restaurant, where all the wines can be enjoyed by the glass. You could also make a weekend of it and stay at the comfortable Weinhotel Maitz.

STYRIA, AUSTRIA

514 Stimulate all your senses on this hike

The almost 9 mi (14 km) long Weinweg der Sinne (Wine Trail of the Senses) makes for a great full-day, interactive excursion through the vineyards around Sankt Anna am Aigen. The start and end point is the local *vinothek*. You'll find your way via signposts with wine bottles or bunches of grapes on them, and can stop at many "stations" that feature information about the soils and landscapes you pass through. There are many opportunities along the way for refreshment, plus stunning views that stretch to Hungary and Slovenia. In short, you'll enjoy a fantastic combination of the great outdoors, wine education, and pleasure.

512 *Left:* Southern Styria contains some of Austria's most beautiful vineyards

515 Drink wine and smell the roses

If you love aromatic wines, you might find
heaven in the village of Klöch at its dedicated
vinothek. Gewürztraminer is the specialty here,
combining with the volcanic soil to create
aromas of roses. Stop at the *vinothek* for tastings
and to buy wines from fourteen local producers.
Take the hiking path that leads you right into
the vineyards.

516 Shop till you drop

Think of almost any Styrian wine you like, and
you'll most likely find it on the encyclopedic list
at Vinofaktur Genussregal wine shop. There are
also forty "stations" where you can taste local
specialties—including wines, schnapps, pumpkin
seed oil, and cheeses. You'll pay a very modest
fee for the tasting experience. The architecture
is modern and creative, adding to the experience.

515   *Above:* The village of Klöch has a *vinothek* that offers tastings

STYRIA, AUSTRIA

517 Imbibe at a castle on a volcano

Eastern Styria is known as "Vulcanland" (Volcano Land), and the castle of Kapfenstein is built right on the peak of a long-dormant crater. The castle is owned by the Winkler-Hermaden family, who also make outstanding wines and run a restaurant on the site. Stay a night or two at the grand Schloss Kapfenstein Winkler-Hermaden and tour the estate.

STYRIA, AUSTRIA

518 Dine at a mecca to Styrian wine

There are few places in the world where you'll find such an exhaustive collection of Styrian wines as Weinbank. You can choose from two dining options: a fine-dining restaurant or the more spacious bistro-style wine bar. Many wines are available in impressive verticals, with vintages that are long sold out at the wineries and basically impossible to find anywhere else.

517 *Above:* The vineyards of Kapfenstein are built on the peak of a long-dormant crater

STYRIA, AUSTRIA

Party like a Styrian at these four fabulous festivals

519 Schilchertage

Western Styria is famous for its pin-sharp rosé wine Schilcher, produced from the local Blauer Wildbacher grape. Drink both still and sparkling versions at the annual Schilchertage festival in Stainz each August. Copious amounts can be enjoyed together with traditional food, music, and dancing.

520 Gamlitz Weinlesefest

The Gamlitz Weinlesefest (Vintage Festival) is a great excuse to enjoy a glass of Sturm, a hugely popular, sweet, partially fermented grape beverage that is only available for a few short weeks in the year. Roasted chestnuts and Styrian folk music will keep you partying for the four days of this annual October fest.

521 Schilcherberg in Flammen

The vineyards around Deutschlandsberg are illuminated by fires and fireworks for one night toward the end of each July. Schilcherberg in Flammen (Schilcher vineyards in Flames) celebrates the patron saint of the vines, Saint James (Der Heilige Jakobus), and uses the imposing castle as its centerpiece. The fireworks over the castle are a spectacular sight!

522 Steirische Weinwoche

Revel in the colorful, local celebration of Steirische Weinwoche in the southern Styrian town of Leibnitz at the end of August. At the five-day festival dedicated to wine, you can taste from an array of local wineries. Live music and food stalls add to the fun, and the Styrian wine queen is crowned during the event.

522

GRAZ, AUSTRIA

523 Experience Austria's largest folk festival

No festival of Styrian culture is more important than Aufsteirern, which takes place in Graz every mid-September. For three days, the entire city is filled with folk music and dance performances, fashion shows for traditional "tracht" clothing, and of course, a bumper dose of traditional foods and wines. Feeling adventurous? Audience participation is very much encouraged!

GRAZ, AUSTRIA

524 Quench your thirst

Cozy up with a great selection of Styrian white wines and Burgenland reds at the quiet courtyard Klapotetz Winebar in Graz's historic center. The wine card features producers both large and small, with more mainstream styles and some rare bottles for those who want to get their wine geek on.

523 *Above:* Join in the celebrations of the Aufsteirern folk festival

TOKAJ, HUNGARY

525 Immerse yourself in sweet wine

Few wine regions are as steeped in history or as filled with ancient cellars as Tokaj, which has been revered for its lusciously sweet wines for a millennia or more. Head to the village of Hercegkút and its UNESCO World Heritage listed cellars, which poke hobbit-like out of the volcanic hills. The town of Tokaj itself is also a good starting point—many wine cellars lie within the city limits. Drive out into the vineyards to experience Tokaj's climate—so important for the development of the so-called noble rot (botrytis), which gives the sweet wines their particular taste and complexity.

TOKAJ, HUNGARY

526 Discover more about the sweet nectar

For a deeper understanding of the Tokaj region, visit Tokaj's World Heritage Wine Museum, spread over three stories of a converted house. There are many interactive exhibits where you can virtually travel around the area. The focus of the impressive museum is Tokaj, but additional exhibitions cover other wines of the world. You can also benchmark your nasal abilities with an aroma-testing game.

TOKAJ, HUNGARY

527 Revel in a lively wine festival

Travel to Erdőbénye in August, when for one long weekend the village comes alive with Tokaj's top wine and gastronomy festival: Bor, mámor, Bénye. Organized jointly by around a dozen local wineries, there are makeshift stages and lounges set up all around the village for jazz and world music performances. It is one of the region's liveliest wine festivals, with great local musicians, food, and wines from Erdőbénye, and includes a guided tasting and many other events.

TOKAJ, HUNGARY

528 Visit a famous Tokaj winery

The Disznókö winery has history as one of Tokaj's biggest names since 1732, with seriously impressive cellars dug 30 ft (9 m) underground. The estate is particularly famed for its Tokaj Aszú (the sweet botrytis-affected style) and the even sweeter and more concentrated Eszencia. Arrange a vertical tasting, where you can buy vintages dating back to 1992.

TOKAJ, HUNGARY

529 Taste dry wines

If you've had enough of Tokaj's sweet bounty, visit the small Szóló winery, which produces a number of quirky wines, including the wonderful dry Furmint and Hárslevelű, plus a pét-nat (a naturally sparkling style) and some wines aged in amphorae. Tímea Éless created the winery from vineyards inherited from her grandfather, and now farms everything organically.

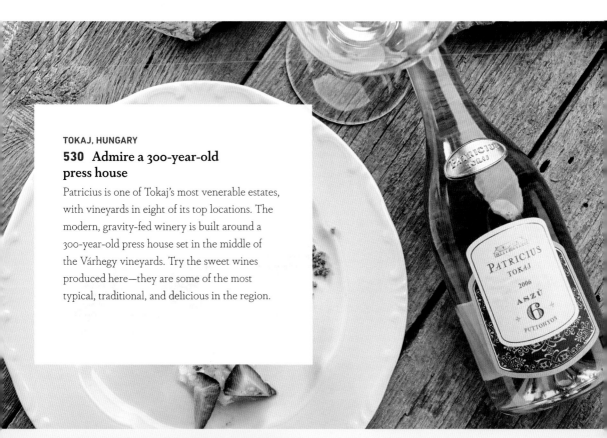

TOKAJ, HUNGARY

530 Admire a 300-year-old press house

Patricius is one of Tokaj's most venerable estates, with vineyards in eight of its top locations. The modern, gravity-fed winery is built around a 300-year-old press house set in the middle of the Várhegy vineyards. Try the sweet wines produced here—they are some of the most typical, traditional, and delicious in the region.

530 *Above:* Patricius winery is one of Tokaj's most respected estates

EGER, HUNGARY

531　Visit a winery in an old quarry

Bolyki Pinceszet is a quirky winery built in an old stone quarry. The buildings alone make this producer worth a visit. Don't miss the idiosyncratic art displays and wine labels, which add to the fun. The wines themselves are also delicious and typical examples of the region.

EGER, HUNGARY

532　Become fearless with Bull's Blood

The Eger wine region is home to the famous red-blend Egri Bikavér (Bull's Blood), which legend has it makes the drinker fearless. Wineries are clustered around Szépasszony-völgy (Valley of the Beautiful Women). It is a convenient thirty-minute walk from Eger town—or you can take the Dottika tourist train for an easy option. There are more than 200 cellars sited along the road into the valley, so it's child's play to taste and compare wines from a number of producers.

BUDAPEST, HUNGARY

533　Sink your teeth into a "book"

For a different kind of dining experience, try KönyvBár & Restaurant, where every week the chef "cooks a book." That's to say, it takes inspiration from anything from Dr. Seuss to George Orwell and bases a tasting menu around the book's characters. The cooking provides a modern take on Hungarian traditions. You can also indulge in an excellent selection of handcrafted wines from Hungary and neighboring countries, with which the outstanding food is paired.

533 *Above: KönyvBár & Restaurant offers book-inspired menus*

534 Hang out at a hip, live music venue

Make your way to a wine bar that really has it all: Doblo has oodles of ambiance and atmosphere, excellent live music (often acoustic or jazz), and the wine list is a dream, with many artisanal and up-and-coming producers on the list. Want to sample widely? The bar offers a number of wine-tasting options. You'll find this lively bar in Budapest's old Jewish quarter.

BUDAPEST, HUNGARY

535 Enjoy a peerless local wines selection

Pick any of DiVino Bazilika's seven wine bars in Budapest, and you're in for a treat. Thanks to its strong links to Hungary's young winemakers association, you can try wines from many up-and-coming producers. Winemakers often drop by, so you can get the lowdown, straight from the horse's mouth.

BUDAPEST, HUNGARY

536 Check out natural Hungarian wines

Mitiszol? Festival is the name of a fair for organic and natural wines that takes place every November at Bálna, Budapest. The list of participating Hungarian winemakers reads like a roll call of every serious artisanal producer, and there is a smaller number of participants from other Central and Eastern European countries. Choose from local and seasonal food options, along with beer and Pálinka tastings.

SOPRON, HUNGARY

537 Meet two sisters making charming wines

Birgit and Katrin Pfneiszl grew up in Austria, but in 2006, decided they wanted to breathe new life into the family's Hungarian wine estate. With winemaking experience from three continents, they've brought excellence, individuality, and charm to their output in Sopron. Be sure to try the Shiraz, Carménère, Malbec, Zinfandel, and Sangiovese blend (Faraway World), which Birgit makes in homage to her previous travels.

SOPRON, HUNGARY

538 Taste top Kékfrankos

If Weninger sounds Austrian, that's because it is—this artisanal winery operates on both sides of the border! Visit this pioneering producer to taste its famed Kékfrankos—it's really pushed the envelope for this variety. Don't miss the delicious rosé named after Franz Weninger's grandmother: Rózsa Petsovits.

538 *Above:* Weninger also produces Steiner Furmint, and have sheep grazing between the vines

SOMLÓ, HUNGARY
539 Savor wines from the "Grand Old Man of Somló"

Fekete winery is iconic due to its previous owner, Mr. Béla Fekete, also known as the "Grand Old Man of Somló." He sold the winery to the current owners (who continue his mission) when he was ninety, but he is still with us. The wines (from local white varieties) are concentrated, tight, and mineral—and age effortlessly for decades. Be sure to try characterful Juhfark, Hárslevelű, and Furmint.

SOMLÓ, HUNGARY

540 Hike up a vineyard-covered volcano

Somló may be Hungary's smallest wine region, but it's also one of the most special. The vineyards are spread around a dormant volcano, and the influence of the volcanic soils on the wines is marked. To really appreciate the special terroir, walk the 2 mi (3 km) Kitaibel trail in Somló's protected landscape area.

SOMLÓ, HUNGARY

541 Get thee to this boutique producer

Somlói Abbey Cellar is a boutique winery that is lucky to have the old vineyards that formerly belonged to an abbey for its raw material. Taste the wines that are made in a natural way, without any additions or modifications, and show the character of their vintages and soils beautifully. The winery has built a cult following for its individual style.

BALATON, HUNGARY

542 Head to this cluster of wineries

There are many reasons to visit the impressive Lake Balaton, one of Central Europe's largest. Make one of them the wineries that cluster around its northern banks, with the town of Badacsony at the epicenter. It's just an hour's drive from Budapest. Get details of accommodation and all the region's wineries from the Badacsony Wine Association.

BALATON, HUNGARY

543 Immerse yourself in wine festivities

For two weeks at the end of each July, Badacsony comes alive with a huge variety of events based around the local winemaking. Named Badacsony Wine Weeks, you can enjoy a full program of music and cultural events, plus craft demonstrations, and of course, copious wine and food tastings.

VILLÁNY, HUNGARY

544 Enjoy full-bodied wines

Villány is one of the warmer, sunnier parts of Hungary, perfect for red wine production. The Gere Attila winery has great examples of Portugeiser and Kékfrankos, plus some oak-matured blends from Bordeaux varieties. Combine a tour and tasting with a stay at the nearby spa hotel owned by the winery.

545 Walk around a romantic vineyard

The small heart-shaped vineyard in the hamlet of
Špičnik is a very pretty spot. The road around
the vineyard was created to mitigate the steep
incline of the land—admire it from farther up the
hill, at the Dreisiebner tavern.

546 Treat your taste buds

Situated very close to the Austrian border, the
slickly designed restaurant Hiša Denk cooks up
a storm of modern Styrian-Štajerskan food. Pair
this with an exceptional selection of wines from
local and nearby producers. Verticals of Radikon
and Batič are just some of the delights, and you
can also stay on-site.

547 Check out a biodynamic enthusiast

Stop at Zorjan, and you'll discover that many elements of the winery are rather unique: white grapes are
fermented in Georgian amphorae (*qvevri*), and often aged for five to seven years before release; Zorjan
works with biodynamics, and employs some quite esoteric practices in the vineyard and the cellar; and
you won't find the year listed on the bottle—Zorjan doesn't want drinkers to have any preconceived
ideas based on the wine's age. A "no mobile phones" symbol on the bottle is taken seriously at the
winery—Zorjan prefers that the wines are enjoyed without distractions or electromagnetic interference.
If you need an English-speaking translator, a neighboring friend can often help.

ŠTAJERSKA, SLOVENIA

548 Gaze upon the oldest-living grapevine

Right in the center of the city of Maribor is a 450-year-old grapevine that still produces fruit. It's listed in *Guinness World Records* and is still very much full of life. It's incredible to think that this vine was planted during a time when the city was held under siege by the Turks. You'll find it located at the Old Vine House museum, where you can indulge in tastings of local wines.

BRDA, SLOVENIA

Meet five of the makers of Brda's best wines

549 Aleš Kristančič

Winemakers don't come much more feted than Aleš Kristančič, who painstakingly built up the Movia brand over several decades. Movia's wines are made with minimal intervention in the cellar. Don't miss an undisgorged sparkling wine, which is often theatrically opened at the estate, and the supernatural "Lunar."

550 Aleks Klinec

Aleks Klinec has one of the biggest smiles in winemaking, and he also happens to be an incredibly skilled winemaker. Klinec works biodynamically in the vineyards, and also farms fruit and vegetables in addition to keeping horses and poultry. His wines are some of Brda's top orange wines—deeply hued with incredible fruit purity and autumnal flavors. Klinec also matures his own hams and salami, which you can consume as part of a serious lunch or dinner at the property's on-site restaurant. Stay for lunch and soak up the stunning views out over the valley from the terrace.

551 Andrej Erzetič

Visit the small family producer of Erzetič, where younger son Andrej Erzetič is now in charge. The winery holds a surprise—Andrej has created a small but perfect *qvevri*-cellar, where these Georgian traditional amphorae are buried underground—just as they would be in Georgian cellars. Andrej uses the *qvevri* to make a delicious line of white and orange wines. Be sure to taste the highlight: the Anfora Belo.

550

552 Janko Štekar and Tamara Lukmann

Fancy some volunteer farm work in beautiful western Slovenia? Janko Štekar and Tamara Lukmann are not just winemakers; they're truly farmers who live off the land, and their sustainable, organic ethic runs through everything. Stay in comfortable accommodation just a couple of miles from the Italian border at Kmetija Štekar. The wines are made in a very traditional, hands-off fashion, and although you can certainly load up the suitcase, they will never taste better than when they are sipped with a backdrop of the sunset over the Collio/Brda hills.

553 Klet Brda cooperative

Klet Brda is a huge winemakers cooperative that has 400 members, and very impressive historic cellars established in 1922. Bottles date back to 1957, and some older vintages are for sale. The winery focuses on the local grape variety Rebula, but also makes a wide range of wines in all colors and styles. Pay a small fee for a tasting of ten wines.

BRDA, SLOVENIA
554 Climb a war memorial for vineyard views

The crest of the hill just above Gonjače provides a perfect viewpoint for miles around. It's also the site of a rather brutalist metal lookout tower; part of a war memorial for the "sons of Brda," who died during World War II. Climb Gonjače Lookout Tower's 144 steps on a clear day, and your reward is a glorious panorama over both Slovenia's and Italy's vineyards.

BRDA, SLOVENIA
555 Celebrate St. Martin's day

There's no better place to enjoy the St. Martin's Day festival than the idyllic hilltop village of Šmartno, itself named after the church of St. Martin. Pay a small entrance fee to receive your tasting glass, then amble around the pretty cobbled streets tasting wines from local producers, who have stalls set up along the streets and in restaurants. Delicious snacking and shopping opportunities abound along the way. The celebration is an annual event, held on St. Martin's Day: November 11.

LJUBLJANA, SLOVENIA
556 Pair Slovenian tapas with wine

When feeling hungry and thirsty in Ljubljana, cart yourself off to Tabar, a stylish, modern restaurant and wine bar. Here, the food takes its cue from a tapas concept, except you'll be dining on appetizing Slovenian dishes! The wine list is a paradise, with great selections from just about every serious artisanal winery in both Slovenia and the Slovenian-speaking parts of Italy just over the border.

LJUBLJANA, SLOVENIA
557 Taste the whole country's wines

Despite its name, the Ljubljana Wine Route is more of a street festival than a route. Twice a year, in June and November, the capital's Stritarjeva Street fills up with stands hosted by wineries from all over the country. Buy a glass for a small fee and walk around and taste to your heart's content.

LJUBLJANA, SLOVENIA
558 Check out a castle with its own vineyards

Take a walk up to the top of Ljubljana Castle, and you'll be rewarded with views of its vineyard, planted in 2016, on terraces to the south side. The Castle Vineyard is homage to the castle's history, since there were almost certainly vineyards here centuries ago. You can also visit the expansive wine bar and shop that is housed in the castle's courtyard.

SOČA VALLEY, SLOVENIA
559 Feed your appetite

Ana Ros's exquisite cuisine has become well known after her appearance on Netflix and numerous awards. But it's not only the food that is superlative at the idyllic Hiša Franko, deep in the Isonzo Valley. The wine list, curated by Ros's husband, Valter Kramar, offers up a dream selection of Slovenia's best artisanal wines, often in multiple vintages. Hiša Franko is a short walk from the small town of Kobarid, which is steeped in rather gruesome history from two world wars; a war memorial is also within easy walking distance. Book into one of the comfortable rooms above the restaurant and make a weekend of it.

559 *Above:* Hiša Franko features some of Slovenia's best artisanal wines

560 Admire jaw-dropping views

Guerila's new winery sits at the top of a breathtaking natural amphitheater of vines, looking a little like something in a James Bond movie. In contrast, the wines made at this high-performing estate are produced with a very gentle hand in the cellar. Be sure to sample local varieties Pinela and Zelen.

VIPAVA, SLOVENIA

561 Drink traditionally made wines

Listening to Primož Lavrenčič of Burja is a great joy—there are few winemakers who can explain their craft as eloquently as he can. Admire his newly built cellar, where gravity is used instead of pumps, and marvel at the mix of ancient (large oak barrels) and modern (concrete "eggs"). Tasting is a real treat—the wines are elegant, assured, and authentic.

VIPAVA, SLOVENIA

562 Soak in winemaking history

The small town of Vipava, in the heart of the beautiful valley of the same name, boasts the small Vipava Museum of Winemaking. Here, you can learn about winemaking in the region and why orange wine is not a new or cultish beverage dreamed up by sommeliers. Vipava has a tradition of at least 200 years of making orange wine (aka skin-fermented white wine, or white wines made like a red wine).

VIPAVA, SLOVENIA

563 Relax in a cozy hilltop wine bar

The pretty hilltop village of Vipavski Kriz has lain, albeit abandoned, since World War II, but now the wine bar, café, and gift shop Darovi Vipavske (Gifts of Vipava) is breathing new life into the village square. The wine list offers an enviable selection of local producers' wines at bargain prices. Enjoy a glass on the terrace, admire the stone architecture of the square, or buy a bottle to take home.

VIPAVA, SLOVENIA

564 Eat in a restored homestead

The restoration of Cejkotova domacija (a centuries-old house) in Goče has been a labor of love for Davorin Mesesnel and his wife. Many other buildings in this village remain semiabandoned and tumbledown. Savor an excellent home-cooked lunch or dinner matched with Davorin's own wines produced on the property. Also visit his small wine cellar across the street, where there's no electricity—it is rather romantically lit by candlelight. Walk off your meal with a trek up to the church on the hill, just above the village, where the views stretch out over the entire Vipava Valley.

563 *Below:* Darovi Vipavske is a wine bar, café, and gift shop

VIPAVA, SLOVENIA
565 Sleep among vineyards

Majerija is a countryside restaurant and boutique hotel with an amazing cellar and impressive verticals of many of Vipava's best producers—Mlečnik and Batič are particularly well represented. Feast your eyes on the exceptional tasting menu featuring local, seasonal dishes. Sleep it all off in one of the peaceful, comfortable rooms that have been cleverly built underground, but have natural skylights.

KARST, SLOVENIA
566 Devour exceptional Čotar wines

Čotar is one of the Karst region's most iconic wineries and produces the traditional macerated style of white wines (aka orange wines). The wines were originally just produced for the family restaurant—then the restaurant was closed to focus just on the wines. Branko Čotar's daughter has since reopened the restaurant as a separate business, so you can now enjoy the family's wines at its source—and with great, local cuisine.

KARST, SLOVENIA
567 Try macerated Vitovska

Joško Renčel's winery isn't state of the art, or even especially photogenic. But the wines that are produced here are some of the Karst region's finest. Make sure you try the particularly fine Cuvée Vincent, and of course the Vitovska.

565 *Above:* The guest rooms at Majerija are underground and have natural skylights

ISTRIA, SLOVENIA

568 Savor delicious food and natural wines

Winemaking has taken over chef-turned-vigneron Andrej Cep's life, but he hasn't entirely turned his back on his old chef's profession. Stare at wonderful views over the Adriatic when visiting his Gordia winery and tavern. Don't miss the outstanding pét-nats and orange wines, and if Cep is in the kitchen, then you're in for a real treat.

ISTRIA, SLOVENIA

569 Pair seafood with orange wines

Reserve a table at Restaurant Neptun—which is popular for its seafood—when visiting Piran. The cuisine is simple, but executed at a high level, and the greatest surprise is the small but excellent selection of Slovenian and Italian orange wines. Try the food-friendly Renčel, Radikon, or Il Carpino wines with your meal.

JUGOVZHODNA SLOVENIJA, SLOVENIA

570 Experience amazing hospitality

When you eat dinner at Domačija Novak, a beautifully restored village house, many of the ingredients will have been foraged by Boris and his wife, Miriam. Everything from bread to jams and smoked meats are produced in-house. Boris's passion is for orange and natural wines, and his cellar boasts an extraordinary collection. Stay in the family's guest rooms and get involved in local activities, such as a fishing trip or cooking class.

569 *Above:* Restaurant Neptun sits between the harbor and main square in the picturesque town of Piran

571 Admire a 500-year-old wine cellar

The cellars of Iločki Podrumi winery were originally built in 1450. There's no wine left from then, but the cellar boasts bottles going back to 1945. Take a tour and experience gripping historical detail and a tasting, and follow it with a hearty meal at the on-site restaurant. There is a lot to see in the area—right next door is the spectacular Principovac Castle and a museum— so book into the accommodation and spend a few days exploring.

572 Walk through Croatia's largest oak forest

Slavonian oak barrels can be found in wineries across Europe and beyond—it's a popular neutral material for large barrels. Spačva forest is a major source for the raw material. It's Croatia's largest forest and spans almost 10,000 acres (4,047 ha). It's possible to walk, drive, fish, and hunt in the forest. Stay in the Kunjevci hunting lodge, which organizes tours.

570 *Above:* Ingredients at Domačija Novak have been sourced from the garden and orchard

ZAGREB, CROATIA
573 Sample Croatia's top wines

Vinart Grand Tasting is one of Croatia's top wine fairs, with around a hundred of the country's best producers in attendance. Join in the side events and tastings during and before the two-day event each March in the capital city to enjoy some of Croatia's best wine. Don't miss the pop-up wine shop, where you can buy wines from all participating producers.

ZAGREB, CROATIA
574 Unearth flights in an old cellar

The *vinoteka* Bornstein is one of Zagreb's best wine addresses, based in a 200-year-old cellar with a strong selection of Croatian wines and knowledgeable staff. Order one of the bar's tasting flights based on regions, or the "tour of Croatia" to taste six wines covering the whole country.

ZAGREB, CROATIA
575 Feast on traditional dishes and wines

Konoba Didov San offers hearty, traditional Croatian fare, including delicious *peka* dishes (meat or fish slow-cooked in a heavy pan on embers). Pair them with wines from top producers such as Kozlovic, Matosevic, Krauthaker, and Tomić.

PLEŠIVICA, CROATIA
576 Taste bubbles from clay

You won't believe that the fresh, delicious yet complex Anfora Brut Nature from Tomac winery was fermented and aged in Georgian amphorae (*qvevri*)—it's possibly unique in this respect. Tomac is based in the Plešivica region close to Slovenia, and makes a range of sparkling wines, plus smaller quantities of still wines using unusual, local grape varieties.

575 *Above:* Dine on *peka*, food that is slow-cooked on embers

ISTRIA, CROATIA

Take a trip to four of the best wineries in Istria

577 Roxanich

Roxanich winery makes some of Istria's most impressive natural wines, including the stunning "Ines in White" blend, and Malvazija Antica—both wonderful examples of the traditional orange wine style. You can enjoy both while staying in Roxanich's wine hotel, with luxurious rooms, a fine-dining restaurant, and a nightclub on the premises.

578 Piquentum

Half-French, half-Croatian Dimitri Brecevič is a busy chap—he's head winemaker at Giorgio Clai, another famed artisanal winery, but his personal winery, Piquentum, is also fascinating. It is housed in a disused World War II water-storage facility, which drips with moisture from the bare stonewalls. It's perfect for aging wine, as you'll discover in Brecevič's outstanding Piquentum bottlings.

579 Kabola

The Markežić family makes a varied range of Malvazija-based wines at its organically certified Kabola estate. Sample the fresh style, an oak-aged Malvazija, and the crowning glory—an amphora-fermented version. The winery is situated in a commanding hilltop position, with views of the surrounding vineyards. Don't miss the amphora garden.

580 Trapan

Sometimes called the wild child of Istrian wine, Bruno Trapan is certainly a lively figure. His tasting room (named "the wine station") is full of playful architectural touches, and the wines are lively too. Farming follows organic principles. Try the Istraditional, a skin-fermented Malvazija, and tasty red blend Nigra Vigro Revolution.

580

ISTRIA, CROATIA

581 Savor seafood and Malvazija

Only what's caught on the day is served at Konoba Batelina, an outstanding restaurant located in the village of Banjole, just outside Pula. There's no better place to enjoy the alchemy of a glass of fresh Malvazija with the wonderful seafood cookery. Choose from specialties such as bottarga or fried fish bones, along with the classics.

ISTRIA, CROATIA

582 Relax on a dream terrace

Motovun is possibly Istria's most scenic hilltop village, with jaw-dropping views over the valley below. Disappear into B5 Wine Bar, buried in a backstreet at the top of the village, and enjoy a wonderful selection of artisanal wines (and craft beer). Step onto the private terrace to savor the sunset to complete the serene experience.

582 *Above:* Soak up a magical sunset wine tasting at B5 Wine Bar

DALMATIA, CROATIA
583 Visit the birthplace of Zinfandel

The mystery about Zinfandel's origins took a team of geneticists four years to resolve. A vine with the local name of Crljenak Kaštelanski (literally "Black of Kaštela") was discovered in one of Kaštela's seven villages—Kaštel Novi—and turned out to be identical to Zinfandel. Take an enticing day trip from nearby Split to the handsome walled villages and their seven forts, where you'll find the local wineries dotted around the villages now replanting their "twin" of Zinfandel.

DALMATIA, CROATIA
584 Taste the power of Postup and Dingač

Dalmatia's two top appellations for the indigenous red variety Plavac Mali are Postup and Dingač. Bura Mrgudić is a family winery that makes outstanding versions of both. Drop into its small cellar in the winemaking village of Potomje—it's a real treat for lovers of full-bodied red wines.

DALMATIA, CROATIA
585 Sip superb Plavac Mali and Grk

Sample Plavac Mali in a beautiful old stone farmhouse at the tiny Vinarija Kriz winery, where father and son work together. Organic viticulture and additive-free winemaking are the focus here, and embody the estate's traditional and sustainable values. Try the elegant and restrained Plavac Mali and the excellent skin-fermented Grk in a stunning vineyard setting.

DALMATIA, CROATIA

586 Stay in boutique luxury

Korta Katerina is one of Pelješac's most impressive wineries. It's situated on the coast and produces nuanced wines from the local Plavac Mali and Possip grape varieties. Wine tasting here is a treat, but make it even more special with a stay at the estate's stunning boutique hotel, with views across the peninsula to the island of Korčula.

DALMATIA, CROATIA

587 Marvel at vines clinging to steep cliffs

The wines from the coastal region of Dingač are famous for their concentration and strength. Take a drive along the road below the vineyards to understand why. The Plavac Mali vines literally bake in the hot Dalmatian sun. Wander through the vineyards and enjoy the uninterrupted views out to sea, but be prepared to admit defeat—human bodies aren't remotely as hardy as these gnarled plants!

SPLIT, CROATIA

588 Devour delicacies from Dalmatia

Once you've finished getting lost in the maze of small streets making up Diocletian's Palace, head to the upmarket restaurant Diocletian's Wine House, right in the heart of the old town. You'll find one of Split's best Croatian wine lists, with practically every serious Dalmatian winery represented, plus offerings from Istria and more.

588 *Above:* Along with traditional Dalmatian cuisine, Diocletian's Wine House dishes up more than fifty Croatian wines

589 Sip wines on the waterfront

Enjoy award-winning wine labels at beautiful Brač's Stina Winery, where waves almost reach the front door of this former cooperative wine cellar. In contrast to the exterior, with its stately reminder of bygone eras, the refurbished interior boasts a slick, modern architectural design. The minimalist style is carried over into the upmarket wines made from local white and red grape varieties, which you can relish at the cellar.

590 Seek wine in a former army bunker

Catch a boat to Vis, and you'll find that everything about this Croatian island is different from the mainland and surrounding islands. The crowds are calmer, the restaurants more upmarket—and the wines have a pronounced freshness and lift. Be sure to sample winemaker Antonio Lipanović's outstanding Plavac Mali. The quirky cellar at Lipanović Winery occupies an old army bunker—a reminder that until 1991, Vis was a closed military base.

591 Taste wines from Europe's sunniest island

Ivo Duboković is one of Hvar's top winemakers. He works with indigenous grapes such as Maraština, Bogdanjuša, and Kuč. Don't miss the outstanding Plavac Mali, which shows a different, fresher character than its mainland cousins. The atmospheric cellar makes a perfect location for tasting. Duboković Winery also produces excellent olive oil and a rose petal liqueur.

KORČULA, CROATIA

592 Discover the feminine Grk

The island of Korčula can feel touristy—at least in the main town—but escape to the beachside village of Lumbarda, and not only do the crowds disperse, but you'll also discover the unique Grk grape variety. It only grows on the village's sandy soils and cannot pollinate itself, since it has only female flowers. It's usually planted in alternating rows with Plavac Mali vines to resolve this problem. Several small wineries around the village make delicious wines from this fragile but fascinating grape, so be sure to sample some of their vino.

KORČULA, CROATIA

593 Taste one of the finest examples of Grk

The Bire family's small winery in Lumbarda makes two of the best examples of Grk on the island: one fresh and one oak-aged. Quantities are tiny, but the quality is top-notch. If you'd like to spend more time in this peaceful village, check out the family's simple *agroturizam*.

DUBROVNIK, CROATIA

594 Enjoy Malvazija in Dubrovnik

Walking through Dubrovnik's beautifully preserved walled center is a treat in itself, but be sure to stop at the cozy Malvasija Wine Bar. The venue makes its own wines and also offers varieties from around sixty local producers, many by the glass. Locally produced olive oil and cured meats round out the experience.

593 *Above:* Bire winery produces Grk, made from an indigenous Croatian grape variety

HERZEGOVINA, BOSNIA AND HERZEGOVINA

595 Drive the Herzegovina Wine Route

Explore Bosnia and Herzegovina's wine land in the region of Herzegovina—and specifically the area surrounding the towns of Medjugorje and Čitluk. Wine culture is somewhat basic, but follow the signposted Herzegovina Wine Route, and brochure, which links thirty-three producers from large to small. You'll find nice, quiet roads, and tasting is possible at most wineries—sometimes for free, sometimes for a small charge. Medjugorje itself offers a bizarre mix of religious ornaments (it's the site of one of the world's foremost Catholic pilgrimages) and the feel of a Wild West frontier town, since its Catholic tourism has expanded like wildfire in recent years.

HERZEGOVINA, BOSNIA AND HERZEGOVINA

596 Visit a biodynamic winemaker

Josip Brkić's handcrafted wines, made from the local Žilavka and Blatina varieties, are some of the most vibrant and thrilling examples from the region. Try them at Brkić—the country's first winemaker to farm biodynamically. Here, chemical treatments in the vineyard are shunned and wine is produced in the most natural way possible. Drop in for a tasting, a cellar tour, and delicious local snacks.

595 *Above:* A vineyard near the Catholic pilgrimage village of Medjugorje

HERZEGOVINA, BOSNIA AND HERZEGOVINA

597 Connect with winemaking history

Tour the handsome complex and tower of Monastery Tvrdoš (near Trebinje). Originally established in the twelfth century, the monastery occupies a commanding hilltop location in the middle of a barren, rocky landscape. Try the red varieties, which are the specialty here, and buy older vintages, which are sometimes available in the shop.

HERZEGOVINA, BOSNIA AND HERZEGOVINA

598 Appreciate upmarket Žilavka and Blatina

Not only is Josip Marijanović one of the region's most affable winemakers, he's also producing some of the most elegant Blatina and Žilavka. Make sure you sample the fruit brandies in addition to the wines when you visit Marijanović, and check its location on the map first, since signage can be easy to miss.

SARAJEVO, BOSNIA AND HERZEGOVINA

599 Soak up the ambiance of this wine bar

Serious wine bars are rare in Sarajevo, with some so-called wine bars little more than cafés. Dekanter is the exception, with a great selection of local wines available by the bottle and a few by the glass. Kick back in the atmospheric wine bar situated on a peaceful corner, just on the edge of the town center.

597 *Above:* Sample Monastery Tvrdoš's red varieties in its atmospheric cellar

FRUŠKA GORA, SERBIA

600 Lose yourself in Serbia's wine capital

Situated between the Fruška Gora wine region and
the Danube, Sremski Karlovci is effectively the wine
capital of Serbia. This elegant city is chock-full of
Habsburg-era architecture and is surrounded by
vineyards on all sides. It's a fascinating city in which
to wander, while contemplating the mix of ethnicities
and cultures that have always defined the area—and
you're never far away from a vineyard or a good glass
of wine. Be sure to seek out Bermet, a typical sweet
wine from the region that was, and still is, traditionally
infused with herbs. Many wineries have their cellars
within the city limits.

FRUŠKA GORA, SERBIA
601 Meet the godfather of Serbian natural wine
If there's one winemaker that's really put Serbia on the map, it's Oszkár Maurer. Working with native grape varieties such as Szerémi Zöld, Kövidinka, Piros Magyarka, Bakator, and Mézes Fehér, Maurer makes a number of characterful and delicious wines, using low-intervention methods. Arrange to have a tour of Maurer's vineyards, which are mostly bush-trained in accordance with the local tradition.

ARAD, ROMANIA
602 Have a glass of Romanian red
If you thought Transylvania was just about vampires, think again—the region also has a number of interesting wineries, such as Balla Géza, near the town of Arad. Be sure to try the excellent Fetească Neagră—one of the area's top local varieties. The winery also offers simple accommodation for up to fifty-seven people, and hosts wine dinners in the cellars (on request and for groups only).

BUCHAREST, ROMANIA
603 Relax in a cozy setting
Spend some quality time in Abel's Wine Bar, which is the perfect place to relax. Abel is the friendly and knowledgeable owner who will recommend wines from a large and mainly Romanian selection. With only around ten tables, the bar is a cozy space to sink a few local glasses.

DEALU MARE, ROMANIA
604 Stare at stunning scenery at this winery
SERVE Winery (short for Societatea Euro Română de Vinuri de Excepţie) was created by Corsican count Guy Tyrel de Poix in 1994 to capitalize on the huge potential of Romania's Dealu Mare DOC wine region. Not only has it done just that, it's also a spectacular location from which to enjoy the area's expansive vineyard panoramas. Be sure to try the rosé wines, a particular focus of the winery.

DEALU MARE, ROMANIA
605 Cycle around the Dealu Mare hills
The rolling hills of the Dealu Mare region play host to some of Romania's top wines. Experience them on an almost 20 mi (32 km) long cycle route where you can create great itineraries that combine a few winery visits with the great outdoors. Alternatively, get a tour operator to sort out a package for you if you don't want to organize your own route.

TRANSYLVANIA, ROMANIA

606 See what Dracula was missing

Appreciate the Transylvanian countryside from the small, quality-focused Liliac winery. Its location is an ideal vantage point with beautiful views over the surrounding foothills (the Carpathian Mountains are nearby)—particularly from its isolated tasting room situated in the middle of the estate's vineyards. Liliac's wines do not disappoint, and include the full family of Fetească: Albă, Regală, and Neagră.

TOP 3

CHIȘINĂU, MOLDOVA

Embark on three Moldovan winery adventures

607 Mileștii Mici

The tunnels under Mileștii Mici winery stretch for an extraordinary 124 mi (200 km)! They form the world's largest wine cellar, with the largest wine collection at around two million bottles—validated by *Guinness World Records*. Vintages date back to 1968. You'll need a car to drive through the different "streets," each named after a different type of wine. The winery's various tours require your own wheels, and space in the car for a guide. Go for the Moldova option that includes a three-course meal and tasting of five wines after the tour.

608 Brănești Cellars

The archeological complex at Orheiul Vechi in Butuceni has numerous attractions, not least a stunning orthodox monastery built into caves. Also largely underground is the winery Brănești Cellars, stretching across 185 acres (75 ha), at a depth of up to 200 ft (61 m) underground. Take the tour where you can taste from the huge variety of wines produced here: sparkling, red, white, sweet, semisweet, and fortified among them.

609 Chișinău Wine Festival

Head to the Chișinău Wine Festival in Moldova's capital in early October. The celebrations kick off once the new year's wine has finished fermenting. There's folk dancing and much local costume on display, plus ample opportunities to taste wines from the many participating producers. The festival concludes with a fireworks display.

609

PLOVDIV, BULGARIA

610 Engage in traditional song and dance

Don't miss the late-November Young Wine Festival in Plovdiv, where you can taste the new vintage from many local winemakers. Traditional song and dance kick off the festivities in the characterful old town, which pulses with life during the three-day party. It's a great excuse to enjoy the historic buildings and an authentic atmosphere. You can buy wine-tasting tokens at every participating venue.

SOFIA, BULGARIA

611 Sample local wines, cheese, and salami

Coupage is a small delicatessen and wine shop that specializes in Bulgarian artisanal products. Friendly, knowledgeable staff offer loads of information about the wines and regions. Take a seat and enjoy a flight of wines with delicious cheese and charcuterie. There are selections from many of Bulgaria's smaller and lesser-known producers.

610 *Above:* Young Wine Festival is one of the largest tourist events in Plovdiv

THRACE, BULGARIA

612 Encounter a young winemaker

Edward Kourian is the mastermind behind the small, artisanal Rossidi winery—part of the new wave in Bulgaria. Taste lighter, more nuanced wines here than most of the mainstream. Rossidi pioneered the production of an orange wine, made from Gewürztraminer and vinified without any added sulfites. It's quite delicious!

THRACE, BULGARIA

613 Taste classical wines from Thrace

Love red wine? Then look up Bessa Valley Winery, situated in the heart of the Thrace region. It has become one of the most important names in Bulgarian wine since 2001, when it was founded. Owner Count Stephan von Neipperg also owns properties in Bordeaux, and you might notice a decidedly French influence in the classic red wines.

THRACE, BULGARIA

614 Admire mountain vistas

Drive two hours south of Sofia to Orbelus winery, which is stunningly situated in the foothills of the Pirin Mountains. The imaginative half-barrel shape of the winery makes a striking impression, and was inspired by a local legend that wine barrels are a gift, fallen from the sky. Enjoy the wines from organically farmed grapes while admiring the stunning views—on a clear day, they stretch to Greece.

SKOPJE, REPUBLIC OF NORTH MACEDONIA

615 Combine wine drinking with storytelling

Antonio Brzanov is famous not just for his wines, but also for his humor and hospitality. His Brzanov Winery in Skopje is small-scale and artisanal, with the estate's rich, hearty Vranec (a local red grape) particularly highly regarded. Arrange to have a wine dinner, or just drop by for a tasting.

SKOPJE, REPUBLIC OF NORTH MACEDONIA

616 Swing by a cozy family property

Just a hop, skip, and a jump from the center of Skopje is Kartal Winery, owned and run by brothers Jordan and Filip Kartalov. Be sure to sample Vranec, the local specialty; the brothers also produce wines from international varieties, such as Cabernet Sauvignon and Chardonnay.

SKOPJE, REPUBLIC OF NORTH MACEDONIA

617 Feast on seafood and local wines

The restaurant Sidro is one of the few places in Skopje that offers a wide selection of local and other Balkan wines. It's deservedly popular for its straightforward fresh fish and seafood dishes, so make sure you book ahead.

615 *Above:* Brzanov Winery produces artisanal wines with creative bottle labels

GOUMENISSA, GREECE

618 Be wowed by peerless Xinomavro wines

The northern Greek appellation of Naoussa is justly famous, but its neighbor Goumenissa also deserves some attention. Call at boutique producer Domaine Chatzivaritis to see how good this region's red wines can be. The winery, built in 2007, opens up to a vast vineyard panorama. The building may be modern, but the wines have a classic quality.

618 *Below:* Domaine Chatzivaritis covers 120 acres (49 ha)

GOUMENISSA, GREECE
619 Rock out with the Tatsis brothers

Stergios and Periklis Tatsis are two brothers who make characterful handcrafted wines at their estate, Domaine Tatsis, in the Goumenissa region. The skin-fermented Malagouzia (a local aromatic white grape) is particularly fine. The brothers are keen motorcyclists and rockers, so don't be surprised if you are greeted by what appear to be Hells Angels on your visit!

NAOUSSA, GREECE
620 Hike, boulder, or ski through vineyards

Not only are Naoussa's vineyards the source of some of Greece's top red wines, they're also situated in prime hiking country. Discover great walking and bouldering opportunities offered by the gently undulating mountain landscape—pleasurably punctuated with wine tasting. There are also two nearby ski resorts in the winter: Seli and 3–5 Pigadia.

NAOUSSA, GREECE
621 Visit Naoussa's maturing wine

These days Boutari is one of Greece's wine giants, with outposts all over the country. Its origins date to 1879, in Naoussa, where it was the first to push high-quality winemaking from the region's red jewel, Xinomavro. Visit the original Boutari winery, which houses some 3,000 barrels of patiently maturing Naoussa wine.

621 *Above:* The winery building of Boutari dates back to 1879

622 Chat with a Naoussa winemaker

Apostolos Thymiopoulos is one of the most respected winemakers working in the Naoussa region. Earth & Sky, his top Xinomavro, is a superb wine designed for aging, but he also makes easier-drinking wines such as Jeunes Vignes. Talk to Thymiopoulos at his Thymiopoulos Vineyards to learn more about this region's stellar wines.

622 *Above:* Thymiopoulos Vineyards is a family business

623 Taste a top Xinomavro wine

If you want to try an exceptional and very typical Naoussa red wine, go no farther than Kotsis Dalamára's cellar. This young producer is one of the leading lights in the region, proving that the tricky Xinomavro grape variety can be tamed with exceptional work in both vineyard and winery.

623 *Above:* Domaine Dalamára welcomes visitors to try its wines

RAPSANI, GREECE

624 Reach the heights of Rapsani vineyards

Ride up Mount Olympus in a 4x4 to Tsantali's Rapsani vineyards. Major wine producer Tsantali has vineyards at a number of different altitudes on Mount Olympus. On the Rapsani Wine Adventure, you can drive up to a height of 2,460 ft (750 m) to see the vineyards that go into the traditional Rapsani blend of three indigenous grape varieties: Xinomavro, Krassato, and Stavroto. The ride up a dirt track in a converted 4x4 is hair-raising but incredibly scenic. At each of the three stops on the ascent, you'll taste Rapsani wines of different quality levels. The marked differences in the wines made from vineyards at different altitudes is fascinating.

ATTICA, GREECE

625 Mix wine tasting with Greek history

Visit the Costa Lazaridi Wine Museum and discover exhibits that date back three centuries. It's a fun way to discover the context for Greek wines, before finishing with a tasting of Domaine Costa Lazaridi's own bottlings. The museum itself covers not only wine, but also distillation and vinegar production.

ATHENS, GREECE

626 Work your way through 200 Greek wines

Greece makes such a huge variety of wines throughout the mainland and islands—but where can you find a good selection in one place? Look no further—Heteroclito is that place! Choose from around 200 different Greek wines at this wine bar, including many small-production gems that you might otherwise never discover.

ATHENS, GREECE

627 Take a dip before you dine

Bring your swimwear to lunch and bag one of the waterside tables at restaurant Bluefish (pro tip: they're downstairs from the main dining area). From there, you can swim right off the terrace! The stretch of sea running alongside the restaurant is private, making this a great way to relax and avoid the crowds. Enjoy immaculately chosen wines and stellar fresh fish cookery afterward.

628 Change your mind about Retsina

Retsina gets a bad reputation for being rustic and prone to creating a great hangover. It doesn't have to be this way! Call into Georgas Family, a pioneering small estate that has biodynamic certification for its farming. Dimitris Georgas will show that the pine resin can be subtly integrated to create a wine of harmony and character.

629 Learn about Nemea's wine

Enter Nemea Wine Land, a tasting room and information center run by the local winemakers association PDO Nemea. You can taste and buy wines from thirty local producers and learn more about what makes the region—right in the center of the Nemea Valley—unique. The center can also help arrange visits to the surrounding wineries.

630 Be charmed by the fragrant Agiorgitiko

Take in ancient ruins when you visit Domaine Papaioannou, which is situated close to ancient Nemea's archeological site. The artisanal winery's vineyards are beautifully laid out with a backdrop of mountains and ancient ruins. Papaioannou focuses on the region's specialty, the delicate Agiorgitiko, which will surely win you over with its soft structure and vibrant red fruit.

NEMEA, GREECE

631 Find good wine in Nemea

It's well worth visiting Domaine Skouras to taste its iconic Megas Oenos, which helped put the Nemea region on the quality wine map in the 1980s. The winery continues to work with a combination of local and international grape varieties, and also innovates with some production in amphorae.

ARGOLIS, GREECE

632 Take your seat in an ancient theater

The Argolis wine region has four recommended wine routes (Argolis Wine Roads), which take in wineries, beaches, and some of the many important ancient Greek sites in the region. Select route four, and you'll come across the ancient theater of Epidavros—a vast, open-air amphitheater that is often almost deserted.

631 *Above:* Domaine Skouras started producing wine in 1986

MANTINIA, GREECE

633 Learn about ancient Greek wine production

Stroll through the vineyards of Domaine Spiropoulos, a winery steeped in history. One of the oldest established in the region, it's built around a beautiful Arcadian tower. Numerous historical sites surround the vineyards. The winery specializes in Moschofilero, an aromatic local grape, which it makes in several versions, including a sparkling wine, which you can sample in its tasting room.

PATRAS, GREECE

634 Enjoy stunning mountain scenery

You will struggle to find a more beautiful location than the organic Tetramythos Winery in Patras, with its vineyards stretching up above 3,000 ft (914 m) in the Aroania Mountains. Sample one of Greece's most elegant Retsinas with winemaker Panagiotis Papagiannopoulos, and don't miss the chance to taste incredibly rare varieties that he's reintroducing. Be sure to load up the car—these wines are a real bargain!

634 *Above: Tetramythos Winery focuses on organic cultivation*

647 *Above:* Manousakis Winery is located in the pretty village of Vatolakkos

AYIOS MAMAS, CYPRUS

648 Sample the world's oldest denominated wine

The village of Ayios Mamas is at the heart of the Commandaria region. Commandaria is a fortified sweet wine similar to Marsala or Muscat of Samos. Taste it at Revecca Winery in the village and visit the museum to learn more about this style, which has been popular since the twelfth century.

ERIMI, CYPRUS

649 Take in 5,500 years of winemaking history

Visit the Cyprus Wine Museum to discover one of Europe's longest winemaking traditions, which dates back around 5,500 years. Once you're done in the small museum, head downstairs for a tasting of local wines, which can also be purchased in the museum shop.

KRASOCHORIA, CYPRUS

650 Taste forgotten grape varieties

Zambartas Wineries is one of a few leading the charge for Cyprus's almost forgotten local grapes. You'll find delicious Xinisteri, Mavro, and Maratheftiko here, along with a warm welcome and a fun tasting. A quick sample of three wines is free—or paid options include a full tour and more conclusive tasting with bites.

PITSILIA, CYPRUS

651 Try a drop from a boutique winery

Tsiakkas Winery is situated in the Troodos Mountains above the village of Pitsilia. This pioneering organic producer makes a range of wines from both international and local grape varieties, and its Commandaria is particularly revered. Drop in for a tasting or book ahead for a full tour.

648 *Above: Commandaria is a sweet dessert wine made from two indigenous grape varieties*

LIMASSOL, CYPRUS

652 Immerse yourself in a local wine festival

The popular Limassol Wine Festival runs for nine evenings each summer, attracting around 15,000 people in total. Wine tasting is free once you've paid the small entrance fee, and there's a free shuttle service from nearby villages. There is music, dancing, comedy, and theatrical performances every night. You'll also get to see a grape-stomping demonstration.

652 *Above:* Limassol Wine Festival takes place over nine evenings every summer

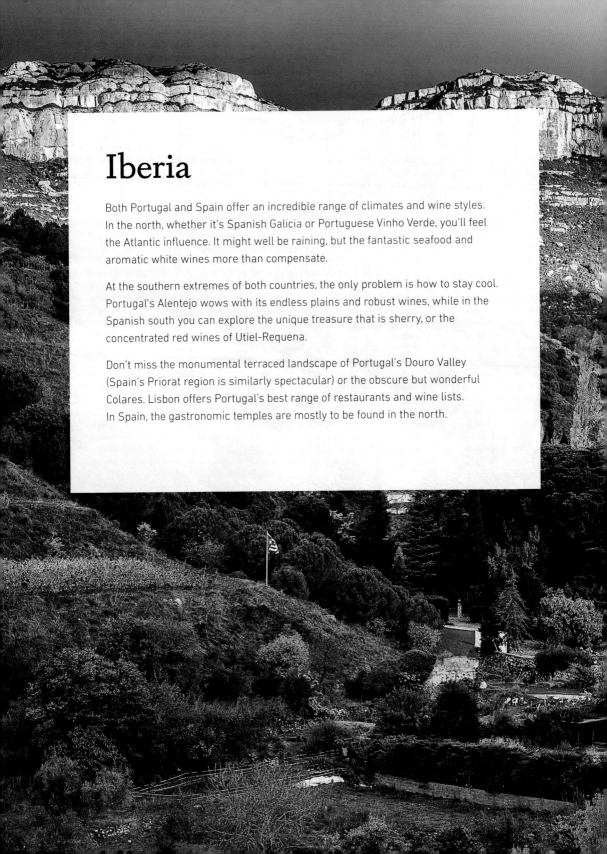

Iberia

Both Portugal and Spain offer an incredible range of climates and wine styles. In the north, whether it's Spanish Galicia or Portuguese Vinho Verde, you'll feel the Atlantic influence. It might well be raining, but the fantastic seafood and aromatic white wines more than compensate.

At the southern extremes of both countries, the only problem is how to stay cool. Portugal's Alentejo wows with its endless plains and robust wines, while in the Spanish south you can explore the unique treasure that is sherry, or the concentrated red wines of Utiel-Requena.

Don't miss the monumental terraced landscape of Portugal's Douro Valley (Spain's Priorat region is similarly spectacular) or the obscure but wonderful Colares. Lisbon offers Portugal's best range of restaurants and wine lists. In Spain, the gastronomic temples are mostly to be found in the north.

BARCELONA, SPAIN

653 Drink in a "Brutal" bar

When in Barcelona, don't miss what is likely its most famous natural-wine venue: Bar Brutal. It's become an institution for anyone who likes the adventurous side of wine; it's a bar with tons of atmosphere and loads of open bottles. So much so that a number of winemakers from around the world—from Gut Oggau in Austria to Patrick Sullivan in Australia—now make a special Brutal wine, often exclusively available in the bar itself. While there, eat in the excellent restaurant Can Cisa—you'll find it using the same entrance.

BARCELONA, SPAIN

654 Enjoy a tipple with tapas

Avoid the tacky tapas joints around the Ramblas and head for La Vinya del Senyor, a lively tapas bar that focuses on wine. Some twenty wines are available by the glass, with an additional 350 by the bottle. Ask the staff for help with recommendations.

BARCELONA, SPAIN

655 Dine or graze with a lengthy wine list

Monvínic is one of Barcelona's dream wine locations, with a huge list of not just Spanish wines, but also of just about every other important wine nation on the planet. Whether you go for tapas while seated at the convivial bar, or the full tasting menu in the upscale restaurant, the full wine list is available to you.

655 *Above:* You can order from the full list in Monvínic's bar and restaurant

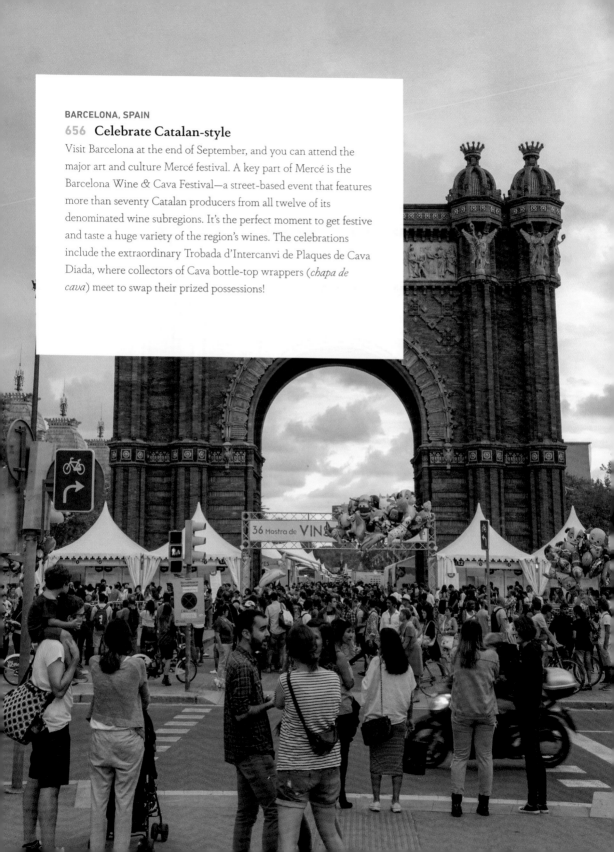

656 Celebrate Catalan-style

Visit Barcelona at the end of September, and you can attend the major art and culture Mercé festival. A key part of Mercé is the Barcelona Wine & Cava Festival—a street-based event that features more than seventy Catalan producers from all twelve of its denominated wine subregions. It's the perfect moment to get festive and taste a huge variety of the region's wines. The celebrations include the extraordinary Trobada d'Intercanvi de Plaques de Cava Diada, where collectors of Cava bottle-top wrappers (*chapa de cava*) meet to swap their prized possessions!

CATALONIA, SPAIN

657 Get on the road in Cava country

Cava isn't a place but rather a style, and it can be produced in several Spanish wine regions. That said, its undisputed home is in Catalonia, with the city of Sant Sadurní d'Anoia very much at the epicenter—it's here where you'll find several Cava-related festivals throughout the year. There are many wineries specializing in these Spanish bubbles in the area, from small to large. Most are well prepared for visitors, and you'll learn about this Champagne-like winemaking method in the most enjoyable fashion—with a glass in hand, of course!

CATALONIA, SPAIN

658 Taste a traditional Catalan wine style

It's easy to get distracted by the beautiful mountain vineyards when you visit Joan Franquet at his winery Costador Mediterrani Terroirs. But don't forget to taste his range of *brisat* wines—an old local tradition of making white wines with skin fermentation; these wines are now often called orange wines. You'll taste a totally different side of Catalan wine here.

658 *Above and right:* Costador Mediterrani Terroirs produces a range of orange wines

TOP 3

CATALONIA, SPAIN

Explore three of the best Catalonia Cava producers

659 Freixenet

Freixenet is one of Spain's top Cava producers, and its winery tours don't disappoint. In ninety minutes you will learn about Cava production, as well as ride a train through the winery's cellars. Freixenet is less than an hour's drive from Barcelona.

660 Cordorníu

Having invented the Cava style, it figures that Cordorníu knows a thing or two about Cava. Tour these historic cellars and then eat lunch or dinner served in the Cava cellars themselves.

661 Raventós i Blanc

Raventós i Blanc is a producer that is pioneering biodynamic agriculture, and also focuses only on native grape varieties (Xarel·lo, Macabeu, and Parellada). The aim is to achieve a pure, elegant style of Cava. Experience one of its luxury tours to find out how well it succeeded.

661

662 Check out an exceptional winery

Parés Balta is a small estate that continues to push itself to higher levels of quality, converting all its vineyards first to organic and then to biodynamic viticulture. Don't miss the highlights, which include the red Mas Elena and the Brut Nature Cava. You can choose from various visiting options, but opt for the scenic 4x4 tour of the surrounding Foix Natural Park, where the vineyards are located, since it's truly beautiful.

663 Discover wines aged underwater

Winemaking doesn't get much more stripped down than it is at Porcellanic—here, nothing is added, not even sulfites. The wines are put into clay bottles for superior aging and then stored underwater as a further protection against temperature changes or oxygen. Porcellanic specializes in wines made from the appley Xarel·lo, and despite (or because of?) the quirky methodology, the wines are quite delicious, as you'll discover on an in-depth tour of the winery.

664 Touch the skies in Vins Nus vineyards

Winemaker Alfredo Arribas has rescued many old vineyards in the high-altitude Montsant region, which surrounds Priorat like a doughnut. Arribas makes delicious lo-fi wines at his Vins Nus winery. Tour the estate's spectacular vineyards either over a two-hour basic tour or the extended four-hour version.

662 *Above:* Indigena is a Grenache wine produced at Parés Balta

TOP
4

PRIORAT, SPAIN

Visit four of Priorat's top wineries

665 Scala Dei Cellars

This mountainous corner of Catalonia has built an impressive reputation for its structured, serious red wines over the past few decades. Learn about the region's winemaking history at Scala Dei Cellars, at a Carthusian monastery, which is once again active as a producer. The monastery dates from the twelfth century, and in around 1263, monks authored a winemaking manual.

666 Bodegas Mas Alta

Enjoy beautiful vineyard scenery and exceptional examples of Priorat wines made from one-hundred-year-old vineyards at this modern, Belgian-owned winery. Winemaking here has evolved over the years, to better express fruit quality and rely less on oak than hitherto.

667 Clos Figueras

Taste the restrained, elegant wines made by Anne Cannan at this family-owned estate, which also has an on-site restaurant. Cannan shows that despite Priorat's hot, dry climate, the wines can, with care, have a real sense of freshness and lift.

665

668 Clos Mogador

Visit one of Priorat's iconic wineries, where René Barbier forged the reputation of the region in the late 1990s. Although Barbier's winemaking is stripped down, his modern concrete winery is extremely impressive. His Manyetes and Nelin wines are simply peerless.

BASQUE COUNTRY, SPAIN
669 Taste traditionally produced Txakoli

Txakoli—a superlight, fresh white wine—can be a real delight, but it is often produced in an industrial manner. Head to Bengoetxe for a more traditional take—the vineyards are farmed organically, and the youthful spritz in the wines is natural, and not the result of added CO_2.

BASQUE COUNTRY, SPAIN
670 Stay the night in Txakoli country

It's simply a joy to visit Gaintza Txakolina, a winery specializing in Txakoli production. Join the informative and enthusiastic tour and tasting. The coastal views from the winery are beautiful—you might even be tempted to stay in the winery's adjoining hotel!

670 *Above:* Gaintza Txakolina specializes in the spritzy dry white wine Txakolina

SAN SEBASTIÁN, SPAIN

671 Enjoy fine dining with 125,000 bottles

Seek out Rekondo in a town filled with Michelin-starred establishments. Food focuses on seasonal cuisine without unnecessary frills, and then there's the amazing wine list! Rekondo's wine cellar is one of the world's largest, with some 125,000 bottles stored away. Browse the 200-page wine list if you wish—or just ask the sommelier for a recommendation.

BILBAO, SPAIN

672 Pair *pintxos* with a lively wine list

The Basque Country is famous for amazing food and *pintxos* (pronounced "pinchos"), which are larger than a tapas but smaller than a main dish. Settle into Cork, a cozy wine bar and restaurant, where you can enjoy an eclectic list of artisan Spanish wines by the glass or bottle with excellent *pintxos*. Make the most of the knowledgeable and enthusiastic staff.

672 *Above:* Cork is the place to go for delicious *pintxos* and good Spanish wines

RIOJA, SPAIN

673 Uncover 8,000 years of wine history

It's a working winery, but the real draw at Dinastia Vivanco is the 4,000 sq ft (372 sq m) that is dedicated to the Vivanco Museum of Wine Culture. Delve into the extraordinary number of winemaking and wine-related artifacts, spread across six rooms, that detail 8,000 years of wine history. You'll find 220 different grape varieties planted outdoors in the Garden of Bacchus.

RIOJA, SPAIN

674 Sleep in a Frank Gehry–designed masterpiece

Marqués de Riscal is one of Rioja's biggest names. Its Frank Gehry–designed winery is an iconic piece of modern architecture, with beautiful, curved titanium panes similar to the Guggenheim Museum Bilbao. Contemplate this beauty by staying at the on-site luxury hotel—note that only the three top room categories are situated in the Gehry building itself.

RIOJA, SPAIN

675 Visit a family producer in Rioja

Get a fresh take on Rioja at Bodega Miguel Merino. This artisan producer makes wines of great delicacy and individuality, a world away from the mass-produced supermarket styles that dominate the market. The joven styles in particular show a freshness and fruit focus that is often lacking in more mainstream Riojas. Don't miss the rare, delicious 100 percent Mazuelo.

RIOJA, SPAIN

676 Keep it traditional with Urbina

If you've yet to fall in love with traditional Rioja Reserva and Gran Reserva, Bodegas Urbina is the place that will make it happen. Urbina's wines take their time to evolve into multilayered, magical beverages. Don't miss the delicious Urbina Selección 1999.

RIOJA, SPAIN

677 Get soaked in the "Battle of Wine"

It's been the tradition in the town of Haro for centuries: early morning on June 29, the beginning of the San Pedro festival is celebrated with La Batalla del Vino (a huge wine fight). Join in the antics, where nothing is off-limits: squirt guns, buckets, wineskins—anything that can be used to douse your neighbors in wine is encouraged. Traditional dress is white with red accessories—although your washing machine might not thank you later!

678 Go on a tapas crawl

If you're staying in Logroño, it's essential to spend an evening on Calle Laurel (otherwise known as "tapas street"). Saunter from one small café to another—eat *pintxos* and have a small glass of wine at five or six places. Anywhere that looks busy is worth a go, but outfits of note include Bar Soriano, the innovative La Taberna del Tío Blas, and La Tavina (which is also a bottle shop). There are around twenty cafés on the street itself, and many more on the interconnecting side streets. Don't expect to get a seat, since most places are small and busy.

679 Dine in an old wine storage cellar

Eating and drinking at El Rincón del Vino is a pleasure, not only because this traditional restaurant has great cooking, but also due to its excellent wine list. The establishment is housed in an old wine storage cellar, and you can choose from a huge collection of older Rioja vintages that can be drunk at very reasonable prices.

680 Celebrate the harvest in Rioja

Logroño turns into party central for one whole week in late September, when the Rioja Wine Harvest Festival takes over the town. Expect to drink gallons of Rioja wine; enjoy music, dancing, and fireworks; and don't miss the Cabezudos—costumed performers with giant papier-mâché heads, who traditionally carry a whip and scare anyone in their path!

681 Treat your taste buds to lamb

It's first and foremost a winery, but if you're visiting El Lagar de Isilla, the chances are you're here for the restaurant and its specialty: roast suckling lamb (*lechazo* in Spanish). Wine tastings that include lunch in the restaurant afterward are popular, and rightfully so.

682 Taste a Ribera rebel's wine

Alfredo Maestro makes some of the most vibrant and exciting wines from northern Spain in his cellar at Ribera del Duero. He works a number of different vineyards spread around the region and focuses on healthy grapes and a minimal-intervention approach that is in stark contrast to many of his neighbors. Be sure to ask why aliens appear on one of his wine labels!

RIBERA DEL DUERO, SPAIN

683 Try classic red wines

There's more to Tempranillo than just Rioja. You can really feel this grape variety sing in the wines of Dominio de Atauta—one of the region's most renowned producers. Check out the majestic eighty-five-year-old vineyards, too—the producers don't use any chemical pesticides or herbicides here or anywhere else.

683 *Above:* The barren landscapes around Dominio de Atauta rise to 3,280 ft (1,000 m) above sea level

GALICIA, SPAIN
684 Explore beautiful vineyard landscapes
The hidden gorges, rivers, and tiny villages of Ribeira Sacra make it one of northern Spain's gems. Steeply terraced vineyards can frequently be seen high up in the hills. Put on your hiking boots and head for the Sil Canyon, which has a plethora of marked trails that take in wonderful vineyard views, including the Ribeira Sacra Vineyards Trail (PR-G 86). Look up the Ribeira Sacra tourism site for full details and GPS coordinates.

GALICIA, SPAIN

685 Visit a winery returning to old Ribeira Sacra traditions

Dominio do Bibei will leave you with a love of local grape varieties such as Mencía, Mouratón, and Brancellao. The winery will also demonstrate how a light hand in the cellar is needed to get the best out of the grapes. Take the opportunity to admire the beautiful, high-altitude vineyards—the wines are crystalline and delicious.

TORO, SPAIN

686 Step into a tiny cellar with big ideas

Want to learn about the art and science of winemaking? Then embark on a tour at Bodega Valdigal (located near Zamora). It might be the smallest winery within the Toro denominated area (DO), but it has a big personality, as does its owner! Here, wine is still made and aged in an underground stone cellar—as it once was at every single house in the area. You'll also visit the cellar dating from the eighteenth century (and restored in 2006).

TORO, SPAIN

687 Taste the cream of the crop

Find one of the greatest red wines in Toro at Bodegas Pintia. Old vineyards, hand harvesting, and meticulous quality control all help to create its very fine wine. It may come as no surprise to learn that the Vega Sicilia and Alion wineries are under the same ownership.

TORO, SPAIN

688 Indulge in heavenly food and wine

Bodega Divina Proporción is a relatively young estate that focuses on good old-fashioned winemaking and hospitality. Take in an unhurried, informative tour of the winery and then linger for lunch at the excellent restaurant, where the hearty cooking is a perfect match for the wines.

689 Enjoy restrained excellence

Tasting menus at Restaurante Victor Gutierrez are always full of fun, beautiful balance, and subtle nods to the chef's Peruvian heritage. The wine list is sizable, focused on Spain and specifically the local regions, and very well priced. If you don't want to choose, then go for the excellent course-by-course wine pairing.

TOP 4

MADRID, SPAIN

Delight in four of Madrid's best places to find good wine

690 Madridaje

The concept at Madridaje subtly elevates tapas to modern, fine dining and perfectly preserves its soul at the same time. The restaurant is cozy and airy, the owners and staff are friendly, and the wine pairings are frequently inspired.

691 La Caníbal

The wine and craft beer offering at La Caníbal is simplicity itself: there are eight taps for each. The wines are all sourced from artisan growers in the regions surrounding Madrid. La Caníbal describes them as "naked wines," made without additives or "excesses of oak." Expect an excellent, local vibe!

692 Madrid & Darracott

Opened in 2018, Madrid & Darracott has already built a loyal following for its imaginative selection of Spanish wines at all price levels, and for fun, informative wine tastings that happen at the shop on a daily basis. Tastings are conducted in English and Spanish, reflecting the nationalities of the two owners.

693 Vinoteca Tierra

Pull up a stool at one of the barrels in Vinoteca Tierra, and you can enjoy a glass of something delicious. The choice in this wine bar branch in Ronda de Segovia is relatively small compared to its big brother on Calle Ayala; however, the selection of small-production, high-quality Spanish and French wines is excellent.

MADRID, SPAIN

694 Taste excellent Grenache

For the perfect day trip from Madrid, drive about an hour to Bernabeleva winery, on the edge of the Sierra de Gredos mountains. At this small, high-quality operation, all vineyard work is done by hand, with nothing more than its own cow manure as fertilizer. You can really taste the influence of the granite soils on the fine Grenache.

CASTILLA-LA MANCHA, SPAIN

695 Change your mind about Airén

If you've ever read about the Airén grape variety, you may have the idea it's a bit dull. But Esencia Rural (a small winery in Toledo) is out to show you the opposite. You can sample complex, fascinating wines produced from old bush-trained, dry-farmed (unirrigated) vines, and vinified without intervention or additives. Taste Sol a Sol to experience the most extreme, dark, savory version of Airén, fermented with its skins for a whopping fourteen months.

694 *Above: Bernabeleva is a winery where the work is done by hand*

696 Discover great natural wines

Surrounded by century-old vineyards, Bodega Cueva is a small artisanal winery located inland from Valencia. The wines are made in an old-fashioned way: nothing added, nothing taken out, and no sulfites used at all. They're joyful, easygoing creations that just beg to be drunk. Be sure to try the "orange" Tardana and Macabeo blend.

UTIEL-REQUENA, SPAIN

697 Jump aboard the wine bus!

If you find yourself in Valencia with a Saturday to spare, why not board the Valencia Wine Bus Tour? It takes you to two random Utiel-Requena wineries, with a snack stop in between and a full lunch in a local restaurant before returning to Valencia. It's a great way to sample the range of wines being made in this lesser-known region.

ALICANTE, SPAIN

698 Taste full-bodied wines from Alicante

Seek out Casa Balaguer-Vinessens's full-bodied, lively wines, whose complexity belies their modest price points. The pioneering estate, close to Benidorm, has been showing the world that hot, dry Alicante can do high-quality wine made in a natural way. The winery grows typical grape varieties such as Moscatel and Monastrell.

MURCIA, SPAIN

699 Find good wine in Murcia

Enjoy the Mediterranean climate and see the organic vineyards of Finca Llano Rubio. In a region better known for intensive vegetable farming, the family crafts delicious wines using traditional methods: wild fermentation and no filtration or added sulfites. The wines are bottled under the brand Viña Enebro.

ANDALUSIA, SPAIN

700 Drink an alternative to sherry

Discover the fascinating and delicious unfortified white wines of Muchada-Léclapart. This winemaking project was born out of the friendship of Spanish winemaker Alejandro Muchada and French Champagne producer David Léclapart. They farm a few acres of old Palomino Fino and Muscat grapes in the sherry region to make their wines.

ANDALUSIA, SPAIN

701 Dance, sing, stomp, and drink!

Make your way to the small town of Cómpeta, which holds a famous harvest festival named Noche del Vino (Night of the Wine) on August 15 every year. Contrary to its name, the festivities kick off in the morning with a procession to celebrate the arrival of the grapes. Accompanied by fandango dancing, it finishes up in Plaza Vendimia. The fun continues into the evening (and the wee hours) at the central Plaza Almijara. You'll see a grape-stomping demonstration, wonderful live music, and flamenco dance performances. It's a popular event, particularly since all the wine is provided completely free! The specialty in this part of Spain is both dry and sweet wines made from the aromatic Moscatel (aka Muscat) grape variety. *Salud!*

SEVILLE, SPAIN

702 Devour dinner with copious wine styles

Feast on carefully sourced local produce and an exhaustive Spanish wine list at Antigua Abacería de San Lorenzo, an upmarket delicatessen-cum-tapas restaurant that is nothing if not authentic. The by-the-glass choice is large, and there are sherries and vermouth in addition to regular wines. Look for the charming quote (in Spanish) from Oscar Wilde on the menus.

SEVILLE, SPAIN

703 Combine homemade vermouth and tapas

Ever wondered what *Star Wars* has to do with a tapas joint in Seville? Wonder no more when you spend time at Vermutería Yo Soy Tu Padre, a pocket-size *vermut* bar selling its own homemade vermouth—it's hard not to have fun here! Chat with the owner, Esteban, and even if he can't convince you to try the excellent *vermut*, there's a great selection of wines to choose from too.

MONTILLA-MORILES, SPAIN

704 Get to know Pedro Ximénez

In Montilla-Moriles, the Pedro Ximénez grape is king, and the region excels at producing rich, concentrated sweet wines. Bodegas Alvear is one of Montilla's leading exponents, and its wines span the gamut from dry fino to luscious and complex wines from soleras (groups of barrels used for the blends) more than 200 years old. Swing by the winery for a charming tour that includes the fermentation room and cellars, and ends with a delightful tasting.

705 Explore the sherry triangle

Three towns form the corners of the so-called sherry triangle: Jerez de la Frontera, Sanlúcar de Barrameda, and El Puerto de Santa María. This denominated area is the only place in the world that can legally produce wines that say "sherry" on the label. Sherry itself is much misunderstood—you'll discover that it can be bone-dry or lusciously sweet—or anything in between! Its production revolves around a particular blending method, utilizing a solera—a collection of barrels containing progressively older wines, which are all gradually refreshed with newer wine as they're emptied for bottling. The sherry capital is undisputedly Jerez de la Frontera (where you'll find big names such as Gónzalez Byass/Tio Pepe and Lustau). Sanlúcar de Barrameda is famous for Manzanilla, one of the lightest and driest styles of sherry, which is directly influenced by the coastal climate. It is a smaller and less touristy town than Jerez de la Frontera. Visit renowned producers such as Barbadillo, Hidalgo La Gitana, and Delgado Zuleta, but best of all go barhopping around the Plaza del Cabildo; here, you'll experience the match in heaven that is a chilled glass of Manzanilla plus a fried-fish tapa. El Puerto de Santa María is the least visited, although it's home to historic producers such as Bodegas Osborne and Bodegas Gutiérrez-Colosía. Ultimately, visit any of these three towns, and you'll find a profusion of cellars, tapas restaurants, and wine bars all ready to service your fortified wine craving.

JEREZ, SPAIN

706 Discover the Spanish solera system

Bodegas Williams & Humbert has one of the largest and most impressive cellars in Spain, and it also houses a sherry museum and large horse stables. Drop into the informative winery, and the tour will teach you how the solera system works. You can choose from several different tour options that will include a tasting of multiple sherry styles and an impressive Andalusian horse display.

JEREZ, SPAIN

707 Gaze upon the vineyards of Sanlúcar's oldest producer

Delgado Zuleta is the oldest producer of Manzanilla; its example is a benchmark. Take a trip to the winery in Sanlúcar de Barrameda, and you'll also be shown around the vineyards— it is one of very few bodegas to include this in a visit. Overall, it's a very educational and informative tour.

JEREZ, SPAIN

708 Deepen your sherry appreciation

To understand the true greatness of sherry, you need to visit a top producer like Lustau. This house is unique in that it produces sherries from all three towns (Jerez de la Frontera, Sanlúcar de Barrameda, and El Puerto de Santa María), so you can really hone in on the individual characteristics. The regular sherries are wonderful, but the house also has special vintage dated bottlings for sale that go back to 1992. Don't miss the chance to taste or buy a Palo Cortado—a rarer style that sits somewhere in between the freshness of a fino and the more oxidative character of an Amontillado.

706 *Above:* Take in an Andalusian horse show at Bodegas Williams & Humbert

MENORCA, SPAIN
709 Go underground at this winery

Treat yourself to a tour and a tasting at Menorca's Bodega Binitford. The entire winery is located underground, cleverly built on the site of an old quarry and shielded from the fierce summer heat. As is typical on this island, the grape varieties are French rather than Spanish (Cabernet Sauvignon, Merlot, and Chardonnay). Binitford also makes vermouth.

TENERIFE, SPAIN
710 Learn about this island's wine

Casa Del Vino de Tenerife is a restored seventeenth-century hacienda that now houses a library and a wine museum. It's well worth a look for some background into winemaking on Tenerife—better still, you can taste a wide range of wines on-site. Finally, repair to its excellent restaurant and enjoy your favorite bottle with lunch.

TENERIFE, SPAIN
711 Take a spin around Tenerife's vineyards

Drive the Ruta del Vino Tenerife (Tenerife Wine Route) to appreciate this volcanic terroir and enjoy views of the many old vineyards planted at up to 3,280 ft (1,000 m) of altitude. The route centers on Tacoronte in the north of the island and takes in nine varied wineries. Don't miss the farmer's and craft market in the town of Tegueste, where some wineries sell their bottles.

TENERIFE, SPAIN
712 Visit a cult winery

Wines such as Trenzado, Vidonia, or 7 Fuentes have built a mini cult following for lo-fi wine fans around the world. Their producer is Suertes del Marqués, a family winery in the north of the island. Created in 2006, it farms very old plots of Listán Bianco, Listán Negro, and other local grapes. Some vineyards are up to 130 years old, and all are at high altitudes in the volcanic soil of the Orotava Valley. The wines are made using indigenous yeasts and without filtration or corrections. Visit to taste the salty, savory flavors of a truly individual Tenerife character.

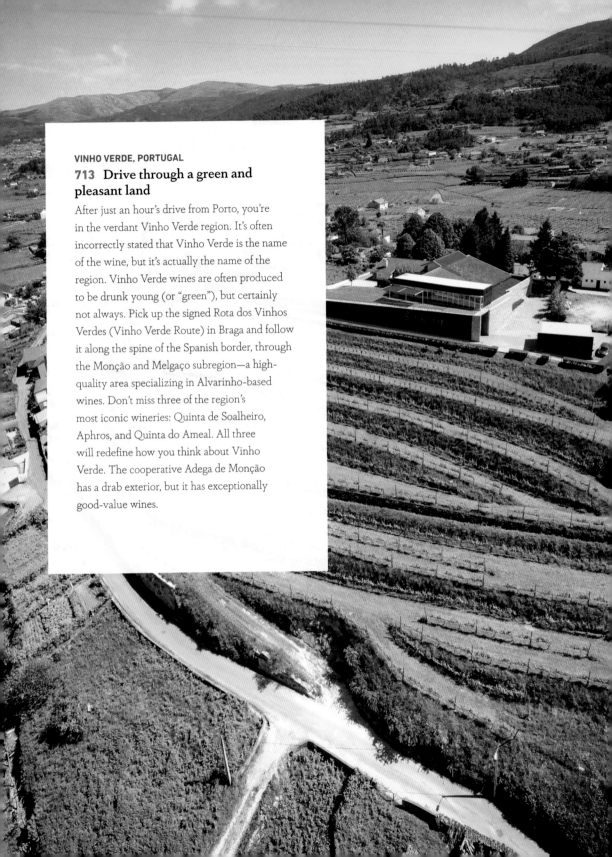

VINHO VERDE, PORTUGAL

713 Drive through a green and pleasant land

After just an hour's drive from Porto, you're in the verdant Vinho Verde region. It's often incorrectly stated that Vinho Verde is the name of the wine, but it's actually the name of the region. Vinho Verde wines are often produced to be drunk young (or "green"), but certainly not always. Pick up the signed Rota dos Vinhos Verdes (Vinho Verde Route) in Braga and follow it along the spine of the Spanish border, through the Monção and Melgaço subregion—a high-quality area specializing in Alvarinho-based wines. Don't miss three of the region's most iconic wineries: Quinta de Soalheiro, Aphros, and Quinta do Ameal. All three will redefine how you think about Vinho Verde. The cooperative Adega de Monção has a drab exterior, but it has exceptionally good-value wines.

VINHO VERDE, PORTUGAL

714 See why harvesting requires a ladder

Look out for the typical high-trellised vines as you drive around the Vinho Verde region. In some cases, they're so high that harvesting the grapes requires an 8 ft (2 m) ladder. There's a particularly large concentration of older trellised vineyards in the area around the village of Fafião, near Braga.

VINHO VERDE, PORTUGAL

715 Treat yourself like royalty

If you're in the Monção area, don't miss the impressive Palácio da Brejoeira—a grand early-nineteenth-century palace. It has impressive formal gardens and a winery that produces one of the region's highest-priced wines.

714 *Below:* High-trained vines in Vinho Verde mean that grape harvesting sometimes requires a ladder

DOURO, PORTUGAL

716 Take the slow train up the valley

Driving around the narrow, mountainous roads in the Douro Valley can be hair-raising and time-consuming. A much more relaxed option is to take the bargain-priced train that saunters up the picturesque valley from Porto all the way to Pocinho. Sit on the right to see the stunning river views and steeply terraced vineyards that cover the hills—many have signs showing which famous port house they belong to. It's hard to imagine just how perilous it was for the port producers of old who had to ship their barrels down the river to reach Vila Nova de Gaia. Régua and Pinhão are among two of the more interesting stops where you might want to spend more time.

DOURO, PORTUGAL

717 Admire centenarian vineyards

Quinta do Crasto is one of the most stunning winery properties located in Cima Corgo (the middle of the Douro Valley). The one-hundred-year-old terraced Maria Teresa vineyards are one of its most prized assets—they're best admired as you drive up the hill to the quinta itself. Later, you can taste the complex wine produced from this vineyard. Ask politely, and you can also take a dip in Crasto's infinity pool, situated right at the top of the estate buildings. It's an idyllic spot with mind-blowing views of the valley.

717 *Above:* The infinity pool at Quinta do Crasto looks out over the Douro Valley

DOURO, PORTUGAL

718 Stay the night at a top quinta

Stay in luxury accommodation at Quinta da
Vallado to fully appreciate this beautiful location
in the Douro Valley. Take a trip up to the quinta's
highest vineyards for its wonderful views. The
quinta also has a small restaurant, which is only
open by appointment.

DOURO, PORTUGAL

719 Taste the lighter side of Douro

See another side of Douro wines when you taste
the light, elegant cuvées made by Rita Marques
at her overachieving Conceito winery. Vineyards
are sited in cooler locations compared to most
Douro properties. Drop in for a vineyard and
winery tour, plus a tasting of its most iconic
wines on Thursdays.

DOURO, PORTUGAL

720 Sleep in luxury in Douro

Taylor's has converted a historic port wine
warehouse, right in the middle of the Douro
Valley, into a luxury hotel: the Vintage House.
It's a splendid spot in which to lodge. Book a
package that combines a two-night stay with
vineyard visits and don't miss the on-site bottle
shop, to ensure you take a little piece of the
valley home with you.

721 Relive Douro's history

Learn about the Douro Valley's world-famous fortified wine at the Museu do Douro (Douro Museum) in Peso da Régua. It's housed in the historic Casa da Companhia building. This two-story museum provides lots of fascinating, historical detail on winemaking in the region. After your thirst has been stimulated, you can taste some wines.

722 Visit caves bubbling with history

Straddling the border of the Douro Valley and Beira Interior, Murganheira winery specializes in sparkling wines (made using the traditional method, as in Champagne). Check out its huge, blue granite cellars that store some three million bottles of wine as it patiently ages. The sparkling wines are some of Portugal's best.

721 *Above:* The Museu do Douro is housed in the historic Casa da Companhia building

DOURO, PORTUGAL

723 Meet an independent port producer

There are very few Portuguese-owned port wine
houses, but Quevedo Port Wine is one of the most
successful. Stop off at its winery and tasting rooms just
outside São João da Pesqueira to learn more about its
port production, and shoot the breeze with the affable
Quevedo family.

PORTO, PORTUGAL

724 Take stock of an architectural gem

Tour Porto's beautiful stock exchange building, the Palácio da Bolsa, which has been at the heart of the port wine industry for a century. It took sixty-eight years to build, and was only completed in 1909. The ornate Moorish decor and glass roof are stunning. The Bolsa is also the site of Porto's biggest wine fair, Essência do Vinho.

PORTO, PORTUGAL

725 Chill out in Porto with great wine

Let Diogo be your drinking guide when you visit Prova Wine, Food & Pleasure. Porto's most laid-back wine bar has a varied and imaginative selection from all over Portugal (and a few from beyond), plus a great jazz soundtrack (sometimes even live). By-the-glass options change frequently.

PORTO, PORTUGAL

726 Savor seafood served with wine

O Gaveto specializes in seasonal and freshly caught produce from the sea—a true classic for seafood cookery. It serves up wonderful shellfish, prawns, and fish of all kinds. Go there in February, and you can feast on bloodsucking lampreys fresh from the tank. You'll love the overarching and excellent selection of local wines!

PORTO, PORTUGAL

727 Encounter port central

The port wine industry is an essential component of Porto. All the major port producers have port lodges (traditionally warehouses, but now focused more on welcoming visitors) in Vila Nova de Gaia, on the opposite side of the river to Porto's center. Visiting a lodge or three is a great way to taste ports from several producers, without the long journeys involved around the Douro Valley. Most lodges don't require reservations to visit, but if you want to upgrade your tasting experience to include more premium bottlings, or ensure a private tour, then you'll need to make arrangements in advance. (Turn the page for details of individual lodges.)

PORTO, PORTUGAL

728 Live it up at a wine weekend

During the third week of February, wine lovers and producers flock to Porto for two major wine fairs. The city throbs with wine-related events and dinners. Visiting both fairs can be combined, since they're just fifteen minutes' walk apart. Essência do Vinho is the larger, more mainstream fair, where hundreds of producers from all over the country congregate in the Bolsa. This is where you can taste wines from many of Portugal's household names—but some smaller producers also participate. You'll need strong elbows to survive the crowds, but it can be fun! Look out for various tutored tastings that take place in the side rooms at the Bolsa during the four-day event. Simplesmente Vinho is a smaller, grittier, artisanal wine fair, with mostly small, independent producers from both Portugal and Spain. With its warehouse setting in Cais Novo and hip music soundtrack, Simplesmente is the one for lo-fi and natural-wine fans, and it's also where you'll discover up-and-coming producers who have yet to become well known. The fair concludes each evening with live music from a local band or performer.

728 *Above:* Porto's Simplesmente Vinho wine fair takes place in Cais Novo

Spend some time at these top ten port lodges in Vila Nova de Gaia

729 Taylor's

Taylor's is one of port's biggest brands, and the tour doesn't disappoint. Here, you take the tour in your own time with an audio guide, before choosing from one of several tasting options.

730 Ferreira

Ferreira was founded in 1751 by a family of winemakers. The guided, informative tour takes you through the impressive cellars before you can relax with a glass or two of port.

731 Poças

Unusually for port, Poças is an independent, Portuguese family-owned house. The cellars are impressive, and the specialty here is wood-aged ports (tawnies and colheitas). You'll see barrels of wines almost a century old, waiting patiently to be bottled.

732 Cálem

The interactive tour at Cálem uses imaginative audiovisual elements to explain the production process. Cálem is part of the Sogevinus Group and makes ports in all styles, from white to tawny to vintage.

733 Graham's

Founded by two Scottish brothers in the nineteenth century, Graham's is known for excellent vintage ports. Its relaxed and unhurried tour (reservation required) is recommended, as is a visit to its riverside restaurant, Vinum.

734 Croft

Unlike many other lodges, Croft isn't located on the riverside. This keeps crowds down and will lend a more relaxed pace to your visit. Croft is focused on bottle-aged styles (vintage, ruby, and reserve), which are all featured in tastings.

735 Corkburn's

The largest of all the port lodges, Corkburn's is very much a working warehouse and includes its own cooperage (barrel-making workshop). This makes the tour much more authentic, and the ports are world-class.

736 Real Companhia Velha

It might be slightly off the beaten track, but Real
Companhia Velha, which was founded in 1756, is
the oldest port house of them all. You'll learn many
fascinating facts about port during the tour, and
tastings often feature premium wines.

737 Casa Kopke

Kopke doesn't offer a tour—instead, you get a
beautiful riverside tasting room and a huge list
of colheitas and tawnies that can be enjoyed by
the glass or in a tasting flight. If you want to drink
something from your birth year, you might just get
lucky here!

738 Churchill's

For a smaller, more intimate
experience, head to Churchill's.
This port house makes
renowned vintage and reserve
styles, and it's well worth having
the premium tasting to
experience its top wines.

738

DÃO, PORTUGAL

739 Survey Dão from its highest peak

The best way to understand a wine region is to
interact with the landscape, so travel to Dão to
find out more. The most major influence on this
wine region's microclimate is Serra da Estrela,
mainland Portugal's highest mountain, and the
huge national park area that surrounds it. The
mountain not only protects the region from the
gusty Atlantic winds, but it also provides a great
deal of its water. There are many hiking trails
within the park area; alternatively, hike or drive
up to Torre, the highest peak, which tops out at
6,539 ft (1,993 m).

DÃO, PORTUGAL

741 Meet a seminal producer

Álvaro Castro is one of the region's, if not the
country's, top winemakers. Visit him at his main
property, Quinta da Pellada, near the Serra
da Estrela Natural Park, to taste his nuanced,
elegant wines and to see the expansive cellars
filled with forthcoming jewels and a considerable
amount of his back catalog.

DÃO, PORTUGAL

740 Taste wine made from 120-year-old vines

A Parisian with Portuguese heritage, Antonio
Madeira has become one of the Dão wine region's
most hyped winemakers. Madeira specializes
in finding old or abandoned vineyards and
recuperating them. For a humbling experience,
visit his oldest plot, which has vines as old as
120 years—and taste the wine (A Centenária)
produced by these hardy senior citizens.

BAIRRADA, PORTUGAL
742 Learn about a saved grape variety

Visit the godfather of Baga, Luís Pato, and find out how he tamed the tricky grape variety that is indigenous to the Bairrada region. You'll taste an amazing number of treatments of the red grape, from Blanc de Noirs to sparkling wines and sweet nectars.

742 *Above:* Luís Pato makes wine derived from the Baga grape variety

BAIRRADA, PORTUGAL

743 Sample wine from a grand hotel

Standing at the gateway to the Buçaco Forest (also sometimes spelled "Bussaco" on signs) is one of Portugal's grand old hotels—the Palace Hotel do Buçaco. You don't have to stay here to admire the property—just call in and enjoy a stroll around the incredibly ornate building and gardens. The attached winery (Buçaco) makes red and white Bairrada wines that are known for their capacity to age for decades. The antique labels and timeless appeal of these wines just add to their mystique and appeal.

BAIRRADA, PORTUGAL

744 Enjoy bubbles in Bairrada

Campolargo is one of Portugal's top sparkling wine producers. Journey to the impressive winery and cellars to taste the wines at source and find out why Bairrada is such a great region to make bubbles. You can select from a range of different tour and tasting options at the Quinta de S. Mateus building.

ALENTEJO, PORTUGAL

745 Choose from a vertical, barrel, or blind tasting

Herdade do Esporão may be one of Portugal's largest wineries, but it's also one of the most innovative. Visit the historic Alentejo winery Herdade do Esporão, with its medieval tower, impressive restaurant, and reservoir. Don't miss the chance to taste the stunning wines from its new *talha* (a Portuguese type of amphora) project, made in 200-year-old amphorae. A huge range of tour and tasting options allow you to find out as much as you wish!

745 *Above:* Discover the many tour and tasting options at Herdade do Esporão

ALENTEJO, PORTUGAL

746 Unearth an old winemaking method

If you've made it to the village of Reguengos de Monsaraz, visiting José de Sousa winery is a must. Its historic amphora cellar has some 120 *talhas*, which are all still in use—apart from the half dozen that exploded from the force of fermentation years ago! Some of the antique vessels date back two hundred years.

746 *Above:* José de Sousa winery has an impressive display of amphorae

ALENTEJO, PORTUGAL

747 Drink straight from the clay

Those amphorae that line the walls of the Casa de Monte Pedral restaurant (in the village of Cuba) aren't just for show! The restaurant (previously a large cooperative winery) makes its own wine, which will be served to you straight from the *talha*, along with its tasty, traditional food.

ALENTEJO, PORTUGAL

748 Orientate in Alentejo with a tasting

Learn more about Alentejo's venerable winemaking traditions at the Alentejo Wine Route tasting room, situated in the handsome walled city of Évora. Taste half a dozen local wines for a nominal fee, and also get advice on who to visit and which parts of the huge wine route to tackle.

COLARES, PORTUGAL

749 Visit the beating heart of Colares wine

Discover the Adega Regional de Colares, the cooperative cellar of this small seaside wine appellation, which is soaked in history. The huge barrel hall, with rows of massive mahogany barrels, evokes a bygone era when the capacity of 220,000 gal (1,000,000 L) was needed. Built in 1931, the winery buildings have an understated grandeur, and the wines are quite unique.

COLARES, PORTUGAL

750 Tour a historic cellar

It's hard not to be smitten with the 1808 warehouse that is home to Adega Viúva Gomes. The tiled exterior is beautiful, and the interior offers wonderful period detail and antique fittings. Situated in Almoçageme, Viúva Gomes isn't a museum, but a working cellar and winery. Nonetheless, you'll find stocks of old Colares wine that go back to 1934—a vintage that is still for sale!

COLARES, PORTUGAL

751 Check out Colares's unique vineyard landscape

There's a lot to see in the Sintra-Cascais National Park area, which hugs the most westerly coastline in Europe. As well as the forest, mountains, and the Pena Palace, the denominated Colares vineyards are a must-see. These bizarre landscapes feature cane and wicker windbreaks, and vines that lie flat on the ground, with their roots painstakingly dug into the sandy soils. The windy Atlantic climate simply doesn't permit normal viticulture. This vineyard landscape is precious—the development of luxury holiday homes in the region almost wiped it out; the area has reduced substantially over the years. Thankfully, the area is now protected against further development, and demand for the wines of Colares has started to grow slowly, from an all-time low in the 1990s. The Adega Regional de Colares can organize tours of the vineyard area, or check online for GPS coordinates.

749 *Right:* Adega Regional de Colares is the oldest cooperative winery in Portugal

LISBON, PORTUGAL

752 Taste Atlantic freshness in these wines

Quinta de Chocapalha is where you'll find a leading light in Lisbon wines—Sandra Tavares is the winemaker at this family estate. Admire the vineyard views over the Serra de Montejunto foothills and the Tagus River, and notice the Atlantic influence on the wines, which overflow with verve and freshness.

LISBON, PORTUGAL

753 Celebrate life at this wine fair

Fancy going to a wine fair where you wander from stand to stand along the sun-soaked quayside by the Tagus River? Vinho ao Vivo (annually on the first weekend in July) offers this idyllic experience, with a brilliant selection of artisanal wines from Portugal and beyond, curated by local wine importer and bar Os Goliardos and restaurant Á Margem. The restaurant is right by the quay and offers a special menu during the fair.

LISBON, PORTUGAL

754 Sample Portuguese flavors

The superseasonal and local dishes at restaurant Prado provide a modern twist on Portuguese cuisine. There's nothing heavy about the food here: flavors are defined, lively, and fresh. Immerse yourself in the wine list—it features well-selected organic, biodynamic, and natural gems from Portugal and beyond. The space is airy and stylish.

754 *Left:* The light and airy space of restaurant Prado

LISBON, PORTUGAL

755 Buy some wine gems from yesteryear

Garrafeira Nacional is a dangerous wine shop to browse in—there are so many interesting and rare vintages from regions such as Madeira, Colares, and Douro that you're liable to leave clutching many more bottles than planned! This is the place to go if you're looking for that birth-year bottle.

LISBON, PORTUGAL

756 Enjoy a glass while you shop

Comida Independente is an *enoteca*-style wine shop–cum-wine bar, where you could enjoyably browse the shelves for hours or just sip contentedly at the counter. So, pull up a stool, order a glass from the esoteric and ever-changing list of artisanal European wines, and opt for a plate of delicious cured meats or cheese.

SETÚBAL, PORTUGAL

757 Experience art, wine, and passion

It's difficult to know where to start at Bacalhôa. The palace was owned by the royal family in medieval times, but is now the site of an impressive winery and one of the world's largest private art collections. It's all due to the passion of owner José Berardo, whose tastes include a Japanese garden, and major exhibitions of African and Art Deco art. Then there are the wines, including Setúbal's specialty— aromatic and luscious Moscatel. Allow for several hours to get the most out of a visit!

755 *Above:* Garrafeira Nacional is stocked with many rare vintages

MADEIRA, PORTUGAL

758 Visit a dynamic Madeira winery

Many wineries have their tasting rooms in
central Funchal, but for a more informative
and personal tour, head to Vinhos Barbeito,
just outside the town. It is one of the most
progressive Madeira producers, and its wines
are an absolute delight. Visit to enjoy a tasting
of its delicious wines.

MADEIRA, PORTUGAL

759 Taste one-hundred-year-old wine

D'Oliveiras, or Pereira D'Oliveira as it's
officially known, is one of the oldest Madeira
shippers still in existence. Its stocks of vintages
that go back to the 1900s are unparalleled. Visit
its tasting room in Funchal and sample younger
wines (twenty- to thirty-year-old blends) for
free. If you're serious about purchasing, you
can also try older vintages.

758 *Above:* Vinhos Barbeito was founded in the 1940s by Mário Barbeito

AZORES, PORTUGAL

760 Marvel at a volcanic vineyard landscape

Viticulture on Pico Island is challenging. Instead of soil, the vines are planted in black volcanic rock and sand. The winds and seawater spray are hazardous, hence the traditional *currais* (vineyard plots with walls built out of the rock), which shield clusters of bush-trained vines. To enjoy this unique landscape, drive the ER1 coast road around Criação Velha parish.

AZORES, PORTUGAL

761 Learn about Pico's winemaking

Although the museum's name is unwieldy, the Landscape of the Pico Island Vineyard Culture Interpretation Centre (CIPCVIP) offers a great orientation into the island's very particular winemaking and farming. You can also partake in wine tastings from a selection of local producers at the museum and go on an organized tour of the vineyards and lava fields (*lajidos*).

760 *Above:* Vineyards and the stratovolcano Mount Pico on Pico Island

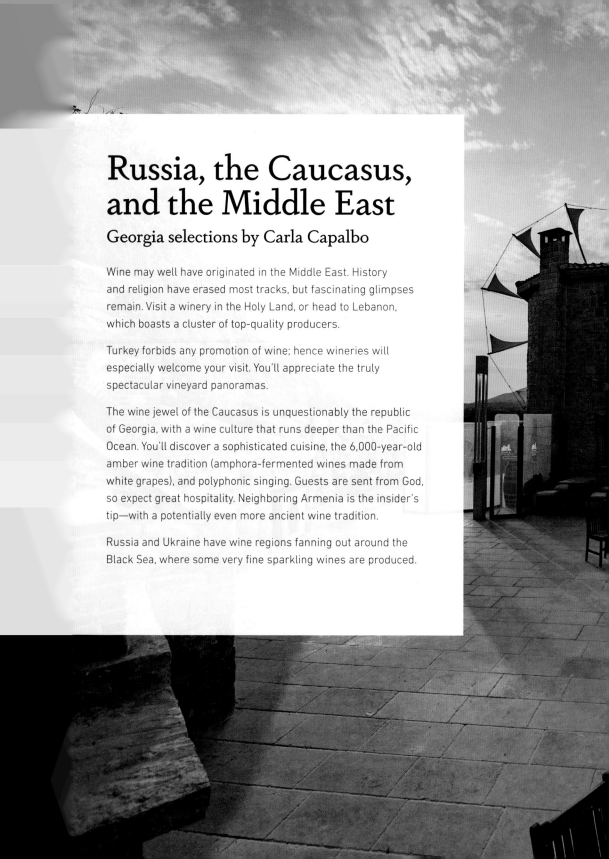

Russia, the Caucasus, and the Middle East

Georgia selections by Carla Capalbo

Wine may well have originated in the Middle East. History and religion have erased most tracks, but fascinating glimpses remain. Visit a winery in the Holy Land, or head to Lebanon, which boasts a cluster of top-quality producers.

Turkey forbids any promotion of wine; hence wineries will especially welcome your visit. You'll appreciate the truly spectacular vineyard panoramas.

The wine jewel of the Caucasus is unquestionably the republic of Georgia, with a wine culture that runs deeper than the Pacific Ocean. You'll discover a sophisticated cuisine, the 6,000-year-old amber wine tradition (amphora-fermented wines made from white grapes), and polyphonic singing. Guests are sent from God, so expect great hospitality. Neighboring Armenia is the insider's tip—with a potentially even more ancient wine tradition.

Russia and Ukraine have wine regions fanning out around the Black Sea, where some very fine sparkling wines are produced.

KAKHETI, GEORGIA

768 Immerse yourself in the spirit of wine

Winemaking is still being practiced today within the walls of Alaverdi Monastery, Kakheti's most influential monastery, in a tradition that began here in 1011. A small vineyard of local varieties flanks the fine medieval church with its soaring steeple. Book a wine tour at Alaverdi Monastery (they run daily), and for hungry visitors, there's also a café that features the monks' honey and yogurt.

KAKHETI, GEORGIA

769 Watch *qvevri* being made

Zaza and Remi Kbilashvili are from one of Kakheti's oldest *qvevri*-making families. They hand make the large clay vinification vessels using a kiln right under their house. While watching their craft, expect to drink wine and *chacha* (a Georgian spirit made from grapes), and eat food cooked by local women.

768 *Above:* The fortress-style Alaverdi Monastery has its own wine cellar

KAKHETI, GEORGIA

Stay in three of Kakheti's most luxurious wine hotels

774 Schuchmann Wines Château & Spa

Spend a couple of nights at Schuchmann Wines Château & Spa and indulge in a wine-themed package. "Saperavi" includes a wine mask; wine bath; and full-body, grape-seed scrub. Afterward, relax in the estate's wine bar and try the excellent *qvevri* wines made by one of Georgia's top winemakers: Giorgi Dakishvili. German owned, the winery sits in the heart of Kakheti's wine country, in the Alazani Valley, and offers comfortable rooms.

775 Radisson Collection Hotel, Tsinandali Estate Georgia

The Radisson Collection Hotel, Tsinandali Estate Georgia is a welcome addition to the wine-crazy region of Kakheti. Book a night or two at this stunningly designed hotel that opened in 2018 beside the nineteenth-century palace and wine cellars of Alexander Chavchavadze. A wine lover's dream, you will be offered tastings from Prince Alexander Chavchavadze's personal wine cellar collection itself!

776 Kvareli Eden Wine Spa

Kvareli Eden Wine Spa, near Georgia's biggest wine-producing region, is the perfect place in which to unwind. Choose from a range of treatments derived from vines, grapes, and their seeds; grapes contain polyphenols, which are powerful antioxidants. The spa and hotel are housed in a luxury resort with pools and gardens.

775

KARTLI, GEORGIA

777 Meet a husband-and-wife *qvevri* team

One of Georgia's pioneer *qvevri* winemakers, Iago Bitarishvili has championed white Chinuri, a grape variety from Kartli, in award-winning wines. His wife, Marina Kurtanidze, has inspired other women to make *qvevri* wines. Contact the husband-and-wife duo to organize a tour that includes a tasting and a delicious meal at their home.

KARTLI, GEORGIA

778 Count 400-plus native grape varieties

Arrange a visit to the Scientific-Research Center of Agriculture (SRCA), an impressive viticultural institute near Saguramo. It houses the principal collection of native Georgian grapevines, with around 437 varieties growing in its extensive vineyards. Vines are reproduced for sale and research, including in microvinifications.

RACHA, GEORGIA

779 Admire a special Georgian church

One of Georgia's hidden gems, the small and beautiful eleventh-century church of Nikortsminda can be found on the way to the forested northern region of Racha. It's decorated with frescoes and elaborate stone carvings, many of which incorporate the grape, whose wine is a symbol of the blood of Christ.

778 *Above:* More than 400 grape varieties grow at the Scientific-Research Center of Agriculture

MTSKHETA, GEORGIA
780   Retrace Queen Tamar's footsteps

With its strategic position along ancient trade routes, the UNESCO Uplistsikhe Cave Town today offers a tantalizing insight into cave-city life in the Middle Ages, when 20,000 people lived here, including artisans and merchants. Queen Tamar commissioned wine cellars and a royal chamber, all now sadly ravaged by time and the elements. Touring the site is possible only for the able-bodied, due to the state of the ruins, but it's fascinating to explore the remaining rock-cut structures.

MTSKHETA, GEORGIA
781   Follow the holy steps of Saint Nino

Nowhere in Georgia is the national obsession with the grape and its vine as apparent as in churches. Mtskheta's important Svetitskhoveli Cathedral is no exception. Here, you'll find grape motifs inside and out, in stone carvings and in Saint Nino's grapevine cross (with its downward-sloping arms) held together, legend has it, with the saint's own hair.

780 *Above:* Uplistsikhe Cave Town was ravaged by Mongols in the thirteenth century

TBILISI, GEORGIA

782 Behold authentic regional houses

Take in a unique viewpoint on Georgian rural history at Tbilisi's Open Air Museum of Ethnography. Founded in 1966, it brings together real houses from each of the Georgian regions, lovingly transported and rebuilt in a large park above the city. Some date back to the nineteenth century and include rooms in which *qvevri* have been buried.

TBILISI, GEORGIA

783 Analyze 8,000-year-old winemaking traditions

With pride of place on Rustaveli Avenue, the Georgian National Museum showcases the many layers of the country's cultural history. Go for the priceless golden jewelry, stone-age anthropological remains, and the collection of ancient clay vessels in which wine was first made in Georgia, in at least 6000 BC.

TBILISI, GEORGIA

784 Find the best wines underground

If natural wines made in *qvevri* are your passion, head straight to Vino Underground. This small wine bar with food, close to Freedom Square, was Tbilisi's first to feature these handmade wines and was started by a group of artisanal producers. Nowhere else will you find as complete a range of wines made from myriad native Georgian grape varieties using low-intervention viticulture. Some are so rare, only a few hundred bottles are produced. Drink here by the glass or bottle and accompany your multihued wines with a small daily menu cooked to order. Or enjoy them with assorted local artisanal cheeses and charcuterie made from Georgian pigs bred by Nathan Moss.

784 *Above: Vino Underground specializes in natural wines*

785 Go to not one, but two wine fairs

On the second weekend of May each year, two wine fairs bring Tbilisi to the wine forefront. The sometimes chaotic but fun Zero Compromise Natural Wine Festival at the Silk Factory Tbilisi on Merab Kostava Street features the ever-growing natural-wine movement of small-scale family and organic producers. In contrast, the New Wine Festival combines wine tastings, food, and traditional music in the spacious Mtatsminda Park, located high above Tbilisi and offering wonderful views of the city. Can't decide which one to go to? Then go to both!

786 Feast on Georgian flavors

Dine at restaurant Azarphesha—a stone's throw from Freedom Square in the city center—and you'll be treated to delicious Georgian food that's been given a modern twist. The wines are fantastic, too, chosen for being made in *qvevri* and using low-intervention viticulture. There's also the chance to have a *tamada* (or toastmaster) and polyphonic singers—just ask the staff.

787 Get pampered at this luxury spa

In the heart of Tbilisi, near the sulfur baths, Sam Raan Spa & Wellness Center offers luxurious spa treatments derived from the curative vine fruit. Detox in style with a ninety-minute, full-body scrub using grape seeds. Many other treatments are available too.

IMERETI, GEORGIA

788 Join a rural winemaking family for a tasting

You'll need to make an appointment to visit Archil Guniava's intimate vineyards and *qvevri* cellar, which flank his house in the small village of Kvaliti, near Zestafoni—but it's well worth the effort. His wines, of local white Tsolikouri and red Otskhanuri Sapere grapes, are a tribute to the personal attention of this wonderful vigneron. Guniava and his hospitable family offer a warm welcome and also feed guests.

IMERETI, GEORGIA

789 Admire Georgia's medieval splendor

The monumental Monastery of Gelati and its medieval church are highlights of Georgia's Golden Age and are a UNESCO World Heritage Site. King David the Builder had an academy here at which philosophy and winemaking were taught, as ancient *qvevri* excavated here attest. Find the impressive site near Kutaisi and don't miss David's tomb in the small gatehouse beside the church.

IMERETI, GEORGIA

790 Watch clay wine jars being made

Zaliko Bozhadze is one of Georgia's master *qvevri* makers. His pottery studio at Maqatubani, on the main road through Imereti from Khashuri to Kutaisi, is a must for wine lovers wanting to see firsthand how these giant coil pots are made and fired. You'll be watching traditional art, believed to be unchanged for more than 8,000 years, and recognized by UNESCO.

790 *Above: Zaliko Bozhadze makes giant qvevri at Maqatubani*

IMERETI, GEORGIA

791 Meet a Georgian wine revolutionary

Nobody in western Georgia has been as influential in keeping the *qvevri* winemaking tradition alive as Ramaz Nikoladze. He encouraged many others to start bottling and selling their wines. His are some of Georgia's most thrilling, especially his amber Tsolikouri. His wife, Nestan, is a fantastic cook, so get in touch to arrange a tour.

SAMTSKHE-JAVAKHETI, GEORGIA

792 Explore a twelfth-century cave city

Visit one of Georgia's biggest attractions and discover wine cellars dating from the twelfth century. Looking up at the vast cave monastery complex of Vardzia, it's hard to believe 10,000 soldiers (many with horses) lived inside it, eating, praying, and even drinking wine that was held in its carved-out cellars. At the time, Vardzia was invisible, hidden from view by the mountain, but it was part destroyed by an earthquake in 1283, exposing its innards.

SAMTSKHE-JAVAKHETI, GEORGIA

793 Greet a grape explorer

Winemaker Giorgi Natenadze has spent years on a mission: to find grape varieties from the southern region, Samtskhe-Javakheti, that went missing due to Ottoman and Soviet occupations. He's managed all this and more. Visit Natenadze's Wine Cellar and the ancient stone terraces he's repopulating with rare grapes like Chitiskvertskha and Akhaltsikhuri Tetri.

SAMTSKHE-JAVAKHETI, GEORGIA

794 Hike up to an ancient winemaking village

The tiny village of Chachkari is now inhabited by only a handful of old folk, but its role producing wine in the twelfth century for the cave city of Vardzia was crucial. Walk around to spot the few pluri-centennial vines that still grow there, alongside ancient stone crush pads, as testaments to Chachkari's former vinous glory.

793 *Left:* Natenadze's Wine Cellar utilizes rare grapes

SAMEGRELO, GEORGIA

795 Experience Georgian hospitality

Keto Ninidze and her husband, Zaza Gagua, live in the countryside near Martvili. They each make natural wines from local Megrelian varieties, including Ojaleshi, Dzelshavi, and Orbeluri. He bottles his wines under the Vino M'Artville label; her label is Oda Family Marani. They also run a fantastic restaurant from their home, in a traditional oda (local house)—it really is worth booking a table here for the scrumptious food! It is cooked in part in a freestanding room made of woven hazelnut branches called a *patskha*. Inside it, cornmeal *ghomi* (like polenta) and roast chicken are cooked over an open fire. Don't miss the addictive Megrelian khachapuri: a circular cheese-filled bread that is also topped with melted cheese. It goes fabulously with the wines.

SAMEGRELO, GEORGIA

796 Step back in time in Samegrelo

Salkhino is the location of the Dadiani family's summer residence—this noble family ruled western Georgia in the nineteenth century. It once contained many *qvevri* and is still surrounded by a beautiful park. You can visit the park, but the palace is usually closed to visitors. It sits close to Martvili, near a monastery that still makes wine, and the monks may open their cellar to you for a tasting.

GURIA, GEORGIA

797 Try a Black Sea wine

Zurab Topuridze of Iberieli winery is the go-to man for learning about the delicious wines of the Black Sea region of Guria, where he has an estate. He's a champion of Chkhaveri, a light-bodied red grape that is native to the coastal area. He also makes fruity Saperavi in Kakheti. Both are low-intervention wines made in his personal cellars in clay *qvevri*. You're welcome to visit the estate, but you'll need to book a couple of weeks in advance.

ADJARIA, GEORGIA

798 Sample authentic Adjarian food

This Black Sea region offers a unique cuisine influenced by the Ottomans. The Adjarian Wine House is situated in the gardens of an eighteenth-century wine cellar and specializes in local dishes, including kebabs with a fiery plum sauce, stuffed vine leaves, and borano, a melted butter and cheese dish, to eat with local Chkhaveri wines. Be sure to save room for baklava for dessert!

797 *Above: Iberieli's traditional qvevri cellar is situated in the westerly region of Guria*

799 Taste truly fine wines from Armenia

Armenia might just be the birthplace of winemaking, yet its wines were barely known outside the Caucasus for many years. Zorah Wines is close to the biblical Mount Ararat and has led the charge for producing exceptional wines in this small, mountainous country. Zorah was founded by Italian Armenian Zorik Gharibian and cultivates indigenous grape varieties such as Areni Noir, Voskèak, and Garandmak. The vineyards (many very old) sit at the lofty height of 4,500 ft (1,372 m) above sea level and are mostly ungrafted (planted on their own roots). If you can't get to the winery itself, contact Zorah to find out where you can purchase its wines.

800 Visit the world's earliest-known winery

Close to Zorah is the huge and impressive Areni-1 Cave Complex (also known locally as "T'rchuneri/bird Cave"). It's here in 2007 that an archeological find turned out to be a 6,100-year-old winery—the oldest currently known to man! You can tour the caves and experience the true cradle of wine yourself. The site is very much a workspace, since the digs are continuing. It's also famous for having turned up the world's oldest shoe.

801 Explore Armenia wines and more

You'll need to talk with the staff at In Víno EVN, because this wine bar has no list—but there are 850 wines to choose from, including some fifteen or so by the glass. It's no hardship, since this cozy spot overflows with passion and enthusiasm. It's a great place to taste a wide selection of Armenian wines.

ISTANBUL, TURKEY

802   Hang out at a lively Turkish wine bar

Solera Winery is a convivial and well-stocked wine bar in Turkey's capital. It's a great spot to try some excellent Turkish wines, but if you get bored with the domestic product, then there are many other choices. You should also try the food here.

CAPPADOCIA, TURKEY

803   Fly high above the vineyards

The bizarre volcanic rock formations and "chimneys" are what make Cappadocia such an extraordinary sight—even more so when you view them from above. Every morning at around 7 a.m., dozens of hot-air balloons take to the skies with visitors eager to experience this dream landscape. The flight is quite magical, and most tour operators finish the experience with a Champagne breakfast once you're back on solid ground. Cappadocia is a wine region, and depending on the route, you'll be able to see some of its vineyards from the skies.

CAPPADOCIA, TURKEY

804   Meet an eccentric winemaker

Gelveri might just be one of the maddest winery projects anywhere in the world. Udo Hirsch, from Germany, grows forgotten native grape varieties at more than 4,000 ft (1,219 m) above sea level and ferments them in traditional Turkish clay amphorae, which he's salvaged from around the area. Some are more than 700 years old. The resulting wines are literally like nothing you've ever tasted.

BOZBURUN PENINSULA, TURKEY

805 • Harvest grapes at Datça Vineyard and Winery

Situated on the impossibly scenic Bozburun Peninsula, west of Marmaris, Datça Vineyard and Winery is a passion-fueled family project that shows real potential. Try the tasty wines, some of which are made from indigenous Turkish grape varieties, and stroll around the property at your leisure. Better yet, visit during the first week of August, and you can participate in the harvest with the family.

805   *Above:* Datça Vineyard and Winery produces wines made from indigenous Turkish grape varieties

URLA, TURKEY

806 Make your way to Urla Winery

Named after the region, Urla Şarapçılık (Urla Winery) is close to Izmir. With
136 acres (55 ha) of vineyards, it's one of Turkey's major producers. High-quality
wines are made from both international grape varieties such as Chardonnay, and
some interesting local cultivars, including white Bornova Misketi and red Urla Karası.
The winery buildings are impressive, and you can stay at the on-site hotel named Two
Rooms Hotel. Urla Şarapçılık is part of the small Urla Bağ Yolu (Urla Wine Route),
which consists of five active wineries. The others are smaller and also well worth a
visit. They are Urlice, USCA, Mozaik, and MMG.

TOP 3

BEKAA VALLEY, LEBANON

Discover three wine-related attractions in Lebanon's Bekaa Valley

807 Château Musar

Plan a tour of Château Musar—it not only makes Lebanon's most iconic wines, it's also the producer that opened the world's eyes to fine wine from this part of the world. The Hochar family has made its inimitable blend of French Rhône varieties every year since 1930, apart from 1982, when access roads to the vineyards were so badly damaged in the Gulf War that a harvest was impossible. Ask to try the signature red blend Château Musar, which tips its cap to the Rhône Valley and the south of France, but adds in an exotic character that is beguiling and distinctive. The wines can age gracefully for many decades.

808 Baalbek

Appropriately enough, since it's Lebanon's main wine region, the Bekaa Valley also boasts one of the largest and best-preserved temples of Dionysus/Bacchus (the Greek/Roman god of wine) in the world. Combine a visit to the temple of Baalbek with local winery tours. It's less than a two-hour drive from Beirut.

809 Château Ksara

Established in 1857, Château Ksara is one of the Bekaa Valley's longest-established wineries. Red, white, and rosé wines are excellent, and a visit takes in the historic bell tower and observatory, plus a walk through the huge Roman cellars where wines are stored. The winery's restaurant is well worth a stop too.

809

BETHLEHEM, PALESTINE TERRITORIES

810 Drink wine from the Holy Land

Cremisan Monastery is one of the only wineries in the Bethlehem area, with an amazing history and an unexpected tie-in with Italian winemaking expertise. Taste the monastery's fascinating wines made from local varieties, and enjoy the location, set in one of the region's most beautiful valleys.

JUDEAN PLAIN, ISRAEL

811 Try Israel's first orange wines

Yaacov Oryah is one of very few artisanal winemakers in this corner of the world. You can visit and taste his Alpha Omega range—the first orange wines to be produced in Israel. You can also follow his progress as he replants and develops almost lost indigenous grape varieties.

810 *Above:* Cremisan Monastery dates back to the seventh century

Australasia
Selections by Jeni Port

Australia and New Zealand don't have ancient traditions to burden them down—and that means that anything goes when it comes to winemaking. Producers here are free to explore the possibilities of any grape variety or winemaking technique they want. This translates into innovation, experimentation, and frequently delicious liquids in your glass.

New Zealand's relatively cool climate excels with Pinot Noir and Sauvignon Blanc, and you'll find many wineries specializing in these varieties. Australia has a range of mostly warmer regions and diverse specialties. Don't miss the sweet wines of Rutherglen, Barossa's meaty Shiraz, or the unique Hunter Valley Sémillon—a wine from one of the world's harshest wine-growing climates.

The feeling of the great outdoors is unparalleled in this part of the world—and if mainland Australia impresses nature lovers, Tasmania ratchets up the wow factor still farther. Its wines are also exceptional.

QUEENSLAND, AUSTRALIA

812 Go bush in comfort and style

Escape to subtropical wilderness for a weekend of relaxation and indulgence only thirty minutes from Brisbane. Sanctuary by Sirromet is a trio of luxury, tented pavilions set in isolation overlooking a natural lagoon on the Sirromet Wines. Enjoy an eight-course Tasting Plate dinner at Restaurant Lurleen's on the estate or at sister restaurant Tuscan Terrace.

HUNTER VALLEY, AUSTRALIA

813 Delve into a "Graveyard" red

It may have a funny name, but rest assured that Graveyard Vineyard Shiraz, one of Australia's top reds, never set its roots down in a graveyard. Find out more when you go behind the scenes at Brokenwood Wines for a day of insider action, including a tasting of Graveyard Shiraz in situ, followed by lunch and more.

813 *Above:* Brokenwood Wines was established in 1970 in the Hunter Valley

HUNTER VALLEY, AUSTRALIA
814 Fill up with fortified and *fromage*

This is not just any wine and cheese tasting—the historic Audrey Wilkinson Vineyard offers a great fortified wine and cheese tasting. You'll sit in the heart of the winery with barrels of well-matured fortified wine that are ready for tapping, and a plate of locally sourced *fromage* ready for a taste challenge.

HUNTER VALLEY, AUSTRALIA
815 Bring the popcorn and wine

Fancy a night at the movies in front of the big screen against a forest backdrop high above the Hunter Valley? You're in for a great night out with Historic Movies under the Stars. Bring some Hunter Valley Sémillon, chairs, and rugs and enjoy a relaxing night of old movies from the 1920s to the 1950s.

SYDNEY, AUSTRALIA
816 Pay a visit to an innovative wine merchant

Alternative wine guru Mike Bennie and friends set the Sydney wine scene alight when they set themselves up as wine merchants. The store sells some of the craziest new and exciting natural and low-intervention wine, beers, and artisanal spirits imaginable. Check it out at P&V Wine + Liquor Merchants.

816 *Above:* P&V Wine + Liquor Merchants calls itself "a bottle shop for the neighborhood by the neighborhood"

SYDNEY, AUSTRALIA

817 Savor down-to-earth tastes

Make tracks to Dear Sainte Éloise wine bar in
Potts Point for its multi-award-winning wine
list that celebrates the great winemakers of
the world. It gives voice to the young, the
entrepreneurial, and the emerging world of
natural and experimental wines. It is what every
wine bar should be: exciting and welcoming.

SHOALHAVEN, AUSTRALIA

818 Soak up the sun, sand, and . . . grapes!

What a combination! It doesn't get much better than visiting wineries and walking sun-drenched beaches . . . on the same day. Visit the wineries on the Shoalhaven coast, led by Coolangatta Estate and Mountain Ridge Wines, and in between tastings, take the 100 Beach Challenge. There are a hundred unspoiled beaches along this 106 mi (170 km) stretch of coastline waiting to be explored.

CANBERRA, AUSTRALIA

819 Peer at pioneering biodynamic wines

High in the hills of Bungendore, the Carpenter family was an early adopter of organic and biodynamic farming methods in the 1970s. Visit their Lark Hill Winery and see just how good the Canberra district is at growing cool-climate Riesling, Chardonnay, Pinot Noir, and Shiraz. The family also helped pioneer Grüner Veltliner— their faith in which certainly paid off.

CANBERRA, AUSTRALIA

820 Revel where Riesling is queen

Each October, the largest collection of Rieslings from around the world is brought together for judging at the Canberra International Riesling Challenge. The wines are judged over three days and are followed by public tastings and master classes. Participating countries include Canada, the Czech Republic, France, Germany, New Zealand, the United States, and of course, Australia.

CANBERRA, AUSTRALIA

821 Meet a most curious winemaker

Take a glimpse into the other side of winemaking: ancestral-style sparkling Riesling, Gamay made with carbonic maceration, or a Fiano blended with Pinot Grigio and Riesling. The creative force behind Ravensworth Wines is Bryan Martin. You'll find his wines at Canberra wine bars such as The Canberra Wine House or Bar Rochford.

CANBERRA, AUSTRALIA

822 Treat your taste buds

Some top wine commentators think this is
Australia's best Shiraz—do you agree? A trip
to Côte-Rôtie in 1991 changed everything for
winemaker Tim Kirk. He returned to Clonakilla
and set about co-fermenting Shiraz with a dash
of Viognier. The result was an instant classic: an
elegant, red-berried, floral beauty with a fine
structure. Seek out the Shiraz Viognier to taste
for yourself.

CANBERRA, AUSTRALIA

823 Craft pottery in the vines

Create your own sushi set in a three-hour
pottery class at Four Winds Vineyard. There is
no need for previous experience. This is a fun
day out for everyone and includes a table for
leisurely grazing, wine, and tuition to Hillgrove
Pottery. Take home a set that includes a plate,
soy sauce bottle, bowls, and chopstick holders.

822 *Above:* The well-protected vines at Clonakilla produce what some commentators regard as Australia's finest Shiraz

RUTHERGLEN, AUSTRALIA

Get involved in these three wine-related activities

824 Campbells Wines

Become a master blender for a day and blend your own fortified wine with the winemaker at Campbells Wines, located just outside Rutherglen. Sourcing base wines from the Campbells solera, you'll blend a Muscat—the sweetest and most intense of all—and the best part is you get to take it home with you! While you're there, don't miss the Rutherglen Durif and Cabernet Sauvignon.

825 Pedal to Produce

Rent a bike in Rutherglen and take in the beauty of the region and its unique wines as you embark on Pedal to Produce, a culinary biking route. Pick up a map at the Rutherglen Wine Experience and Visitor Information Centre, and you're off on your gourmet cycling adventure! Start with a sparkling Shiraz at Anderson Winery, followed by Jones Winery & Vineyard for a French-inspired lunch. Then just follow your map and heart.

826 All Saints Estate

Don a blindfold and let your senses take over as you delve into the rich, wonderful world of Muscat during a blind tasting at All Saints Estate. Muscat is a magical fortified wine that is forever associated with northeast Victoria, and this estate has some of the oldest blended Muscats in Australia. You'll taste three of them in the private family cellar.

824

RUTHERGLEN, AUSTRALIA

827 Don't be confused by the name

What is Topaque and why does it taste so good? A journey to Rutherglen will reveal more. Topaque is a fortified wine that's been made from the Muscadelle grape since the 1860s. Long known as Tokay, a name change became inevitable after the signing of the Australia-EU wine trade agreement in which makers gave up the use of Tokay and other protected names. Producers then came up with the entirely original "Topaque." Some consumers still aren't convinced—some makers too. You will sometimes see "Muscadelle" on labels. Whatever the name, the taste remains a delight, with luscious flavors of dried fruits, honey, raisin, and toffee.

RUTHERGLEN, AUSTRALIA

828 Feel the history of Morris Wines

The floors are dirt, the barrels aged. The patina of 160 years of history is everywhere: you can feel, see, and taste it at Morris Wines. Under the guidance of five generations of Morris winemakers, the winery is home to styles that made the region famous: Shiraz, Durif, fortified, Muscat, and Topaque.

RUTHERGLEN, AUSTRALIA

829 Ascend your luxury tower

A romantic tower built for two—with winding, narrow staircases leading to the top bedroom and views across vines and open country—can be yours at Mount Ophir Estate, just outside Rutherglen. The tower is but one accommodation option at this historic winery and vineyard—it dates back to 1891.

830 *Above:* Chrismont is a multimillion-dollar hilltop cellar door, restaurant, and guesthouse complex

KING VALLEY, AUSTRALIA

830 Don't miss *aperitivo* hour in Cheshunt

Raise a glass of Chrismont's Prosecco, take in the views, and relax. It's always *aperitivo* hour in this beautiful part of the King Valley. The Pizzini family at Chrismont has a proud Italian heritage—enjoy great food and wine in this multimillion-dollar hilltop cellar door, restaurant, and guesthouse complex.

KING VALLEY, AUSTRALIA

831 Get to know your grapes

Take a taste test of grapes created specifically for Australia's hot, dry conditions at Brown Brothers. The grapes have funny names like Tarrango, Mystique, and Cienna, and the flavors are familiar . . . but different. The company has been a tireless promoter of Australia's homegrown grape varieties and crossings of grapes, such as Touriga Nacional x Sultana (Tarrango).

KING VALLEY, AUSTRALIA

832 Travel on the road to fun

Join King Valley's Prosecco Road for a day's exploration of a grape closely connected to the people and the region. The self-drive food and wine adventure takes in five top producers: Brown Brothers, Chrismont, Dal Zotto, Pizzini, and Sam Miranda. You'll taste different styles from ancestral to vintage, rosé, and more.

DOOKIE, AUSTRALIA

833 Walk into a history lesson

Experience the lore of an ancient people and the traditions and stories of the traditional owners of the land in which the vines of Tallis Wine thrive. Join an elder of the local Yorta Yorta people on a bush walk on the Rock Correa track, highlighting the First People of Australia's connection to the land, fauna, and flora.

NAGAMBIE LAKES, AUSTRALIA

834 Enjoy Shiraz beside the Goulburn

Follow the mighty Goulburn River as it twists and turns through thoroughbred horse and farming country to the gates of Mitchelton winery. Taste its award-winning Shiraz, feast at its restaurant The Muse, visit the largest commercial Aboriginal art gallery in Australia, and take in a boat ride to nearby Tahbilk. End the day at the luxurious boutique hotel.

833 *Above:* Tallis Wine's first harvest was in 2000

NAGAMBIE LAKES, AUSTRALIA

835 Sip carbon-neutral wines at Tahbilk

With a glass of Marsanne in hand, take a walk through one of Australia's oldest and most beautiful winery estates, Tahbilk, which translates as *tabilk-tabilk*, "Place of Many Waterholes." The zero-carbon, light-touch producer boasts an original 1860 winery, wetland walk, and restaurant. Taste the Tahbilk range of wines made with minimal touch and maximum flavor, and the 1860 Vines Shiraz, made from the estate's oldest vines.

HEATHCOTE, AUSTRALIA

836 Gorge at a cellar door

Come for a wine tasting at Vinea Marson and stay for a plate of antipasti and Italian-style hospitality. Mario Marson offers wines with a savory sensitivity, such as Prosecco, Friulano, Pinot Bianco, and Nebbiolo. Enjoy with crusty bread, estate-grown olive oil, and cheeses, including Drunken Buffalo cheese made with Vinea Marson Nebbiolo skins.

BENDIGO, AUSTRALIA

837 Go glamping in the vines

You will find the wild Aussie bush beckons just outside your tent at Balgownie Estate Winery Retreat & Restaurant Bendigo. Glamping here comes complete with the sounds and smells of the great outdoors: the scent of eucalyptus and the noisy call of the laughing kookaburra. It's located an hour north of Melbourne, and you can enjoy a bush setting with top food and wine on hand.

837 *Right:* Balgownie Estate Winery Retreat & Restaurant Bendigo

MACEDON RANGES, AUSTRALIA

838 Get lost . . . and found at Hanging Rock

Shrouded in mystery and intrigue, Hanging Rock waits to be explored. Take a picnic and enjoy a walk to the top of this prehistoric volcanic rock formation with panoramic views across the Macedon Ranges. Finish with a visit to Hanging Rock Winery, a pioneering sparkling wine producer in the region.

MACEDON RANGES, AUSTRALIA

839 All aboard this vinous train adventure

Escape to the verdant hills of the Macedon Ranges and visit a winery with its own railway station. Passing Clouds Winery, in the picturesque country town of Musk, installed its own train station and line from nearby Daylesford. Enjoy the ride and finish with lunch served *la famiglia* style. Check train departure times before you travel.

838 *Above:* The prehistoric rock formation Hanging Rock is located near Hanging Rock Winery

YARRA VALLEY, AUSTRALIA

840 Discover the perfect art and wine match

A great Yarra Valley winemaker and one of the greatest collections of modern Australian art ever curated come together in one location: TarraWarra Estate. Owners Marc and Eva Besen combine their two great loves here. Explore modern artists such as Drysdale, Dobell, and Williams before lunch, and a tasting of the outstanding Chardonnay and Pinot Noir.

YARRA VALLEY, AUSTRALIA

841 Visit a very small winery

It's not the biggest cellar door you'll ever visit, but Yarra Yering ranks among the Yarra Valley's best. Former Winemaker of the Year Sarah Crowe fashions expressive Pinot Noirs and Shiraz and strives to perfect the art of blending with her Dry Red No. 1 and No. 2.

YARRA VALLEY, AUSTRALIA

842 Feast on fabulous food and wine

The rich, plentiful land of the Yarra Valley awaits with a day of hedonistic food, wine, and cheese experiences at De Bortoli Wines. Take a stroll through the vines and be the first to try soon-to-be-released wines from the barrel, and a tasting of De Bortoli's own cheeses and wines, followed by a three-course lunch in the Italian-inspired restaurant Locale.

YARRA VALLEY, AUSTRALIA

843 Sing it out loud!

A Day on the Green comes every year to the outdoor amphitheater at Rochford Wines. International artists like Stevie Nicks, Robbie Williams, and Bryan Ferry alternate with great Australian artists during the summer months. Book in advance and enjoy a day of great music, Rochford food, and wines.

842 *Above:* De Bortoli Wines is a fourth-generation family estate

MELBOURNE, AUSTRALIA

844 Go back to school

Make wine or drink wine at Noisy Ritual, an
urban winery by day, hip wine bar–cum-music
venue by night. It produces wines such as
pét-nat rosé, skin-contact Sauvignon Blanc,
and Pinot Noir, all sold on the premises. It also
hosts a series of winemaking workshops.

MORNINGTON PENINSULA, AUSTRALIA

845 Follow the Farmgate Trail

Embark on the Wine Food Farmgate Trail to
forage for the very best of the seasonal bounty
to be found on the Mornington Peninsula. You'll
roam from Benton Rise Farm and Green Olive
at Red Hill to the Main Ridge Dairy, Pure
Peninsula Honey, Ripe 'n' Ready Cherry Farm,
and Sunny Ridge Strawberry Farm. Finish
with a well-deserved espresso at Tully's Corner
Produce Store.

MORNINGTON PENINSULA, AUSTRALIA

846 Eat, drink, sleep, and repeat

The goat's milk, magnesium, and rosewater
bath is ready to go, and the glass of Peninsula
Chardonnay is poured. Enjoy a spot of luxury
with a night at the luxurious Jackalope Hotel
overlooking the Willow Creek Vineyard. Your
food options range from the informal Rare
Hare Wine & Food Store to the deluxe Doot
Doot Doot.

844 *Above:* Noisy Ritual was started in 2014 by two friends

MORNINGTON PENINSULA, AUSTRALIA

Discover four of Mornington Peninsula's best wineries

847 Montalto

Only have a day on the peninsula? Pack everything you need to know about wine growing and making in this exciting wine-producing maritime region with a Mornington Peninsula Discovery Tasting at Montalto. Educational and fun, the tastings follow the role of grapes, growing, and making, followed by lunch. Don't miss the outstanding, permanent outdoor sculpture collection on display.

848 Quealy Winemakers

In the beginning one person saw a future for Pinot Gris on the Mornington Peninsula where others scoffed. Now, Kathleen Quealy of Quealy Winemakers has the last laugh. See and taste why the grape is among the peninsula's most exciting. Then visit her son Tom McCarthy's Kerri Greens Winery in Red Hill South to experience the low-intervention future of winemaking. With French winemaker Lucas Blanck, McCarthy explores Chardonnay, Pinot Noir, and, unusually for the peninsula, Riesling and Gewürztraminer. Blanck's Alsatian background comes in handy when producing dry and expressive aromatic whites.

849 Pt. Leo Estate

Spend a day on the beach, and later make your way to Pt. Leo Estate to wind down for a relaxing lunch, a glass of Chardonnay, and a wander around the multimillion-dollar Sculpture Park. The outdoor gallery stretches more than 334 acres (135 ha) with sixty major works on display, from a 23 ft (7 m) cast-iron head to a mirror labyrinth.

850

850 Foxeys Hangout

Maker of sparkling wines at Foxeys Hangout, Michael Lee offers a one-on-one tutorial into the mysteries of the bubble at the important final stages of disgorgement, and the addition of the dosage before corking. You get to determine how many grams of sugar should be added to your own bottle of bubbles, together with the selection of a base wine.

BALLARAT, AUSTRALIA

851 Go west to Eastern Peake

Discover real, no-fuss winemaking at Eastern Peake, a small father-and-son wine venture. Australia's 2018 Young Winemaker of the Year Owen Latta and his father, Norm, are Pinot Noir fanatics, and are pioneering Project Zero wines, farmed organically with zero preservatives or sulfur additions. It's white-knuckle winemaking at its best, and produces fantastically exciting wines.

GRAMPIANS, AUSTRALIA

852 Venture down into these cellars

Go down where the sun never shines, where thousands of bottles of sparkling wine bide their time. The underground cellars of historic Seppelt Wines (more than 2 mi/3 km long) were excavated by out-of-work gold miners around 1868. Don't take the tour if you're claustrophobic!

852 *Above:* Dine in the atmospheric underground cellars at Seppelt Wines

COONAWARRA, AUSTRALIA

853 Sleep with the gum trees

You don't get much closer to the source of Coonawarra's fine wines than sleeping among the red gums at Bellwether Wines. Winemaker Sue Bell turned the 1868 Glen Roy Shearing Shed into her winery and restaurant/cellar door in 2009 and added six glamping campsites. Book into A Table of Twelve experience at the winery with a six-course tasting menu that includes matching wines.

853 *Above:* As well as being a winery, Bellwether Wines comprises a produce garden, kitchen, and campground

COONAWARRA, AUSTRALIA

854 Explore the wine cellars of your dreams

Coonawarra is renowned for its Cabernet Sauvignon; a combination of climate and terra rossa soils producing concentrated wines capable of long-term aging. Each July, the winemakers of Coonawarra open their private cellars for aged wines to put on at their cellar doors. Don't miss this rare treat!

CLARE VALLEY, AUSTRALIA

855 Meander through Riesling villages

Walk, run, or ride the Riesling Trail through the beautiful wine villages of the Clare Valley. Converted from a disused railway line, the 22 mi (35 km) track runs between Auburn and Clare. As you make your way through Leasingham, Watervale, Penwortham, and Sevenhill, stop for a break at local wineries for tastings of the region's most noted white grape.

BAROSSA VALLEY, AUSTRALIA

856 Savor some personal history

One of the rarest wine experiences on the planet can be yours at Seppeltsfield, home to a collection of fortified wines dating back to 1878. The Taste Your Birth Year Tour takes you through the majestic Centennial Cellar, which houses an unbroken lineage of every vintage of tawny fortified Shiraz back to 1878.

BAROSSA VALLEY, AUSTRALIA

857 Lose yourself in the music and wine

Do you like to party? Then venture to one of the A Day on the Green concerts. You'll find names such as James Blunt, Elton John, and Jason Mraz spending an Australian spring and summer playing at various Aussie wineries. Peter Lehmann Wines in the Barossa Valley, one of fourteen participating wineries, brings old-style country hospitality to a fun day out, with a featured artist performing once a year.

BAROSSA VALLEY, AUSTRALIA

858 Feel the serenity

Gain a new perspective on one of Australia's most beautiful wine regions, the Barossa Valley, with a sunrise hot-air-balloon adventure. You'll soar high above vines, cottages, hamlets, and rolling hills. The valley's wine industry dates back to the 1840s, and the region is home to some of Australia's oldest wine names, including Yalumba, Seppeltsfield, and Henschke.

BAROSSA VALLEY, AUSTRALIA

859 Learn about the importance of the wineglass

Discover why the wineglass adds so much to the wine-tasting experience at the multimillion-dollar St. Hugo Cellar Door's St. Hugo & Riedel Masterclass. Find out how the shape of a wineglass, or the angle the wine falls into your mouth, dictates the degree of your tasting appreciation and enjoyment.

858 *Above: Barossa Valley vineyards can be viewed on hot-air-balloon experiences*

ADELAIDE, AUSTRALIA

860 Stumble upon the home of Penfolds

The Penfolds story started at the Magill Estate Cellar Door, just 5 mi (8 km) from Adelaide.
Dr. Christopher and Mary Penfold planted vines in 1844, but the production of Grange Shiraz in
the 1950s really put the estate on the map. Visit a spectacular cellar door space that offers tours and
tastings that are both conducted in English and Mandarin. There are many options, including the
Magill Estate Heritage Experience, Twilight Tour and Luxury Degustation Dinner, and The Ultimate
Penfolds Experience (with tastings of Penfolds wines, including Grange). Then wander over to the
Magill Estate Restaurant for a truly indulgent lunch or dinner.

ADELAIDE, AUSTRALIA

861 Discover more than just cricket

A world-class wine needs a world-class venue
to show it off, and they don't come much bigger
than the Hill of Grace Restaurant at the Adelaide
Oval cricket ground. Expect fine dining in a
world-class sports stadium with an array of
South Australian wines to match the local
produce. Henschke Hill of Grace takes pride
of place!

860 *Above:* Penfolds also produces a Cellar Reserve range

McLAREN VALE, AUSTRALIA
862 Find sustainable world tourism

Gemtree Wines holds an award for the Best of Wine Tourism. Find out why as the organic/biodynamic wine producer invites you to visit its sustainable tasting room to taste wines that are preservative-free, vegan-friendly, and extremely tasty. Shiraz and a new superstar, Tempranillo, lead the way.

McLAREN VALE, AUSTRALIA
863 Stay at McLaren Vale's Hotel California

Staying at and visiting Inkwell Wines is a multinational experience—there's an American-born winemaker, a Brazilian-born viticulturist, and the winery and vineyard are on California Road. Stay in the Hotel California Road boutique suites and wake up to expansive views across the Inkwell vineyards. Don't forget to indulge in a tasting of Inkwell Wines and the wilder DubStyle lo-fi label.

McLAREN VALE, AUSTRALIA
864 Learn the classics

There are three grapes that best exemplify the history and quality of the wines of McLaren Vale: Cabernet Sauvignon, Grenache, and Shiraz. The trio will reveal all during the Classic McLaren Vale Tasting at Wirra Wirra. Learn from your host, and see, sniff, taste, and talk while grazing on a regional tasting plate.

864 *Above:* Wirra Wirra hosts the Classic McLaren Vale Tasting

McLAREN VALE, AUSTRALIA

865 Free your inner winemaker

It's time to make a winemaker of you! The Blending Bench at d'Arenberg is where you will craft your own personalized Shiraz. With three selections from barrels of premium McLaren Vale Shiraz in front of you, you get to trial different blends to perfect the final taste. And the best bit? You can keep what you've made!

SWAN VALLEY, AUSTRALIA

866 Enjoy a bush tucker experience

Welcome to Noongar country, the land of the traditional owners. Learn more about Australia's First People and their heritage, food, and culture at Mandoon Estate. Bush Tucker Tasting & Talk takes you through indigenous connection to the land over thousands of years. Freshen up afterward with a tasting of Mandoon's Verdelho, Chenin Blanc, or Sémillon.

865 *Above:* You can experiment with wine blending at d'Arenberg

MARGARET RIVER, AUSTRALIA

867 Stay at a homestead

A house among the vines in one of Australia's prettiest and most sustainable vineyards can be yours for the night. The homestead at Cullen Wines is made of local granite and timber, and was originally built by the founders. Make a weekend of it and bring your friends, for the venue sleeps seven. You can then wander over to the winery for tastings, lunches, and tours.

MARGARET RIVER, AUSTRALIA

868 Try your hand at blending

Leeuwin Estate Winery is one of the pioneers of quality Chardonnay and Cabernet Sauvignon in Margaret River. In the Ultimate Leeuwin Wine Blending & Dining Experience, you will see behind the scenes and get to blend your own Margaret River red wine. Enjoy your handiwork with the five-course degustation lunch, plus other top estate wines.

868 *Above and right:* Leeuwin Estate Winery offers a variety of tastings and experiences

MARGARET RIVER, AUSTRALIA
869 Descend into The Vault

In beautiful Margaret River, the sun and surf await, but there's more! The Cellar Experience is a historical tour through Vasse Felix, founded in 1967, with a walk among the vines and then a tasting of the region's best wines: Cabernet Sauvignon and Chardonnay. Held in The Vault, the tasting includes older vintages and a lunch to finish.

MARGARET RIVER, AUSTRALIA
870 Get wise to lo-fi wines

The Lo-fi Wine Trail is perfect for the intrepid wine drinker—it's full of minimal-intervention, wild yeast, and no-added-anything wines. Join this day tour, and visit a group of winemakers normally off the beaten track, who generally don't have cellar doors or distributors: Blind Corner, Goon Tycoons, Stormflower, Dormilona Wines, and more.

MARGARET RIVER, AUSTRALIA
871 Master the wine essentials

Embark on an immersive wine experience at Voyager Estate. You'll learn about trellising and grape growing in the vineyard, the secrets of blending in the winery, and food and wine matching led by a trained sommelier. The Wine Essentials Day is just that: a full day in which you have access to all areas.

TASMANIA, AUSTRALIA

872 Enter a winery of the future

Follow the River Derwent—or catch a ferry—to Moorilla for a day's exploration of Tasmanian wine history. Moorilla Decanted is a relaxed and intimate wine tasting with knowledgeable wine experts in the underground chambers of one of Tasmania's pioneering producers. There will be new releases and a harking back to rare wines of the past.

TASMANIA, AUSTRALIA

873 Snag a memorable wine experience

Fly-fishing in the unspoiled rivers and secluded fishing spots of Tasmania is a national pastime. Never fly-fished before? Don't worry—Josef Chromy Wines, in conjunction with RiverFly Tasmania, offers one-on-one instruction in the art of fly-casting, and fishing at its own private fishery. All equipment is supplied, and lunch and wine tasting are included.

873 *Above:* Josef Chromy Wines is a picturesque setting for fly-fishing

TASMANIA, AUSTRALIA

874 Live it up at Taste of Tasmania

Stuck for New Year's Eve ideas? The Taste of Tasmania comprises of six days of celebration during the last week of December and early January with the best Tassie food, wine, artisanal spirits, music, entertainment, and more down by Hobart's wharf precinct. Watch competitors finish the Sydney to Hobart Yacht Race while you enjoy a local wine at one of the harbor-front wine bars. Wander down to Princes Wharf No. 1 Shed for tastings, master classes, food, wine, and live music. Hobart always turns on great weather for the occasion. Stay for a New Year's Eve extravaganza!

TASMANIA, AUSTRALIA

Stay at one of these three unique Tasmanian places

875 Stillwater

Find yourself at the pristine waterfront setting of Stillwater, where an 1830s flour mill has been reborn as one of Australia's leading restaurants—with a list devoted to the wines of Tasmania. You'll find bright Rieslings, complex Chardonnays, and supple Pinots from all over the island on the 200-strong listing curated by sommelier and co-owner James Welsh. Why not treat yourself to the luxury accommodation at Stillwater Seven? You'll have your own private guest bar and exclusive access to the restaurant's kitchen.

876 Saffire Freycinet

The east coast of Tasmania is wild, isolated, and rich in natural bounty. Stay at Saffire Freycinet luxury resort and enjoy world-class, locally sourced food and wine, plus a raft of local experiences: beekeeping in a private apiary overlooking the Hazards mountains, oyster farming (and eating), and immersion in maritime ecology, as well as a country walk with a local indigenous guide.

877 Swinging Gate Vineyard

At night, you can count the stars of the southern hemisphere in the sky above; come morning, you'll wake at first light to the morning chorus of birdcalls and the other sounds of nature stirring. This is what you'll get to experience at Swinging Gate Vineyard's Domescapes—a dome-shaped tent with a full skylight that allows panoramic views of the surrounding vineyards by day, and starry skies by night. It's the perfect way to get away from it all.

875

TASMANIA, AUSTRALIA
878 Meet Pinot d'Pig

It's true—Holm Oak Vineyard's general manager is called Pinot d'Pig. He's a big, handsome bundle of love, and apart from the fine-edged Riesling, Chardonnay, and Pinot Noir produced at Holm Oak Vineyard . . . he's the star attraction! He's a domestic pig and Instagram sensation. Stop and say hi, and bring an apple—Pinot loves apples as much as he loves people.

TASMANIA, AUSTRALIA
879 Join a wine crusader in his quest

Winemaker Joe Holyman lives on a farm in the Tamar Valley. He's a quiet family man, not given to making bold philosophical wine arguments, but a tasting with him and his Stoney Rise/Holyman wines will give you hope about the future of minimum-intervention and sustainable wine growing. It doesn't get more real than a tasting with Holyman in his airy tasting area overlooking the vines.

TASMANIA, AUSTRALIA
880 Cross paths with a sparkling wine superstar

Just minutes outside the Tasmanian capital city of Hobart lies Stefano Lubiana Wines, the winery of quiet, unassuming winemaker extraordinaire Stefano Lubiana. He is taking Tasmanian sparkling wine to the next level, with wines such as Grande Vintage aged on lees for nine years. Book a tutored tasting, which includes museum wines, and stay for lunch at the Lubiana Osteria, with a menu that beautifully encapsulates Lubiana's biodynamic wine and food approach.

TASMANIA, AUSTRALIA
881 Embark on a ghostly adventure

Journey on the ferry *Spirit of Tasmania* to northwest Tasmania, and then it's just minutes from the dock to the newest—some say the coldest—wine subregion in the state, Cradle Coast. Almost perennially green and lush, and with views across Bass Strait, Ghost Rock Wines is the area's first commercial winery. Book a tasting with winemaker Justin Arnold, who specializes in lively, savory Pinot Noir. His wife, Alicia Peardon, conducts classes at the Hundred Acres cooking school. Stay for lunch and enjoy a grazing menu featuring local farm-to-table produce.

TASMANIA, AUSTRALIA

882 Fly over Tasmania's vineyards

The rugged beauty of Australia's Apple Isle is best seen and enjoyed from the air. Book a seaplane to the Meadowbank vineyard for a three-hour escape into Derwent Valley wine country. Above & Beyond charter flights leave from Hobart's waterfront and follow the famous River Derwent to the Meadowbank vineyard and farm. Meadowbank first planted vines in 1976 and is an all-round Tassie specialist—from wild-fermented Riesling to pure, intense Chardonnay and Pinot Noir.

TASMANIA, AUSTRALIA

883 Heli over the vines

Soar through the majestic Tamar Gorge, wing your way over Lake Trevallyn, and touch down at a vineyard or two. Helicopter flights depart from the Peppers Silo Hotel in Launceston and can include extras such as dropping into a Tamar Valley Vineyard for a private tasting or picnicking in the vines with glasses of premium Tassie sparkling. Flights are through Unique Charters/Peppers Silo Hotel.

882 *Above:* Meadowbank is a farm and vineyard in Tasmania

TASMANIA, AUSTRALIA
884 Support local farmers

Feel the history within the walls of an old cannery factory in the Huon Valley that once exported local produce to the world from the Port Cygnet wharves. It's now the center of the vibrant Cygnet rural community. Eat at the Cannery Kitchen and Bar, and you will help local farmers who are getting over the effects of the 2019–20 bushfires. The dark, textural interior is perfect during a Tassie winter. In summer, head for the outdoor beer garden. Next door is Sailor Seeks Horse—it's one heck of a winery name and winery!—and the wines, including award-winning Pinot Noir, feature on the list.

TASMANIA, AUSTRALIA
885 Join a walking and tasting tour

Venture into heaven on earth with a wander through a garden, vines, and scenery in one of Tasmania's more isolated vineyard cellar doors. Entry to Waterton Hall Wines at Rowella is by prior arrangement. The Historic Walking & Tasting Tour takes in the historic barn, garden, homestead, Vineyard House, and Boathouse on the Tamar River. Taste the wine grown just feet from you, and enjoy a firepit barbecue. Patting Basil, the four-legged marketing manager, is free!

TASMANIA, AUSTRALIA

886 Experiment with food-and-wine pairings

What to match with the plumpest, tastiest dish of Tasmania, the
Pacific oyster? Venture down to Home Hill Winery's restaurant for
the imaginative offerings. Maybe coconut vinegar and mango caviar
or smoked maple bacon and black walnut ketchup? Home Hill
Kelly's Reserve Chardonnay is the natural accompaniment. The
restaurant serves up some of the best food in the state, all sourced
locally, including mussels, lamb, dry-aged duck, and Meander
Valley pork.

886 *Above:* Try out new food-and-wine pairings at Home Hill Winery's restaurant

887 Grasp the fundamentals of making sparkling wine

There are around 44 million tiny bubbles in a bottle of sparkling wine. Learn all about their magic and how they got there—and then make your own during a course at Josef Chromy Wines. You'll work with the winemakers to choose your wine and then add the liqueur, cork, and the wire. Then it's yours! The next time you order a Josef Chromy sparkling, you can choose your own dosage rate for a truly personalized drink. A two-course lunch with wine is included on the course.

888 Find a German grape grown in Tasmania

How cold is southern Tasmania for grape growing? You are about to find out! Wrap up warmly when you go to Bream Creek Vineyard's cellar door at the Dunalley Waterfront Café. Winemaker Fred Peacock is acknowledged as one of Tasmania's best, so when he planted Schönburger at Bream Creek—a grape crossing created in Germany—people paid attention. Seek it out for tasting. The grape is largely unknown in Australia but thrives in the cold, exuding an exotic spice-filled fragrance from the glass. Peacock produces a dry style and a late-harvested dessert wine.

889 Complete a sparkling master class

Where better to learn more about the art of sparkling wine than at pioneering producer Clover Hill Wines? Cellar door manager Ian White guides you for ninety minutes. The Cuvée Exceptionelle Blanc de Blancs and Cuvée Prestige Blanc de Blancs are always highlights. Finish with an antipasti platter and glass of wine in the winery's al fresco area.

TASMANIA, AUSTRALIA

890 Taste in a surreal all-white venue

Head to the coolest place to be in Hobart when the sun goes down: Institut Polaire. Here, natural winemaking meets artisanal gins meets clean, effortless food in one amazing space decorated completely throughout in Antarctic white. Nav Singh, owner and winemaker at Domaine Simha, and his master distiller–marketer wife, Louise Radman, offer a totally sustainable *avant-garde* wine—and spirit—experience at their cool hangout. You'll find Paysan, a Riesling pét-nat, and low-tech wines made in oak and clay amphorae. Spirits include the celebrated Süd Polaire Antarctic dry gin. Wine-, gin-, and whiskey-tasting experiences can be had at Institut Polaire at weekends.

TASMANIA, AUSTRALIA

891 Hang out at a local market

Visit Australia's favorite community market, a place that combines Tasmanian environmental awareness, art, and crafts with the talents of a bustling dynamic city. The Salamanca Market is open on Saturdays and crawls around historic Salamanca Place, near Princes Wharf, and overlooks Sullivan's Cove on the Hobart waterfront. Tall trees provide shade in summer as you wander 200 stalls with everything from homemade wares and antiques to food and wine.

TASMANIA, AUSTRALIA

892 Venture to the Devil's Corner— if you dare!

All wineries should have a lookout like the one at Devil's Corner's cellar door on Tasmania's east coast. It is within easy walking distance of the winery. Buy some wine (Devil's Corner specializes in Riesling and Pinot Noir) and food (from Tombolo Café) and enjoy a picnic on the lawns before a short climb to the top of the Lookout. There, soak up the expansive views across The Hazards Vineyard and the Tasman Sea.

TASMANIA, AUSTRALIA

893 Take in a twilight vineyard tour

Spot wedge-tailed eagles—or *bunjil*, as the indigenous people of Australia call the country's largest bird of prey—on a twilight vineyard tour at the beautiful Bay of Fires Wines estate. Based at Pipers River on the northern tip of Tasmania, the tour (which runs during winter) will bring you up close to some of Australia's furriest and cutest marsupials, including the possum and the platypus. The walk is a two-hour, all-terrain stroll, complete with headlamps and the odd glass of wine. On clear nights there's a little astronomy included in the talks, which take in sustainable vineyard practices and one of Australia's most important resources: water.

TASMANIA, AUSTRALIA
894 Interpret sparkling wine

Pipers Brook subregion is where you will find some of the best vineyards in the state producing Chardonnay and Pinot Noir grapes for sparkling wines or, as the Tasmanians like to say, sparkling Tasmanoise. The Wine Room and Interpretive Centre at Jansz Tasmania was one of the first cellar doors to embrace an interactive hi-tech approach to learning more about the production of sparkling wines. Processes and technical terms are explained, and then it's on to a tasting and maybe a cheese board.

TASMANIA, AUSTRALIA
895 Follow the Tamar Valley Wine Route

In Launceston with some spare time? The Tamar Valley Wine Route awaits, with 106 mi (170 km) of wine roads across the northeastern vineyards to explore. Your wine tour takes in around thirty cellar doors. Wine purchases made along the way can be delivered to your home from the last winery you visit.

TASMANIA, AUSTRALIA
896 Try a food BYOB

In Australia bring your own booze (BYOB) is popular. At Puddleduck Vineyard in Richmond, you can bring your own food for a barbecue! But you don't have to if you don't want to, since vineyard platters are available. The winery concentrates on a small selection of Tassie classic grapes: Riesling, Fumé Blanc, Chardonnay, Pinot Noir, and sparklings. You can also go on a vineyard and winery tour.

894 *Above:* The Jansz Tasmania Wine Room and Interpretive Centre

WAIHEKE ISLAND, NEW ZEALAND
897 Experience a touch of Provence

Maybe it's the scent of lavender, the olive groves, or the ivy-strewn winery buildings, but Stonyridge Vineyard on the holiday island of Waiheke evokes images of Provence. Located in a beautiful valley close to Onetangi Beach and Putiki Bay, Stonyridge is the dream of winemaker Stephen White, who rose to international prominence with Larose, a Cabernet Sauvignon and Merlot blend. You can take a yoga class on the winery's yoga deck or, at other times, you can sit there with a glass of wine and a shared food platter. In summer, Sunset DJ Sessions are held every Saturday afternoon. The island is only a forty-minute ferry ride from Auckland, so what are you waiting for?

AUCKLAND, NEW ZEALAND
898 Choose from a wine list with no "messing"

Delve into a restaurant experience where the ingredients shine in their utter simplicity. At Pasture in Auckland, chef and owner Ed Verner curates a small wine list featuring only New Zealand and Australian wines that he says haven't been "messed" with. Every wine is low intervention or natural. It's a challenge Verner thrives on. Pasture only seats six people, and customers sit at the chef's bar, close to the open kitchen, for the three-hour tasting menu.

GISBORNE, NEW ZEALAND
899 Find where the clean, green Kiwi wine image was born

Sustainable. Low intervention. Taste the wines that encouraged a winemaking nation to think twice about organic and biodynamic wine growing. At Millton Vineyards & Winery, James and Annie Millton showed what was possible in the early 1980s with their highly successful Chenin Blanc, and along the way inspired fellow wine producers to follow suit. Taste the wines and finish with Amrita, a certified organic, cloudy grape juice made from Muscat grapes and is 100 percent grape juice and nothing else.

897 *Above:* Laid-back Waiheke Island is home to Stonyridge Vineyard

HAWKE'S BAY, NEW ZEALAND

900 Cast your eyes upon dazzling winery architecture

Elephant Hill winery rises from its place of rest, an aqua-colored monolith that not so much interrupts the Hawke's Bay coastline as absorbs it. Clad in an aged copper material that will only intensify with weathering and age, it is a remarkable piece of winery architecture that beautifully illustrates the owners' reputation for sustainability and innovation. The complex is sleek and graceful throughout. Visit the cellar door for a tasting or stay in one of the guest rooms. The winery partners with Elephant Family, an international charity committed to the conservation of the endangered Asian elephant.

HAWKE'S BAY, NEW ZEALAND

901 Feast among the vines

Dine against the jaw-dropping beauty of Te Mata Peak and among the vines at Craggy Range Vineyard, one of the North Island's premier wine producers. Your meal at Craggy Range Restaurant celebrates everything local—from the vegetables and herbs, fresh from the kitchen garden, to locally sourced venison, mackerel, octopus, flounder, and New Zealand's famous quality lamb. And the wines? Look out the window—that's where they grow. Seek out Chardonnay, Syrah, Merlot, and Cabernet blends off the famed Gimblett Gravels Vineyard.

HAWKE'S BAY, NEW ZEALAND

902 Enjoy great wine at this celebration

The numbers at the Hawke's Bay Wine Celebration are impressive: close to forty Hawke's Bay wine producers, 200 wines under one roof, and just one night in which to taste and learn more about the region. It's one of the sunniest in the country where Chardonnay, Syrah, and Cabernet Sauvignon rule. The traveling wine bazaar moves to Wellington and Auckland each September.

HAWKE'S BAY, NEW ZEALAND

903 Explore the oh-so-versatile wine grape

Explore the wine grape's multifaceted states and vinous
personalities—from balsamic vinegar to quality table wine and
barrel-aged spirit. The journey takes place behind the scenes
at Pernod Ricard's Church Road Wines, with a glass in hand,
naturally, and finishes with a guided tasting of current-release
wines. The spacious winery also plays host to a fine restaurant
for a post-tasting treat.

903 *Above:* Church Road Wines was the first in New Zealand to craft Bordeaux-style red wine

MARTINBOROUGH, NEW ZEALAND

904 Celebrate wine in Martinborough

The flavors of Martinborough Pinot Noir are among the most generous and long living in New Zealand—something worthy of exploring at the region's annual Toast Martinborough, a wine, food, and music festival. Come mid-November each year, this is the place to be. Around ten wineries participate from the big names Escarpment, Ata Rangi, and Palliser Estate to the smallest, including vegan-wine producers Tirohana and Luna Estate.

MARTINBOROUGH, NEW ZEALAND

905 Soak up some exciting Pinots

When in Martinborough, be sure to call at Te Kairanga—which translates in Māori as "where the soil is rich and the food is plentiful"—and we might also add, "and where the Pinot Noir excels." Te Kairanga Wines—known as TK—is one of the premier producers of Pinot Noir in the region with extensive resources to call upon: 260 acres (105 ha) in four distinct vineyard settings. The Cottage cellar door, originally built in the 1800s, is in a beautiful spot above the Huangarua River. Don't miss the farmers market, which it hosts each summer.

MARTINBOROUGH, NEW ZEALAND

906 Don your apron at this winery

Try your hand at making authentic Italian fresh pasta or tiramisu. Learn the tricks of baking, how to navigate classic spicy Indian flavors, or the secrets of traditional French and Catalan cuisine. The simple but often hard-to-make things in the kitchen are taught at Carême Cooking Classes at Palliser Estate. Classes are held throughout the year at the winery's on-site cooking school and conducted by chef Jo Crabb. After the cooking comes the wine and an indulgent lunch.

906 *Left:* Palliser Estate is located in Martinborough

MARTINBOROUGH, NEW ZEALAND
907 See one winery's composting methods

Smell the authenticity—and the compost—at Ata Rangi, a leader in sustainable biodynamic wine growing and a founding member of Sustainable Winegrowing New Zealand (SWNZ). Grape stalks, skins, and seeds from winemaking are used as compost for the vines. Cofounder Clive Paton is the force behind the Aorangi Conservation Trust, planting more than 70,000 trees in his effort to reintroduce threatened native birds back to the forest environment. He also works with Project Crimson to save the native rātā flower, the inspiration behind Ata Rangi's young Crimson Pinot Noir wine label. Share a glass of Crimson and a natter with Paton at the cellar door.

908 Discover the story of a French vine

Few tales in wine are taller than the mystery of the gum-boot clone. In the 1970s a Kiwi rugby player was stopped by customs officers upon his return to New Zealand from France. Caught red-handed with cuttings of Pinot Noir stashed in his gum boots, he claimed they came from the world's most famous Pinot Noir vineyard, Domaine de la Romanée-Conti, in Burgundy. The vines were confiscated by customs officer Malcolm Abel, who also happened to be a winemaker. Rather than destroy the vines, Abel paid for them to be quarantined and eventually planted them in his vineyard. Many other winemakers took cuttings, and today, the Abel Clone of Pinot Noir is planted throughout New Zealand. Try Escarpment Vineyard's Kupe and imagine Burgundy.

907 *Above:* Ata Rangi is a founding member of SWNZ

WELLINGTON, NEW ZEALAND

909 Hang out at this hip Kiwi bar

Chandeliers, a stuffed peacock or two, antique mirrors, and crazy, rococo furniture collide in a busy, sometimes bizarre, decorative scheme that proves as irresistible as the cocktail and wine lists. With its pulsating energy and international vibe, Hippopotamus could be in London or New York. Make your own martini or G&T with a New Zealand gin, be inspired by a smoky Negroni or a New Zealand–inspired cocktail (including something called an NZ Hanky Panky), plus local beers, wines, and an international cast of spirits.

WELLINGTON, NEW ZEALAND

910 Join a walking tour in the Kiwi capital

Cruise the streets of the country's restaurant capital, where the locals take their food, wine, and especially the coffee, very seriously. Choose Zest Food Tours' Wellington Walking Gourmet option, where your friendly guide will first lead you to a city-based coffee roaster for a heart-starter caffeine. For the next four and a half hours there will be chocolates, a purveyor of local art, a Greenwich Village–style food and wine market, and a stylish café.

NELSON, NEW ZEALAND

911 Visit this clean, green winery

Enter a world where New Zealand's clean, green image is alive and thriving, and continues to inspire fellow winemakers and astound drinkers around the world. Neudorf Vineyards co-owner and winemaker Tim Finn helped establish the SWNZ scheme that aims to increase biodiversity in the vineyard and best practice in the winery. Neudorf Chardonnay, the first among equals, is one of the best in the world.

MARLBOROUGH, NEW ZEALAND

912 Enjoy the wildlife at Brancott Estate Wines

Brancott Estate Wines produces extremely exciting wine. This is the birthplace of Sauvignon Blanc in Marlborough (in 1979), and it is one of the most photographed vineyards in the world—you'll understand why when you visit and see the wide, flat expanse of vivid green set against rising hills. You will also discover the estate's strong sustainability message in an up-close encounter with the kārearea, New Zealand's endangered native falcon. Being one with the land means living together with its beautiful creatures, and there are few more beautiful and impressive than the kārearea in midflight over Brancott Estate Wines. Enjoy a demonstration of its power and presence, and learn more about the Marlborough Falcon Trust and the falcon's ongoing protection. Although no longer open to the public for tastings, you can book the estate's former restaurant and cellar door for private functions, and still enjoy the exceptional wines produced at Brancott.

MARLBOROUGH, NEW ZEALAND

913 Imbibe at a farmers market

Marlborough's farmers market is an authentic, community-driven market showcasing the produce of the land. Held every Sunday morning in Marlborough's main city of Blenheim, more than fifty stalls are devoted to local foods. Head along to find everything from apricots and orchard fruits to nuts and wild venison—and of course wine!—to be enjoyed and bought. Soak up the rich community vibe.

MARLBOROUGH, NEW ZEALAND

914 Seek a seafood culinary match

The green-lipped mussel is the perfect partner with a glass of zesty Marlborough Sauvignon Blanc—its saline, sea-spray qualities are the best foil for the grape's herbaceous exuberance. Find out how the two come together brilliantly at de Burgh's Bistro, Hotel d'Urville, one of the best restaurants in the region. The mussels, some of the largest in this shellfish family, couldn't be fresher, since most of the country's green-lipped mussels are sourced from the nearby Marlborough Sound.

912 *Above:* Brancott Estate Wines is one of the most photographed vineyards in the world

MARLBOROUGH, NEW ZEALAND

Visit three of Marlborough's top wineries

915 Dog Point Vineyard

Go for the wine—stay for the peace and quiet! Here in your own little slice of heaven, atop a small hill with views across to the Richmond Range and Wairau Plains, you have the choice of vineyard accommodation: The Bell Tower on Dog Point or the more intimate French-inspired cottage, The French Barn. Take a walking route and explore nearby vineyards, then finish with a tasting at Dog Point Vineyard. Privacy and relaxing country quiet are assured.

916 Framingham Wines

Framingham Wines' chief winemaker has a PhD in organic chemistry; follows a sustainable, organic approach; and is obsessed with Riesling.

Dr. Andrew Hedley and the Framingham team are a little different, and Riesling drinkers everywhere appreciate him for it. Framingham Rieslings, from some of the oldest vines in the area, positively star in a place where Sauvignon Blanc rules. Drop in for a complimentary tasting, a vineyard or cellar walk, or a winery tour to discover their wonderful wines in person.

915

915

CENTRAL OTAGO, NEW ZEALAND

918 Live it up at a Pinotphiles bash

Few wine conferences are as much fun and so downright educational—not to mention scenic—as the Central Otago Pinot Noir Celebration, held every January. Attend the three-day event and explore one wine style along with copious tastings, discussions, dinners, and the odd bit of drinking. Also take in the wide, green lands and ice-capped mountains of a wine region that casts itself as one of the more serious places in the world to grow Pinot Noir.

CENTRAL OTAGO, NEW ZEALAND

919 Traipse through a cluster of vineyards

The beauty of Cromwell is too good to explore by car. Take to the walking path that winds between vineyards and orchards, known as the 4 Barrels Walking Wine Trail. It comprises of four leading vineyards: Misha's Vineyard, Aurum Wines, Scott Base, and Wooing Tree Vineyard. The trail is a 5 mi (8 km) loop passing by Lake Dunstan and allowing time for lunch and a tasting at each winery.

CENTRAL OTAGO, NEW ZEALAND

920 Eat where the locals eat

Dine at the Bannockburn Hotel, and you'll find pub food with a twist. The local wine list is definitely a step up from the usual country hotel offerings—it features an extensive Central Otago wine selection of sixty wines by the glass. And you never know—at the next table could be a well-known Central Otago winemaker or two. Order beer-battered flake and a glass of Central Chardonnay.

917 Tohu Wines

Embrace Māori culture and the connection to land with New Zealand's first Māori-owned winery, Tohu Wines. The company celebrates *tūrangawaewae* (sense of place), and is best known for its single-vineyard wines under the Whenua label. A busy cellar door in Marlborough is the perfect place to learn about this fascinating enterprise, which, like Māori people, is defined by the land.

917

CENTRAL OTAGO, NEW ZEALAND

Explore the wines of these six Central Otago producers

921   Gibbston Valley Winery

The shires, back roads, and craggy outcrops of Central Otago are a cyclist's delight. Gibbston Valley Winery offers bike rentals and bike tour packages. Top cycling experiences such as the Arrow River Trail are all within reach of the winery by day. By night, stay at the winery's lodge and spa and dine in. Vinotherapy treatments are a specialty.

922   Cloudy Bay Vineyards

The most beautiful "shed" in the whole of New Zealand is made of glass, wood, and stone. Explore the wines behind the famous Cloudy Bay Vineyards name, from the company's original vineyards in Marlborough to its exploration of Pinot Noir from its Central Otago vineyard, culminating in the super-premium Te Wahi (the place).

923   Peregrine Wines

In the wake of Central Otago's Crown Range lies a shimmering, silvery wing that's almost flat against the landscape. Under the "fly" roof is Peregrine Wines' winery and cellar door, named after the architecture inspired by New Zealand's native peregrine falcon. Call in for a tasting, and you'll find bright Chardonnays, complex Pinots, and a stunning Riesling.

924   Aurum Wines

Be led down the organic path of winemaking practice in a private tasting with the winemaker at Aurum Wines. Lucie Lawrence, a third-generation winemaker, is a strong advocate for sustainable practices and biodiversity in the vineyard. Can you taste the difference? In one hour you'll explore the flavors of wine made without preservatives or additives. Aurum Organic Amber Wine is made using ancient techniques, including fermentation and a lengthy time on skins with the wine drained through a muslin cloth. The taste is an explosion of emotions.

921

926

925 Rippon Vineyard & Winery

Brambles, black cherries, crushed raspberries—
your glass of Rippon Pinot Noir will delight and
surprise with its intensity and purity. Take a deep
breath of the clean mountain air, hold your gaze
on the shimmering blue water of Lake Wanaka,
and sip contentedly. Few vineyard scenes in the
world compare to the majesty of Rippon's
biodynamic vineyards.

926 Greystone Wines

Leave your worries behind as you enter Greystone
Wines. Motor past the cellar door, vines, and sheep,
and maneuver up to the hilly rise, where luxury
awaits. The Greystone PurePod is a glass eco-cabin
with all modern amenities, but totally secreted
away in nature. Offering privacy and tranquility,
PurePods are dotted throughout New Zealand. Pour
a glass of wine, look to the heavens, and soak up
the serenity.

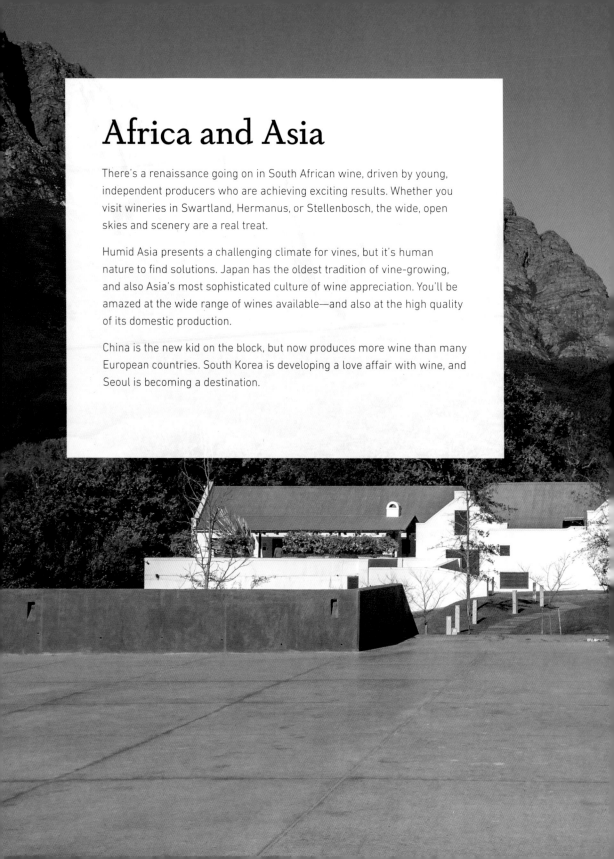

Africa and Asia

There's a renaissance going on in South African wine, driven by young, independent producers who are achieving exciting results. Whether you visit wineries in Swartland, Hermanus, or Stellenbosch, the wide, open skies and scenery are a real treat.

Humid Asia presents a challenging climate for vines, but it's human nature to find solutions. Japan has the oldest tradition of vine-growing, and also Asia's most sophisticated culture of wine appreciation. You'll be amazed at the wide range of wines available—and also at the high quality of its domestic production.

China is the new kid on the block, but now produces more wine than many European countries. South Korea is developing a love affair with wine, and Seoul is becoming a destination.

ESSAOUIRA, MOROCCO
927 Trade in the view for a great meal

The city and the beachfront are amazingly beautiful, but it's hard to find restaurants in Essaouira that rise above touristy mediocrity. Dine at Umia, and you'll find it is the exception—a place with excellent cooking that focuses on lighter, more aromatic flavors; friendly service from the owners; and—most importantly—a solid wine list that focuses on higher-quality Moroccan wines.

CASABLANCA, MOROCCO
928 Enjoy fresh wines from the coast

Situated close to the coast and to Casablanca, Domaine Ouled Thaleb benefits from a slightly cooler climate than inland Morocco. Both white and red wines are assured and refreshing. Established in 1923, this winery still uses concrete tanks for most fermentations—vessels that went out of fashion in the 1980s but that have since become de rigueur again! Be sure to eat at Le Riad des Vignes, its highly rated restaurant.

MEKNÈS, MOROCCO
929 Taste some top Meknès red wines

Sample ripe, fruit-driven reds at Domaine de la Zouina, a beautiful boutique winery close to Meknès. Wines are bottled under two brand names: Volubilia and Epicuria. As with most wine-related activities in Morocco, this estate is French owned. The tours and tastings are informative and convivial, with a refreshing lack of "hard sell" at the end.

OMARURU, NAMIBIA

930 Discover a desert winery

Michael Weder has been conducting a bizarre experiment since 2007: How can you make wine in desert conditions? Kristall Kellerei is his winery, and the experiment is proving successful. Working with grape varieties such as Colombard or Tinta Barocca (both adapted to hot, dry conditions), he's making interesting wines and excellent brandy. Join a tour and tasting and then enjoy a lunch at the winery.

JOHANNESBURG, SOUTH AFRICA

931 Pair pomegranates and Pinotage

The exquisite Middle Eastern cuisine is just one of the attractions at Tanen Wine Bar & Eatery—a great selection of boutique, small-production wines from the Cape is the other. Opt for the wine pairings—two wines are offered per course, and you select the one you prefer after sampling. Relax in the restaurant, which has a wonderful and inviting ambiance.

KRUGER NATIONAL PARK, SOUTH AFRICA

932 Stay in luxury while on safari

You might not expect a great selection of wines on safari in the Kruger National Park, but the selection on offer at Sabi Sabi Private Game Reserve is peerless. This is extremely extravagant territory, so you'll be staying in unrivaled luxury. Expect to enjoy a wine list that features many great and hard-to-find Cape wines (and classics from farther afield) in addition to the spectacular wildlife and tranquil surroundings.

932 *Above:* Earth Lodge at Sabi Sabi Private Game Reserve

ROBERTSON VALLEY, SOUTH AFRICA

933 Stay at a family business in the valley

Head two hours east of Cape Town to reach the warm, dry Robertson Valley region. Weltevrede Wine Estate is at one of its most hospitable addresses: a family-owned winery that also offers self-catering accommodation. The Jonker family crafts full-bodied reds and sweet wines from old vineyards, which you can taste in the candlelit cellar.

SWARTLAND, SOUTH AFRICA

934 Sleep in a dreamy Swartland paradise

Want to wake up to unspoiled views of the Paardeberg Mountains? Fynbos Estate is a 667 acre (270 ha) farm and winery with an old farmhouse and a range of self-catering cottages to accommodate you. Wander among the olive trees and vines, arrange a wine tasting, or go for a walk in the granite-topped mountains.

SWARTLAND, SOUTH AFRICA

935 Catch up with exciting Cape wines

Swartland is one of the Cape's most dynamic wine regions, full of innovative winemakers who constantly push boundaries. It's here that many important trends, such as dry farming, organic viticulture, and earlier picking were first championed. Taste new and old vintages from all the top producers at a party hosted by the organization Swartland Independent Producers in Riebeek Kasteel every November. It's a festive, unpretentious occasion with street food and live music. The event is usually named Swartland Heritage Festival, although in 2019, a one-day version ran as the Swartland Producers Street Party.

SWARTLAND, SOUTH AFRICA

Visit five of the best independent wineries in Swartland

936 Mullineux & Leeu

Chris and Andrea Mullineux only established their Swartland winery in 2007, but these terroir-driven wines quickly became some of the region's most feted. The duo now also makes wine at Leeu Passant in Franschhoek. Wines from both estates can be sampled at the grand Franschhoek tasting room.

937 Môrelig Vineyards (Wightman & Sons)

Andrew Wightman released his first vintage in 2015, and ever since, this truly father-and-son–operated business has been achieving outstanding results from dry-farmed bush vines and a gentle non-interventionist touch in the cellar.

938 Lammershoek

Overlooked by Paardeberg Mountain, this classic Swartland winery has evolved as winemaking duties passed from Craig Hawkins (who left in 2012) to Schalk Opperman, who continues its tradition of making top-quality Chenin and Syrah, plus more unusual varieties, such as Hárslevelű and Tinta Barocca.

938

939 AA Badenhorst

Adi Badenhorst is one of the Cape's seminal winemakers, and he makes outstanding wines using dry-farmed plots of old bush vines. The previously abandoned estate has been lovingly restored by the family, and guests can also stay in the hundred-year-old Winemaker's Cottage.

940 Testalonga

Craig Hawkins has been a hellraiser for Swartland wines in the most positive sense, pioneering earlier picking for fresher wines and, back in 2010, making South Africa's first orange wines. His winery is situated in Piketberg, in Swartland's far north. It's worth a trek to see this beautiful albeit isolated spot.

PAARL, SOUTH AFRICA
941 Discover how ducks help make wine

You'll never think about ducks the same way again after visiting Avondale Estate. This winery works only with natural fertilizers and pest control—and that's where the ducks come in, to protect vineyards from small snails. The wines are complex and flavorsome, and now include two made in Georgian amphorae (*qvevri*).

PAARL, SOUTH AFRICA
942 Taste Cape wine history in a glass

Few Cape wineries are as soaked in history as KWV. Formed as a winemakers cooperative in 1918, KWV finally became a private company in 1997. It's lived through good and bad times, but the wine has endured. Visit the KWV Wine Emporium for a tasting, or tour the famous Cathedral Cellar—a huge barrel cellar with a grand domed ceiling.

PAARL, SOUTH AFRICA
943 Have a sip of handmade wines

SCALI Wines is a small organic winery, where Willie and Tania de Waal live and work in a beautiful Cape Dutch building. Their lo-fi wines are refreshing, quirky, and delicious. Some are produced in such small quantities that they're only available to regular customers or at the winery. If you want to enjoy this peaceful and beautiful spot a little longer, book into the self-catering accommodation.

942 *Above:* KWV's Cathedral Cellar with its towering ceiling

FRANSCHHOEK, SOUTH AFRICA

Check out these three fabulous Franschhoek wineries

944 Babylonstoren

Babylonstoren is a classic Cape Dutch farm with beautiful period buildings that now house the aspirational winery, a restaurant, and a hotel. Stroll around the huge fruit and vegetable garden, whose produce is used extensively in the restaurant.

946 Colmant

Walk up to the top of Franschhoek town to find this Belgian-owned winery specializing in Méthode Cap Classique (Champagne method) sparkling wines. The MCCs are excellent, but just in case you need more bubbles, Colmant also imports Champagnes from three boutique French wineries.

945 Boekenhoutskloof

It's off the tourist trail, but this exceptional estate is famous among wine fans for its Syrah and The Chocolate Block blend. Book a private tasting in the handsome tasting room, and tour the impressive cellars too.

945

945

FRANSCHHOEK, SOUTH AFRICA

947 Jump aboard a wine farm tram

Railway lines were laid in and around Franschhoek in 1904—and were all abandoned by the 1990s. The Franschhoek Wine Tram has revitalized this scenic method of travel, with beautiful 1923 double-decker trams modeled on those used in Blackpool, England. Eight hop-on, hop-off lines are operated, allowing you to choose which wineries you want to visit.

STELLENBOSCH, SOUTH AFRICA

948 Compare the Cape's wines with its competitors

Stellenbosch is a lively university town with plenty of restaurant and bar options—but for wine, there's little better than the Wijnhuis Wine Bar & Grill, with its 500-strong wine list and twenty wines by the glass. Try the Wijnhuis Wijnskrum, where you taste two iconic Cape wines up against a comparably priced equivalent from elsewhere in the world.

STELLENBOSCH, SOUTH AFRICA

949 Dine with a vineyard view

The views are breathtaking, so be sure to enjoy the sunset on the terrace before taking your seat in Tokara's upscale restaurant. The estate's Cabernet Sauvignon and Sauvignon Blanc–based wines feature in wine pairings, or you can select a pairing from other iconic wineries in the region.

949 *Above:* Tokara's restaurant dishes up contemporary cuisine

STELLENBOSCH, SOUTH AFRICA

950 See horses at this winery

Get lucky, and you might see the horses at work at Waterkloof. This biodynamically certified winery is situated in acres of wild fynbos (natural shrubland that's the Cape's equivalent of France's *garrigue*) and surrounded by its vineyards. Dine at the very serious on-site restaurant, once you've finished tasting the excellent wines.

STELLENBOSCH, SOUTH AFRICA

951 Try top South African Cabernet

Johan Reyneke is on a continual drive to improve quality at his Reyneke Wines, first converting his farm to organic agriculture and then to biodynamics. His reserve wines are some of South Africa's most thrilling and are regularly awarded five stars in Platter's *South African Wine Guide*. Reyneke also supports a home-ownership program for its workers, via the Cornerstone project and its associated wines. Arrange to have a wine tasting, vineyard walk, and cellar tour at this high-quality estate.

STELLENBOSCH, SOUTH AFRICA

952 Take a tuk-tuk so you can sip-sip

Spending a day visiting wineries is great fun, but it's best done with someone else at the wheel. Tuk Tuk Stellies offers wine tours on its authentic, specially imported Thai tuk-tuks. Book either a half- or full-day wine tour, and you'll be treated to a 1980s music soundtrack and an enthusiastic guide along the route.

950 *Above:* The spectacular Waterkloof building sits atop the Schapenberg Hills

CAPE TOWN, SOUTH AFRICA

953 Exercise your taste buds

Gather in downtown Cape Town every second
Wednesday of the month with other wine lovers
for #InnerCityWineRoute. It's described by the
organizer Tuning the Vine as "an epic midweek
tasting adventure." A single ticket allows you to
visit the fifteen or so participating wine bars and
restaurants that all offer special wine-tasting
experiences for the night.

953 *Above:* The #InnerCityWineRoute wine-tasting adventure takes place across multiple venues

CAPE TOWN, SOUTH AFRICA

954 Open up at this *enoteca*

Based in Cape Town's Old Biscuit Mill complex, Openwine is an *enoteca*-style wine bar and shop where you're encouraged to taste wines from up-and-coming and artisanal winemakers from all over the Cape. Stay to enjoy a glass and eat snacky foods. You can even bring your own food for a small charge ("foodage").

CAPE TOWN, SOUTH AFRICA

955 Be spoiled for choice at Belthazar

If you love meat, then Belthazar Restaurant & Wine Bar, Grill & Seafood in the lively waterfront area is the place to go. Steaks are a specialty, as are South African game and exotic meats such as wildebeest, ostrich, and springbok. The restaurant serves a massive 250 wines by the glass (almost all of them from the Cape itself), or the full list runs to 600 options by the bottle. Expect impeccable service.

CAPE TOWN, SOUTH AFRICA

956 Dine at an innovative restaurant

Try the cuisine at The Test Kitchen, which takes inspiration from all over the world—lobster salad with Thai aromatics, ceviche, or the flavors of a Middle Eastern curry. It's cleverly assembled into tasting menus that are always delicious, sometimes theatrical (such as barbecued fish steaks served in a clay egg), and frequently innovative. The wine pairings, drawn from a grab bag of the Cape's top artisanal wineries, are inspired. The wine list itself is impressive not just for the range of producers, but also for the number of back vintages.

CONSTANTIA, SOUTH AFRICA
957 Call at an estate dating back to 1685

Klein Constantia is one of the region's most iconic estates, beautifully situated with views out to False Bay. Its sweet Vin de Constance was historically one of the New World's most famous wines. It's still produced today, along with a range of dry Sauvignon Blancs, reds, and sparkling wines. Sample these and more on a cellar tour in the amusingly named Duggie's Dungeon.

CONSTANTIA, SOUTH AFRICA
958 Taste the sweet jewels of Constantia

Sometimes known as "Cape Town's Vineyard," the small Constantia wine region is almost a suburb of the city, lying just on the south side of Table Mountain. Traverse the Constantia Wine Route and discover the ten wineries that form this wine trail. You can easily get around it within a day, either by car or bicycle. Constantia has centuries of winemaking history and has always been famous for its lusciously sweet wines produced from Muscat grapes. The phylloxera louse decimated the region's vineyards at the end of the nineteenth century, and most estates only started producing again seriously in the late 1980s.

957 *Top and above:* Klein Constantia sits on the upper foothills of the Constantiaberg

ELGIN, SOUTH AFRICA

959 Chill out at the Cape's coolest wine fair

Ocean breezes and relatively high-altitude vineyards mean that Elgin Valley's wines are some of the freshest and lightest in the Cape. Verify this for yourself at Elgin Cool Wine & Country Food Festival, held annually in April. It's a great opportunity to taste wines from thirteen producers. Take the whole family to enjoy a program of live entertainment, cellar tours, and art exhibitions. The action centers on the Elgin Railway Market.

ELGIN, SOUTH AFRICA

960 Visit an acclaimed cool-climate producer

Iona Wine Farm's vineyards are quite literally "the coolest vineyard in the Cape," situated at 1,378 ft (420 m) above sea level, and just a few miles from the Atlantic Ocean. See how that influence shows in the restrained, charming Sauvignon Blancs, Chardonnays, and Pinot Noirs that have made this estate famous.

960 *Above:* Iona Wine Farm uses only natural fertilizers and biodynamic techniques

HERMANUS, SOUTH AFRICA

961 Watch wine as well as whales

When you visit Hermanus, don't go just for whale watching—the town is also at the center of a fascinating wine region: the fertile, cool-climate Hemel-en-Aarde Valley. Some fifteen wineries stretch along the valley, making a great itinerary for a day or two's wine tasting. Why not visit them on a flexible wine tour? Wine Hoppers runs a hop-on, hop-off safari-style truck that shuttles between a different selection of wineries, depending on the day of the week.

HERMANUS, SOUTH AFRICA

962 Enjoy craft beverages from Hermanus

If you're in the mood to party, then head to the Hermanus Wine & Food Festival! It is a vibrant gathering not just of wineries, but also craft beer and craft spirit producers from the region, together with loads of food stalls and family-friendly entertainment. The festival has moved from an early-August slot and now takes place at the end of September each year.

HOKKAIDO, JAPAN

963 Indulge in wine and beef

Visit the town of Ikeda in early October for its large wine festival held every year. Buy a ticket to the Ikeda Autumn Wine Festival for unlimited wine tasting—and the consumption of delicious, tasty barbecued beef! It's a great way to taste a wide selection of Hokkaido's wines.

HOKKAIDO, JAPAN

964 Taste small-production wines

For a complete contrast to the area's larger, more corporate producers, visit the tiny Yamazaki Winery, housed in a cozy homestead. The excellent white wines are the main focus, although the winery also produces Pinot Noir and Zweigelt. Production volumes are small, and many wines are available only on-site.

HOKKAIDO, JAPAN

965 Explore a modern-day wine castle

The Ikeda Wine Castle is a bizarre modern concrete structure shaped like a medieval castle, which houses Tokachi Wines' production facility. Tours of the "castle" take you through the various levels of the winery, the brandy distillery, and lastly, a shop, tasting area, and restaurant.

965 *Above:* Tokachi Wines is located inside Ikeda Wine Castle

YAMAGATA, JAPAN

966 Eat sheep in a rural idyll

If you're an adventurous eater, then this restaurant is for you. Head to Sheep, the name of the restaurant—or Hitujiya-Yamagata, named after its location. Here, the sheep are bred specially, and every part of the animal is used in some shape or form. The food is absolutely delicious—so long as you're not too squeamish about what you're eating. Wash it down with a short but excellent selection of natural wines. The restaurant slaughters only one sheep a week, and can in theory close for a day or two if it runs out of meat, so check ahead.

SHIGA, JAPAN

967 Taste these artisanal wines

Hitomi Winery is a small-scale artisanal producer achieving really delicious results from a mixture of international grape varieties and local specialties such as Delaware. Try the DeLa Orange or DeLa Soul to get a flavor of this winery. Winemaker Naoki Yamada has a bright future ahead.

TOCHIGI, JAPAN

968 Visit Japan's natural wine pioneers

Coco Farm & Winery is one of Japan's most progressive wineries, and was one of the first to push the parameters of minimal intervention. The winery produces delicious wines from Koshu, Petit Manseng, and other varieties. A new line of wines has been made from Hokkaido-grown fruit, in collaboration with 10R (Bruce Gutlove). Make sure you don't miss the sensational Pinot Noir!

968 *Above:* Coco Farm & Winery produced its first wine in 1984

TOKYO, JAPAN
969 Shop for wine in a fish market

Iwai Hozumi's mini wine-and-sake shop Shubiduba is right opposite Tokyo's old fish market. Shop here for a great selection of artisanal Japanese wines and some European natural selections. Sakes are also anything but run-of-the-mill. Hozumi normally has a few interesting bottles open if you want to taste or enjoy a glass.

TOKYO, JAPAN
970 Drink impossible wines in the red room

You'll need to persevere to find Akai Mise, a bizarre basement wine bar entirely bathed in red light—but it's worth it. With just a dozen bar seats, it's an intimate experience. Wines are served only by the glass, and include iconic European and Japanese artisanal selections that are hard to find anywhere else— by the bottle, never mind the glass!

TOKYO, JAPAN
971 Delve into a meal with many wine choices

It's nominally a Vietnamese restaurant, but Ăn Đi adds in a healthy dose of Japanese fusion and fine dining. The wine list offers an amazing selection of natural, orange, and handmade wines from around the world. If you're into alternative wine, you'll have a ball here! As with many top Tokyo restaurants, the number of seats is minuscule— reserve well ahead.

971 *Above: Tokyo's Ăn Đi offers a plethora of alternative wines*

YAMANASHI, JAPAN

972 Go winery-hopping in Yamanashi

Yamanashi prefecture is Japan's hot spot for wineries—there are around sixty, many within walking distance of one another. Much of the region is extremely beautiful, with a mountain backdrop and even views of Mount Fuji in some parts. Winemaking has a surprisingly long history here, going back more than a century. Vines are traditionally trained on high trellises, and vineyards are often punctuated with persimmon trees. It's here in Yamanashi that one of Japan's only true native grapes flourishes: the delicate Koshu, which produces light, low-alcohol wines—so much so that many wineries have experimented with ways to plump it up, such as oak aging or skin fermentation. To get there from Tokyo, take the express to Kofu, Yamanashi-shi, or Katsunumabudokyo station. This puts you within spitting distance of well-known wineries such as Marufuji Winery, Maruki Winery, and Château Mercian (Katsunama Winery). Take a taxi from the train station to your first point of call. If you don't speak Japanese, you'll need a translator for most wineries.

972 *Above:* Château Mercian (Katsunama Winery) is one of the spots to visit in Yamanashi

YAMANASHI, JAPAN

973 Visit one of Yamanashi's oldest wineries

Lumiere Winery has been established for 130 years, and certainly keeps its pedigree. The wines are very polished, complex, and assured. Lumiere is one of very few wineries that exports its wines, and since 2008, even has a royal warrant (issued because the wine is purchased by the Japanese Imperial Family). Visit to find out more and to taste its excellent wine—if you need a translator, be sure to give a few days' advance notice.

YAMANASHI, JAPAN

974 Taste superb Koshu wines

Established in 1890, Marufuji Winery has a long history. Current winemaker Masako Mitsuhiro studied in Bordeaux before joining Marufuji in 2005. She's experimenting with a number of new ideas, including a Koshu-based orange wine and a pét-nat. Don't miss Koshu—a Japanese indigenous grape variety. This is what this winery really excels at, and the barrel-aged version is excellent.

YAMANASHI, JAPAN

975 Raise a glass to Mount Fuji

Treat a loved one to a stay at Hoshinoya Fuji—a "glamping hotel" with concrete cabins nestling on the hillside of a forest. Soak up the unimpeded views of Mount Fuji right off your balcony, while feeling connected to nature. The cabins are minimalistic, but extremely comfortable, and there are many outdoor spaces where you can enjoy a campfire or just contemplate the surroundings. An on-site restaurant offers a range of seasonal dining experiences paired brilliantly with local wines, or you can dine on your balcony with only the stars—and each other—for company.

YAMANASHI, JAPAN

976 Explore inside a wineglass museum

Close to Enzan station, Budokobo Wine Glass-Kan is a wine museum with a twist: the main exhibits are 200 different wineglasses from around the world, plus a separate floor exhibiting wine bottle labels and artwork based around grapes. Once you're done in the museum, be sure to check out the café, wine cellar, and craft store.

OSAKA, JAPAN
977 Try this divine food-and-wine pairing

Want to try traditional Japanese *okonomiyaki*—a type of Japanese omelet? Pasania is the place to go! Run by a brother and sister, it is famous for its outstanding *okonomiyaki*. Ask the staff to recommend a wine pairing—it will likely be an orange wine from Radikon, or perhaps a delicate Pinot Noir from Hokkaido. Savor the sensational combinations!

SEOUL, SOUTH KOREA
978 Immerse yourself in Seoul's natural wine

In 2019, natural wine suddenly became a big thing in Seoul. Head to Bar Piknic, which has led the charge for this back-to-basics movement. A coffee bar by day, Bar Piknic morphs into a wine bar at around 6:30 p.m. each evening and offers a great selection of European artisanal goodness selected by sommelier Clément Thomassin. The Alsace native also runs the wine program at the upstairs restaurant Zero Complex, which has a Michelin star.

YEONGDONG, SOUTH KOREA
979 Go on a wine train tour

Ride the wine train from Seoul into the Yeongdong wine region, where you'll visit Château Mani (aka Wine Korea)—the country's only winery producing wine from its own grapes (most Korean wine is made from other fruits). It's a really fun day out, involving plenty of wine tasting on board, a wine footbath, and some walking around Yeongdong itself.

BEIJING, CHINA

980 Taste the diversity of rice wine

Head to the tasting rooms of Nuoyan Rice Wine and prepare to be amazed at the quality and variety of different rice wines from this artisanal producer. Many are aged for multiple years, and there's even a sparkling rice wine to try. An added bonus is that Nuoyan is located in a picturesque Beijing *hutong* (alley).

980 *Above:* Nuoyan Rice Wine is made with natural spring water from a deep well

BEIJING, CHINA

981 Journey back through the ages of Chinese wine

One of the few wineries within Beijing's city limits, Beijing Dragon Seal Wine Museum is based in Haidian District and in 2006 was converted into a museum. The winery dates from 1910 and provides a fascinating glimpse into wine production in China. Wine is still produced there, as you'll see when you visit the expansive cellars.

BEIJING, CHINA

982 Hang out at a deli with good wines

Chez Gérard Boucherie Française is part deli, part shop, part café, and effectively part wine bar. Drop by to purchase tasty French charcuterie, bread, and cheeses and then consume it on the premises at one of the tables. The deli has a good selection of wines and beers to help you wash it down.

BEIJING, CHINA

983 Try Chinese wines in a trendy bar

For a good night out, venture into Pinó, Beijing's first serious wine bar, set in a nice location in one of the *hutongs* near Jiaodaokou Nandajie. There's a great ambiance and a good by-the-glass selection, plus plenty of choices of both Chinese and imported wines. If you tire of the pleasures of the grape, Pinó also offers cocktails and craft beers.

NINGXIA, CHINA

984 Visit China's Napa Valley equivalent

The dusty Ningxia region—where summer temperatures reach 95°F (35°C), but it can drop to -16°F (-9°C) in winter—is China's most hyped wine region by far. The Helan Mountain Grape Culture Corridor is the epicenter—a specially built road that cuts through Helan county and links up countless modern winery buildings. You'll find Chandon China here, and also Château Changyu Moser XV, along with signs to many other producers.

VARIOUS LOCATIONS, CHINA

Check out these top four wineries in China

985 Kanaan Winery

Chinese-German Wang Fang created this winery in the east Helan Mountains, Ningxia, in 2011, and its wines have since won many accolades from wine critics around the world. Kanaan has produced one of Ningxia's first-ever dry Rieslings. Its signature wine is Crazy Fang Cabernet Sauvignon.

986 Château Changyu Moser XV

This winery is a collaboration between one of Austria's top winemakers, Lenz M. Moser, and the Changyu group, which created China's first commercial winery in 1892. Located in Ningxia, the grand Château and winery museum are well worth a visit.

987 Silver Heights

By Chinese standards, Silver Heights in Ningxia is a tiny boutique winery, although it has expanded from producing just a few barrels in 2007 to some 200,000 bottles today. Owner-winemaker Emma Gao Yuan studied in Bordeaux, and her wines (some from organically farmed vineyards) have won many awards worldwide.

988 Grace Vineyard

Established in 1997, this Shanxi-based estate is one of very few to have won acclaim outside China. Famous for its red Bordeaux blends, Grace's young and dynamic CEO, Judy Leissner, has also made headlines: she took the helm when she was just twenty-four. Visitor facilities and guest accommodation are available.

985

988

SHANGHAI, CHINA

989 Discover an Italian flavor in Shanghai

Drink at Enoterra to experience Shanghai's oldest, and quite possibly preeminent, wine bar. The varied selection of bottles is particularly strong on Italy and France, and the Italian theme continues through to the cuisine. Fill up on the popular brunch—and there's no reason why a glass of Prosecco shouldn't accompany it!

SHANGHAI, CHINA

991 Be spoiled at a high-end restaurant

Offering one of Shanghai's most substantial wine lists, Napa Wine Bar and Kitchen keeps its upscale dining options simple: there's a highly seasonal five- or six-course tasting menu, or a short à la carte. This leaves you free to focus on the 900-strong bottle list! Whether you're after back vintages of Bordeaux, an orange wine from Radikon, or a high-end Ningxia Cabernet, it's all here—together with a hundred options by the glass.

SHANGHAI, CHINA

990 Engage in this one-of-a-kind dinner

Savor one of the world's truly unique dining experiences at Ultraviolet, created by chef Paul Pairet. There are only ten seats per night, at a single large table, where you'll dine with other guests. You'll feast on a twenty-course tasting menu paired with iconic wines (often from seriously mature vintages) and other craft beverages, combined with a multisensory show—audio, visual, smell, taste, and touch—to create a complete experience. It's wowed guests since opening in 2012, and has been awarded three Michelin stars.

YUNNAN, CHINA

992 Visit the world's highest-altitude vineyards

If you're an intrepid traveler, this is one to add to your bucket list. Meaning "flying above the clouds," Ao Yun is a premium winery located near Shangri-La, in the foothills of the Himalayas, so it can be a bit of a mission to get to. With the organic vineyards ranging from 7,218 ft (2,200 m) to 8,530 ft (2,600 m) above sea level, the quality of the Cabernet Sauvignon and Cabernet Franc is unique. To get to this remote corner of the world, you'll need to take a four-hour ride in a 4x4—but it'll be worth it for the exceptional wines that you'll taste when you get there. Ao Yun is owned by LVMH (Möet Hennessey).

990 *Above:* The Ultraviolet dining experience awakens all the senses

KHAO YAI, THAILAND

993 Go wine tasting in Thailand

GranMonte Vineyard and Winery occupies a stunning spot in Asoke Valley, with a mountain backdrop. Winemaker Nikki Lohitnavy trained in Australia and is Thailand's first and only female winemaker. She is achieving great results in Thailand's challenging climate. Her Syrah is particularly impressive, as is the new range of minimal-intervention wines. Join one of the excellent winery tours, where a small train takes you through the vineyards.

BANGKOK, THAILAND

994 Indulge in natural and orange wines

Satisfy your natural and orange wine cravings at About Eatery, an upscale Italian restaurant and wine bar in Bangkok's busy Sukhumvit area. The cuisine is seriously impressive, as is the wine list, which offers serious, handcrafted wines from all over Italy and beyond.

994 *Above: The wine at About Eatery is sourced from small artisanal growers*

CHON BURI, THAILAND

995 Visit one of the longest-established Thai wineries

Discover "new latitude winemaking" at Silverlake Vineyard, a beautifully situated winery, which started bottling in 2005. Thai owned, but with an Aussie winemaker at the helm, Silverlake focuses particularly on its estate-grown Shiraz (other varieties are made from bought-in grapes). Visit and tour the vineyards, lake, and garden, before enjoying lunch at its restaurant.

BANGKOK, THAILAND

996 Relax in a speakeasy-style wine hangout

Head to peaceful Dusit and seek out Kangkao—a supercool, stripped-down natural-wine bar that brings a touch of New York minimalism to Bangkok. Atmospheric lighting and a short but exciting wine list will lure you in. If you get tired of wine, Ku Bar (through which you must enter) serves amazing cocktails.

MAHARASHTRA, INDIA

997 Try some Italian flair with your Indian wine

With expertise from Tuscan winemaker Piero Masi, Fratelli Vineyards was bound to get off to a good start. This premium winery currently makes some of India's most convincing red wines, plus one of its only zero-dosage sparkling wines (from Chenin Blanc). Call in to try the delicious wines—and stay the night in one of the winery's four guest rooms.

NASHIK, INDIA

998 Swing by a pioneering Indian winery

When Rajeev Samant established Sula Vineyards in 1999, it was the only winery in the region. Now there are more than thirty! Visit and taste to find out how classic grapes like Viognier and Shiraz have adapted to India's climate. Check the calendar to ensure that your visit won't be on one of the state's eleven dry days—you won't be able to taste wine at this time.

NASHIK, INDIA

999 Taste sparkling wines made by a master

Famed Champagne producer Moët & Chandon (Moët Hennessy) has opened a number of wineries around the world, including Chandon in India (established 2013). Making high-class sparkling wine, Chandon uses Chenin Blanc in its brut blend and Shiraz for rosé. Visit to taste the differences in some of India's most premium bubbles.

MUMBAI, INDIA

1,000 Wine, dine, and dance in Mumbai

There are few serious wine offerings in Mumbai, but check out Wine Rack (in the Lower Parel) for its ample wine selection. With around 300 bottles to choose from, there's a good variety of Indian wines, and solid coverage of wine regions worldwide. The space is convivial and inviting, and cocktails and a DJ notch things up later in the evenings.

Index

Picture credits

t = top, b = bottom, l = left, r = right, m = middle, tl = top left,
tr = top right, bl = bottom left, br = bottom right